Phenomena

Phenomena

SECOND EDITION

21 Extraordinary Stories—with Exercises for Developing Reading Comprehension and Critical Thinking Skills

Henry Billings
Melissa Billings

JAMESTOWN PUBLISHERS
a division of NTC/Contemporary Publishing Group
Lincolnwood, Illinois USA

ISBN 0-89061-106-8

Published by Jamestown Publishers,
a division of NTC/Contemporary Publishing Group, Inc.
4255 West Touhy Avenue,
Lincolnwood (Chicago), Illinois 60712-1975, U.S.A.

9 10 11 12 13 14 15 16 113 09 08 07 06 05

CONTENTS

UNIT THREE

To the Student

One dictionary defines a phenomenon as "an unusual, significant, or hard-to-explain fact or happening; a marvel." *Phenomena* is the plural form of *phenomenon*.

As you might expect, the articles in this book will introduce you to some intriguing events and people. You will probably learn something from every article. You will come away from many of them with unanswered questions. You may be intrigued or puzzled. You may be skeptical or amazed. But you will not be bored.

All the articles tell about actual events. As you read and enjoy them, you will also develop your reading skills. *Phenomena* is for students who already read fairly well but who want to read faster and to increase their understanding of what they read. If you complete the 21 lessons—reading the articles and completing the exercises—you will surely increase your reading speed and improve your reading comprehension and critical thinking skills. Also, because these exercises include items of the types often found on state and national tests, you will find that learning how to complete them will prepare you for tests you may have to take in the future.

How to Use This Book

About the Book. *Phenomena* contains three units, each of which includes seven lessons. Each lesson begins with an article about an unusual event, person, or group. The article is followed by a group of four reading comprehension exercises and a set of three critical thinking exercises. The reading comprehension exercises will help you understand the article. The critical thinking exercises will help you think about what you have read and how it relates to your own experience.

At the end of the lesson, you will also have the opportunity to give your personal response to some aspect of the article and then to assess how well you understood what you read.

The Sample Lesson. Working through the sample lesson, the first lesson in the book, with your class or group will demonstrate how a lesson is organized. The sample lesson explains how to complete the exercises and score your answers. The correct answers for the sample exercises and sample scores are printed in lighter type. In some cases, explanations of the correct answers are given. The explanations will help you understand how to think through these question types.

If you have any questions about how to complete the exercises or score them, this is the time to get the answers.

Working Through Each Lesson. Begin each lesson by looking at the photographs and reading the captions. Before you read, predict what you think the article will be about. Then read the article.

Sometimes your teacher may decide to time your reading. Timing helps you keep track of and increase your reading speed. If you have been timed, enter your reading time in the box at the end of the lesson. Then use the Words-per-Minute Table to find your reading speed, and record your speed on the Reading Speed graph at the end of the unit.

Next complete the Reading Comprehension and Critical Thinking exercises. The directions for each exercise will tell you how to mark your answers. When you have finished all four Reading Comprehension exercises, use the answer key provided by your teacher to check your work. Follow the directions after each exercise to find your score. Record your Reading Comprehension scores on the graph at the end of each unit. Then check your answers to the Author's Approach, Summarizing and Paraphrasing, and Critical Thinking exercises. Fill in the Critical Thinking chart at the end of each unit with your evaluation of your work and comments about your progress.

At the end of each unit you will also complete a Compare/Contrast chart. The completed chart will help you see what the articles have in common. It will also give you an opportunity to explore your own ideas about what makes a happening truly phenomenal.

SAMPLE LESSON

THE YEAR WITHOUT A SUMMER

It was 1816, and the spring in New England was cold and damp. The farmers grumbled a bit because their crop planting was delayed. Such chilly springs in New England, however, are not unusual. Anyone who takes up farming in that part of the United States has to expect the worst. But even the old hands were not prepared for the summer of 1816.

2 June started out nice and warm. It made the farmers forget the frosts and snows of May. But on June 6, and for the next five days, snow and hail returned. Several inches of snow covered the newly planted fields. It was so cold that a fire was necessary to keep warm indoors. It felt like mid-November rather than early June. People had to wear winter hats and coats.

3 Finally, more normal weather returned. The farmers tried to repair the damage done by the killing frost and snow. In July, however, a second blast of cold arrived. It was not as severe as the June cold, but this was July, and July was supposed to be the hottest month of the year. Ice and cold again killed the crops. From July 5 to July 9 the temperature hovered near freezing.

Unusually cold winter weather damages a Florida orange crop.

4 Warm, summerlike weather finally came on July 12. The weather stayed pleasant until August 20. Around this time the farmers began to harvest those crops that had survived the cold spells of June and July. Then came the most incredible cold of all. Frost again killed crops in New Hampshire and Maine. The mountains of Vermont were covered with snow. In fact, it snowed every month that year in Vermont. The corn crop was ruined. In Canada, even the normally hardy wheat crop was wiped out.

5 The story was the same in Europe. Crop failures and food shortages plagued the people. Record-cold temperatures were recorded. Unseasonable snows fell. In the years to come, 1816 would be known as "The Year Without a Summer."

6 Not everything was bad that year, however. The famed English artist J. M. W. Turner painted some of his best paintings in 1816. He is particularly noted for the brilliant sunsets, green suns, and blue moons he included in these paintings. Turner was not color-blind or trying to be different. He painted what he saw in the real world, and in 1816 the sky was full of odd colors and strange lights.

7 What caused this frigid summer with the strangely colored sky? Scientists blame the volcanic eruption of Mt. Tambora, in Indonesia—half the world away. The explosion was so great that the height of this volcanic mountain was reduced by 5,000 feet. Many cubic miles of ash and

The giant ash cloud formed by the eruption of Mount St. Helens, July 22, 1980

dust were hurled into the air. They gathered into a huge cloud in the upper atmosphere. This cloud then began to circle the globe. It prevented some of the sun's rays from reaching the Earth. It also caused some spectacular sunsets and weird colors in the sky.

8 No one is certain just how much blame belongs to Tambora for the unusually cold summer of 1816. Some of the cold might have been the result of normal weather changes. But other volcanoes, such as Krakatoa in 1883 and Gunung Agung in 1963, have also been accused of causing unusual weather. In 1982, El Chichon in southern Mexico exploded. Many scientists believe that its impact on world weather will be felt for many years to come.

If you have been timed while reading this article, enter your reading time below. Then turn to the Words-per-Minute Table on page 71 and look up your reading speed (words per minute). Then enter your reading speed on the Reading Speed graph on page 72.

Reading Time: Sample Lesson

_______ : _______

Minutes *Seconds*

A Finding the Main Idea

One statement below expresses the main idea of the article. One statement is too general, or too broad. The other statement explains only part of the article; it is too narrow. Label the statements using the following key:

M—Main Idea **B—Too Broad** **N—Too Narrow**

B 1. Unusual weather can result from many different factors. [This statement is true, but it is *too broad*. The story is about the specific influence of one volcano on the weather during one year.]

N 2. During the cold summer of 1816, the wheat crop in Canada was wiped out. [This statement is *too narrow*. It tells you nothing about Mt. Tambora and its impact on the weather that year.]

M 3. Scientists believe that volcanic ash and dust from Mt. Tambora may have caused the cold and snow in the summer of 1816. [This statement is the *main idea*. It tells you what the reading selection is about—the summer of 1816. It also tells you about how volcanoes may cause unusual weather.]

15 Score 15 points for a correct M answer.

10 Score 5 points for each correct B or N answer.

25 **Total Score:** Finding the Main Idea

B Recalling Facts

How well do you remember the facts in the article? Put an X in the box next to the answer that correctly completes each statement about the article.

1. During the first few days of June 1816, New England weather was
   - ☒ a. nice and warm.
   - ☐ b. cold and snowy.
   - ☐ c. chilly and overcast.
2. Compared with the June cold wave, the July cold wave was
   - ☐ a. worse.
   - ☐ b. about the same.
   - ☒ c. less severe.
3. In 1816, it snowed every month in
   - ☐ a. Europe.
   - ☐ b. England.
   - ☒ c. Vermont.
4. J. M. W. Turner's paintings included
   - ☐ a. a view of Tambora.
   - ☒ b. green suns and blue moons.
   - ☐ c. bowls of fruit.
5. Mt. Tambora is located in
   - ☐ a. Canada.
   - ☐ b. New England.
   - ☒ c. Indonesia.

Score 5 points for each correct answer.

25 **Total Score:** Recalling Facts

C Making Inferences

When you combine your own experience and information from a text to draw a conclusion that is not directly stated in that text, you are making an inference. Below are five statements that may or may not be inferences based on information in the article. Label the statements using the following key:

C—Correct Inference **F—Faulty Inference**

C 1. New England is known for having a relatively short growing season. [This is a *correct* inference. You are told at the beginning of the story that chilly springs and delayed plantings are common in New England.]

F 2. The farmers of New England give up on their crops if the planting and early growing season goes badly. [This is a *faulty* inference. In 1816 the farmers kept trying to grow something even after the cold waves of June and July.]

C 3. Some crops can survive cold weather better than others. [This is a *correct* inference. You are told that the normally hardy wheat crop in Canada didn't make it. This implies that wheat can usually stand a lot of cold—more than most crops.]

C 4. The summer of 1817 was warmer than the summer of 1816. [This is a *correct* inference. If it were not warmer, the summer of 1816 would not have been unusual.]

F 5. Every time a volcano explodes it has a serious impact on the weather in New England. [This is a *faulty* inference. Only the major volcanoes, which throw up huge amounts of dust and ash, have a serious effect on the world's weather. Scientists are not even sure how much Tambora was to blame for the summer cold of 1816.]

Score 5 points for each correct answer.

25 **Total Score:** Making Inferences

D Using Words Precisely

Each numbered sentence below contains an underlined word or phrase from the article. Following the sentence are three definitions. One definition is closest to the meaning of the underlined word. One definition is opposite or nearly opposite. Label those two definitions using the following key; do not label the remaining definition.

C—Closest **O—Opposite or Nearly Opposite**

1. The farmers <u>grumbled</u> a bit because their crop planting was delayed.

____ a. relaxed
O b. praised
C c. complained

2. Then came the most <u>incredible</u> cold of all.

C a. unbelievable
____ b. freezing
O c. ordinary

3. In Canada, even the normally <u>hardy</u> wheat crop was wiped out.

____ a. tall
C b. tough
O c. fragile

4. What caused this <u>frigid</u> summer with the strangely colored sky?

C a. extremely cold
____ b. lengthy
O c. hot

5. Crop failures and food shortages <u>plagued</u> the people.

_____ a. frightened

__C__ b. cursed

__O__ c. blessed

15	Score 3 points for each correct C answer.
10	Score 2 points for each correct O answer.
25	**Total Score:** Using Words Precisely

Enter the four total scores in the spaces below, and add them together to find your Reading Comprehension Score. Then record your score on the graph on page 73.

Score	Question Type	Sample Lesson
25	Finding the Main Idea	
25	Recalling Facts	
25	Making Inferences	
25	Using Words Precisely	
100	**Reading Comprehension Score**	

Author's Approach

Put an X in the box next to the correct answer.

1. The author uses the first sentence of the article to

☐ a. inform the reader about weather conditions in New England.
☒ b. describe the qualities of the spring of 1816.
☐ c. compare the spring and the summer of 1816.

2. Which of the following statements from the article best describes the summer of 1816?

☒ a. "Ice and cold again killed the crops."
☐ b. "Warm, summerlike weather finally came on July 12."
☐ c. "The weather stayed pleasant until August 20."

3. From the statement "but other volcanoes, such as Krakatoa in 1883 and Gunung Agung in 1963, have also been accused of causing unusual weather," you can conclude that the author wants the reader to think that

☐ a. unusual weather is just the result of normal changes.
☐ b. Tambora had nothing to do with the unusual weather in 1816.
☒ c. Tambora probably had something to do with the unusual weather in 1816.

4. The author probably wrote this article in order to

☐ a. warn the reader about El Chichon's impact on world weather.
☒ b. explain how major events, such as volcano explosions, can affect weather.
☐ c. inform the reader about farming in New England.

__4__ Number of correct answers

Record your personal assessment of your work on the Critical Thinking Chart on page 74.

Summarizing and Paraphrasing

Put an X in the box next to the correct answer for question 3. Follow the directions provided for the other questions.

1. Look for the important ideas and events in paragraphs 3 and 4. Summarize those paragraphs in one or two sentences.

   Sample answer: Frigid blasts of cold in early July and late August ruined crops throughout New England and Canada.

2. Complete the following one-sentence summary of the article using the lettered phrases from the phrase bank below. Write the letters on the lines.

Phrase Bank:
a. theories about what caused the strange weather
b. a description of the unusual cold
c. its effect on crops

The article about the summer of 1816 begins with __b__, goes on to explain __c__, and ends with __a__.

3. Read the statement about the article below. Then read the paraphrase of that statement. Choose the reason that best tells why the paraphrase does not say the same thing as the statement.

   Statement: In 1816, English artist J. M. W. Turner filled his paintings with spectacular sunsets and weird colors because that is what he actually saw in the sky.

   Paraphrase: Turner used his imagination to create the brilliant sunsets and other odd colors he included in his paintings.

☐ a. Paraphrase says too much.
☐ b. Paraphrase doesn't say enough.
☒ c. Paraphrase doesn't agree with the statement about the article.

__3__ Number of correct answers

Record your personal assessment of your work on the Critical Thinking Chart on page 74.

CRITICAL THINKING

Critical Thinking

Put an X in the box next to the correct answer for questions 1, 2, 4, and 5. Follow the directions provided for the other question.

1. Which of the following statements from the article is an opinion rather than a fact?

☒ a. "The famed English artist J. M. W. Turner painted some of his best paintings in 1816."
☐ b. "In 1815 Tambora blew its top."
☐ c. "No one is certain just how much blame belongs to Tambora for the unusually cold summer of 1816."

2. From the article, you can predict that if a huge volcanic eruption occurs,

- ☐ a. a famous artist will fill his or her paintings with strange colors.
- ☐ b. New England will once again endure a year without a summer.
- ☒ c. it will have an impact on the weather.

3. Choose from the letters below to correctly complete the following statement. Write the letters on the lines.

According to the article, the eruption of Mt. Tambora caused __c__ to __a__, and the effect was __b__.

a. form a huge cloud in the upper atmosphere

b. some of the sun's rays could not penetrate the cloud and reach Earth

c. many cubic miles of ash and dust

4. Of the following theme categories, which would this story fit into?

- ☐ a. Weather is always unpredictable.
- ☒ b. People are often at the mercy of nature.
- ☐ c. Farming is a risky undertaking.

5. What did you have to do to answer question 1?

- ☒ a. find an opinion (what someone thinks about something)
- ☐ b. find a cause (why something happened)
- ☐ c. find an effect (something that happened)

__5__ Number of correct answers

Record your personal assessment of your work on the Critical Thinking Chart on page 74.

Personal Response

What new question do you have about this topic?

____

____

____

____

Self-Assessment

I'm proud of how I answered question number _____ in section _______ because

____

____

____

____

Self-Assessment

To get the most out of the Critical Reading series program, you need to take charge of your own progress in improving your reading comprehension and critical thinking skills. Here are some of the features that help you work on those essential skills.

Reading Comprehension Exercises. Complete these exercises immediately after reading the article. They help you recall what you have read, understand the stated and implied main ideas, and add words to your working vocabulary.

Critical Thinking Skills Exercises. These exercises help you focus on the author's approach and purpose, recognize and generate summaries and paraphrases, and identify relationships between ideas.

Personal Response and Self-assessment. Questions in this category help you relate the articles to your personal experience and give you the opportunity to evaluate your understanding of the information in that lesson.

Compare and Contrast Charts. At the end of each unit you will complete a Compare and Contrast chart. The completed chart helps you see what the articles have in common and gives you an opportunity to explore your own ideas about the topics discussed in the articles.

The Graphs. The graphs and charts at the end of each unit enable you to keep track of your progress. Check your graphs regularly with your teacher. Decide whether your progress is satisfactory or whether you need additional work on some skills. What types of exercises are you having difficulty with? Talk with your teacher about ways to work on the skills in which you need the most practice.

UNIT ONE

THE WILD BOY OF AVEYRON

The Farmhouse, *painted by Jean Baptiste Oudry, shows how a French farm looked in the early nineteenth century.*

It was early in the morning, on January 9, 1800, that the Wild Boy of Aveyron was captured. He was found digging for vegetables in the garden of a tanner who lived near Aveyron, in southern France. The tanner managed to capture the Wild Boy, but once he had caught him, he was unsure what to do with this amazing creature.

2 The boy was small, only about four feet tall, but he looked like he was about 11 or 12 years old. He had dark, matted hair and yellowed teeth. He did not speak, but only made strange cries and odd noises. Although the boy did walk upright, the tanner thought that he looked more like an animal than a person.

3 For clothing he wore only the tattered remnants of a shirt, and his whole body was covered with scars. When the tanner took him into his house, it became clear that he was not "housebroken." As the boy warmed himself by the fire, the tanner offered him a plate of food. On the plate were breads, cooked and uncooked meats, fruit, and raw potatoes. The boy grabbed the potatoes and threw them into the fire. Before they were fully cooked, he reached his hand right into the flames and pulled them out. He ate them while they were still steaming hot. He would not touch the rest of the food.

4 When the commissioner of the town heard of the Wild Boy, he rushed to the tanner's house. After watching the boy, he sensed that this was a most unusual case. The boy, he decided, should be sent to Paris where the government could take over his care.

5 First, though, the boy was taken to a nearby town. He was kept there for five months, until all the parents in the area who were searching for missing children had had a chance to look at him. No one claimed him.

6 In those early months, the boy kept up much of his animal behavior. When clothes were put on him, he tore at them until he had pulled them off. He often squatted, but refused to sit in a chair. Whenever he had the opportunity he tried to run away. So, when he was taken out for a walk, he was kept on a leash. Still, even restrained by a leash, he loved to go outside. The temperature might be freezing, but he showed no signs of noticing the cold, even when completely naked.

7 Aside from his walks, the boy appeared to be interested in only one thing: food. He always sniffed his food suspiciously before eating, and he refused to try most new dishes. He ate mainly potatoes, sometimes with peas or beans. The only drink he would accept was water. It took him four months to learn to eat meat, and then he would eat it either raw or cooked—it didn't make any difference to him.

8 The boy usually ate as much as he could. He often stole food from the table to take back to his room. Once, when he had been given more food than he could eat, he grabbed the leftovers and carried them outside. He buried the food in the garden, just as a dog might bury a bone. Soon the boy grew soft and fat.

9 Meanwhile, people tried to find out about the boy's background. When the tanner had caught him, the boy had not been totally wild. After all, he had known how to cook potatoes. And he had been

A portrait of the Wild Boy of Aveyron, 1801

wearing a ragged shirt. So perhaps this boy was not so very wild after all.

10 Researchers found that, in fact, the boy had been living in the wild for at least three years. He had first been seen in 1797 in a town more than 70 miles from the tanner's cottage. There, several people had seen a wild boy running naked in the mountains. The sight of people frightened him, and he had run away each time he saw them.

11 Early in 1798, he was captured and put on display in a town square. He escaped, and hunters later caught him again. That time he was brought to the home of an old widow. She dressed him in a shirt and showed him how to cook potatoes. After a week he ran away again.

12 For the next two years, he prowled around the outskirts of many small towns. Slowly, he learned to trust people. He began to walk right into farmhouses. There he would wait quietly until he was given some food, and then he would disappear.

13 Although the police tried, they could learn nothing more about the boy's early life. A long scar across his neck suggested foul play. Some people thought that his neck had been cut and he had been left for dead in the woods. But why? And by whom? These questions would never be answered.

14 When the Wild Boy of Aveyron finally reached Paris, he was put in a school for deaf mutes. A priest there took on the task of trying to train him. This priest was famous for his work with deaf mutes. But he soon grew impatient with the Wild Boy. Before long he stopped trying to teach him. The boy became an outcast, even among the deaf children. Except for the visitors who came to stare at the Wild Boy, he was totally neglected.

15 Late in 1800, however, a young doctor named Itard arrived at the school. He grew very interested in the Wild Boy. Convinced that the boy was not an idiot or a savage, Itard named him Victor. He spent the next five years trying to teach Victor how to talk.

16 Itard also appointed a woman, Madame Guérin, as Victor's caretaker. This woman cooked and cleaned for Victor and was very kind to him. With a caretaker and a teacher, Victor began to make progress. He learned how to do simple tasks, such as setting the table and dressing himself. Before long he stopped wetting his bed and learned to keep his room tidy. He responded to hugs and loved to be tickled. Victor even learned to recognize the letters of the alphabet.

17 But Victor could not learn how to speak. Possibly his vocal cords had become paralyzed. Because he'd lived in the woods with no people to talk to, he hadn't used them for years. Perhaps they had simply not developed. In any event, after five years Itard gave up. He wrote two papers about Victor but then he forgot about him.

18 With Itard gone, people stopped calling the boy Victor. They just referred to him as The Savage. He and Madame Guérin were moved into a small house, where they lived until 1828, when Victor died. No one bothered to make a note of the cause of his death. And today, because no record was made, no one knows where Victor was buried.

19 The Wild Boy of Aveyron was not the only child ever to be found in an untamed state. In 1920, two young girls were discovered in a cave in India. They were curled up with two wolf cubs. One girl died soon after being captured. The other lived for nine years, just long enough to learn how to walk and say a few words. In 1970, a boy was seen running wild with a herd of gazelles in France. Whenever the herd rested, the boy sniffed and licked the animals just as any gazelle would do.

20 No one can fully explain the phenomenon of children living in the wild. How do they manage to survive? When captured, they appear to be severely retarded. But have they been living in the wild because they are retarded and have been abandoned, or do they seem retarded because they have been abandoned and have lived in the woods for so long? These are questions that remain unanswered.

If you have been timed while reading this article, enter your reading time below. Then turn to the Words-per-Minute Table on page 71 and look up your reading speed (words per minute). Then enter your reading speed on the Reading Speed graph on page 72.

Reading Time: Lesson 1

________ : ________

Minutes *Seconds*

A Finding the Main Idea

One statement below expresses the main idea of the article. One statement is too general, or too broad. The other statement explains only part of the article; it is too narrow. Label the statements using the following key:

M—Main Idea **B—Too Broad** **N—Too Narrow**

_______ 1. Before the Wild Boy of Aveyron was captured, he had been living in the woods in southern France for at least three years.

_______ 2. Some children, such as the Wild Boy of Aveyron, have been found living in the wild, and no one knows how they came to be living in the woods or how they manage to survive.

_______ 3. Some children are raised in situations that are very different from the lifestyles most people are used to.

_______ Score 15 points for a correct M answer.

_______ Score 5 points for each correct B or N answer.

_______ **Total Score:** Finding the Main Idea

B Recalling Facts

How well do you remember the facts in the article? Put an X in the box next to the answer that correctly completes each statement about the article.

1. When the Wild Boy was captured by the tanner near Aveyron,
   - ☐ a. he refused to drink water.
   - ☐ b. his body was covered with scars.
   - ☐ c. he was afraid of fire.
2. People who searched for information about the boy after he was captured near Aveyron found that
   - ☐ a. he had been abandoned when he was a baby.
   - ☐ b. hunters had once tried to kill him.
   - ☐ c. he had first been seen three years earlier in a town 70 miles away.
3. The two girls in India were found
   - ☐ a. cooking potatoes over an open fire.
   - ☐ b. hiding from a pack of wolves.
   - ☐ c. curled up with wolf cubs in a cave.
4. Under the instruction of Itard, Victor learned to
   - ☐ a. perform simple tasks such as setting the table.
   - ☐ b. eat meat.
   - ☐ c. say a few words.
5. Madame Guérin
   - ☐ a. taught Victor how to cook potatoes.
   - ☐ b. kept Victor on a leash.
   - ☐ c. cared for Victor until he died.

Score 5 points for each correct answer.

_______ **Total Score:** Recalling Facts

C Making Inferences

When you combine your own experience and information from a text to draw a conclusion that is not directly stated in that text, you are making an inference. Below are five statements that may or may not be inferences based on information in the article. Label the statements using the following key:

C—Correct Inference **F—Faulty Inference**

_____ 1. The Wild Boy did not survive in the woods by hunting and eating wild animals.

_____ 2. Even before he began living in the woods, Victor would only eat potatoes.

_____ 3. Victor was happier living in Paris than he had been in the woods.

_____ 4. During his years in the woods, the Wild Boy faced many hardships.

_____ 5. After Itard left, Madame Guérin continued to take care of Victor only because she was ordered to.

Score 5 points for each correct answer.

_____ **Total Score:** Making Inferences

D Using Words Precisely

Each numbered sentence below contains an underlined word or phrase from the article. Following the sentence are three definitions. One definition is closest to the meaning of the underlined word. One definition is opposite or nearly opposite. Label those two definitions using the following key; do not label the remaining definition.

C—Closest **O—Opposite or Nearly Opposite**

1. For clothing he wore only the <u>tattered</u> remnants of a shirt, and his whole body was covered with scars.

_____ a. checkered

_____ b. ragged

_____ c. well-kept

2. He often <u>squatted</u>, but refused to sit in a chair.

_____ a. stood

_____ b. jumped

_____ c. crouched

3. For the next two years he <u>prowled around</u> the outskirts of many small towns.

_____ a. terrorized

_____ b. sneaked around

_____ c. walked boldly through

4. A long scar across his neck suggested <u>foul play</u>.

_____ a. a violent act

_____ b. a game

_____ c. an accident

5. But have they been living in the wild because they are retarded and have been abandoned, or do they seem retarded because they have been abandoned and have lived in the woods for so long?

_____ a. neglected

_____ b. well cared for

_____ c. beaten

_____ Score 3 points for each correct C answer.

_____ Score 2 points for each correct O answer.

_____ **Total Score:** Using Words Precisely

Enter the four total scores in the spaces below, and add them together to find your Reading Comprehension Score. Then record your score on the graph on page 73.

Score	Question Type	Lesson 1
_____	Finding the Main Idea	
_____	Recalling Facts	
_____	Making Inferences	
_____	Using Words Precisely	
_____	**Reading Comprehension Score**	

Author's Approach

Put an X in the box next to the correct answer.

1. What does the author mean by the statement "when the tanner took him into the house, it became clear that he was not 'housebroken'"?

☐ a. The Wild Boy was terrified of being enclosed in a house.

☐ b. The Wild Boy began breaking items in the house.

☐ c. The Wild Boy relieved himself on the floor.

2. What is the author's purpose in writing "The Wild Boy of Aveyron"?

☐ a. to inform the reader about children living in the wild

☐ b. to express an opinion about the people who took care of the Wild Boy

☐ c. to emphasize the similarities between animals and untamed children

3. From the statements below, choose those that you believe the author would agree with.

☐ a. Itard lost interest in the Wild Boy after he realized that the child would never learn to speak.

☐ b. The Wild Boy was grateful for being rescued from the wild.

☐ c. When he was first found, the Wild Boy was physically and emotionally retarded.

4. The author tells this story mainly by

☐ a. telling the story of one wild child.

☐ b. telling stories about several different wild children.

☐ c. using his or her imagination and creativity.

_____ Number of correct answers

Record your personal assessment of your work on the Critical Thinking Chart on page 74.

Summarizing and Paraphrasing

Put an X in the box next to the correct answer for question 3. Follow the directions provided for the other questions.

1. Complete the following one-sentence summary of the article using the lettered phrases from the phrase bank below. Write the letters on the lines.

Phrase Bank:
a. the efforts made to civilize him
b. his life and death alone with Madame Guérin
c. the child's capture in 1800

The article about the Wild Boy of Aveyron begins with __________, goes on to explain __________, and ends with __________.

2. Reread paragraph 16 in the article. Below, write a summary of the paragraph in no more than 25 words.

____

____

____

____

Reread your summary and decide whether it covers the important ideas in the paragraph. Next, decide how to shorten the summary to 15 words or less without leaving out any essential information. Write this summary below.

____

____

____

3. Choose the best one-sentence paraphrase for the following sentence from the article:

   "He always sniffed his food suspiciously before eating, and he refused to try most new dishes."

- ☐ a. The Wild Boy wouldn't eat anything new because he thought the townspeople were trying to poison him.
- ☐ b. The Wild Boy was suspicious of new foods and new smells.
- ☐ c. The Wild Boy thought the food the townspeople offered him didn't smell very good.

________ Number of correct answers

Record your personal assessment of your work on the Critical Thinking Chart on page 74.

Critical Thinking

Put an X in the box next to the correct answer for questions 2 and 4. Follow the directions provided for the other questions.

1. For each statement below, write O if it expresses an opinion or F if it expresses a fact.

________ a. Children who live in the wild are severely retarded.

________ b. If the Wild Boy had not been kept on a leash, he would have run away.

________ c. The Wild Boy's parents cut the child's throat and then left him for dead in the woods.

2. From the article, you can predict that if someone had captured the boy seen running with the gazelles, the child would have

- ☐ a. died.
- ☐ b. become soft and fat.
- ☐ c. tried to escape.

CRITICAL THINKING

3. Choose from the letters below to correctly complete the following statement. Write the letters on the lines.

   In the article, __________ and __________ are alike.

   a. the priest who worked with deaf mutes

   b. Victor

   c. Itard

4. What was the effect of Madame Guérin's kindness toward Victor?

☐ a. He learned how to say a few words.

☐ b. He began to respond to hugs.

☐ c. He became an outcast.

5. Which paragraphs from the article provide evidence that supports your answer to question 3?

____

________ Number of correct answers

Record your personal assessment of your work on the Critical Thinking Chart on page 74.

Personal Response

How do you think you would feel if you were a wild child and someone captured you?

____

____

____

____

Self-Assessment

What concepts or ideas from the article were difficult?

____

____

____

____

Which were easy?

____

____

____

____

LESSON 2

VOODOO MAGIC

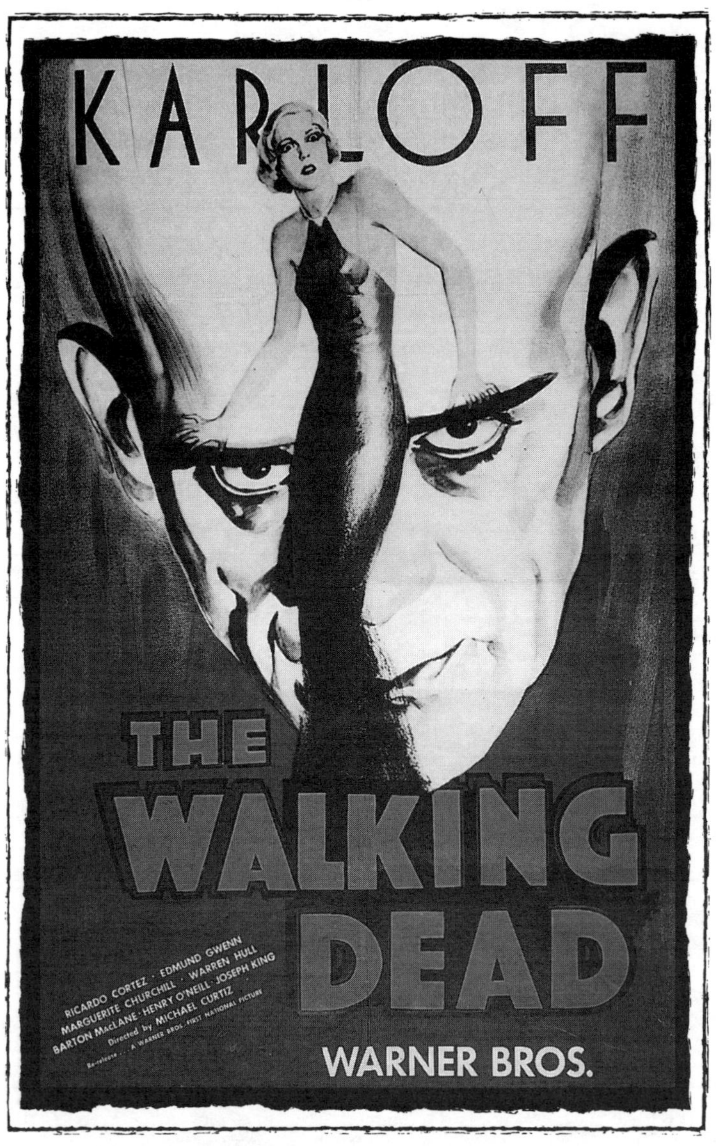

In the 1936 Warner Brothers movie The Walking Dead, *Boris Karloff plays a man wrongfully executed who is brought back to life.*

Can a person be scared to death? Can a person really die from nothing but sheer terror? Many of us may doubt it, but here is one case that is hard to explain.

2 In 1969, a 22-year-old woman ran into a hospital in Baltimore. She was screaming wildly that she was about to die. What was her illness? There was none. Yet, the woman insisted that she was going to die. Her reason was a simple one. She said that she was hexed.

3 The woman told doctors that she had been born in Georgia on Friday the 13th. Perhaps because of the unlucky date, the midwife who delivered her had put her under a voodoo curse. This same midwife also cursed two other baby girls born on the same day.

4 One girl's curse was to die before she turned 16. The girl died in a car accident at the age of 15. The second girl's curse was to die before her 21st birthday. This girl was shot and killed during a gunfight in a night club. She would have turned 21 the very next day.

5 Was it mere coincidence that these two women died when the midwife had

declared they would? To most observers, this is the only sensible explanation. After all, the midwife was nowhere near the scene of either death. But the woman who ran into the Baltimore hospital blamed the deaths of these two girls on the midwife's curse. She believed that voodoo magic had caused the tragedies.

6 The woman told the doctors at the hospital of her own curse. According to the midwife, she was doomed to die before the age of 23, and her 23rd birthday was only three days away. She was convinced that she would die before that day.

7 The doctors performed tests on the woman, but could find nothing wrong. Still, just to be safe, they admitted her to the hospital. But a hospital bed was not safe enough. The next morning the woman was found dead in her room. No cause for her death was ever discovered.

8 What killed this woman? Some people believe that she was the victim of "voodoo death." Dr. Walter B. Cannon, of Harvard University, has stated that extreme terror may kill a person. Great stress can cause the blood pressure to drop sharply. This reduces the flow of blood to the body. Vital organs, such as the heart, are affected. If the change is drastic enough, the result can be death.

9 Such extreme cases are rare, of course. There are only a few things in life scary enough to produce such a strong reaction. But voodoo seems to be one of them.

10 Voodoo is a kind of religion that originally came from Africa. Magic plays a major part in this religion. Today it is most often performed on the Caribbean island of Haiti. There it thrives on the strong native belief that the spirit world is the most important world. This belief is so powerful that it dominates the culture of Haiti. People are sure that nothing is beyond the reach of voodoo magic. They believe that curses can cause all sorts of evil things to happen.

11 Belief in the power of voodoo magic certainly accounts for some of the incredible tales that surround it. Just like the woman in the Baltimore hospital, some people believe so strongly in a curse that they actually cause it to come true. But voodoo is more than a set of ideas that people believe. Sometimes a curse is given a little outside help. Voodoo priests, or houngans, sometimes secretly use drugs to work their evil deeds.

12 The most famous act that houngans perform is the creation of zombies. For this they use all aspects of voodoo magic. Zombies are believed to be "walking dead." They are said to be the resurrected bodies of people who died. These bodies are used for slave labor. They can move and work, but, according to native beliefs, they have no souls or minds. They are under the complete control of their master.

13 In one case, a voodoo priest was attracted to a certain young woman. When he found that the feeling was not

This image represents a powerful voodoo medicine. Voodoo influences are still felt in various areas throughout the world, including Haiti and Brazil.

mutual and, in fact, that she was engaged to marry someone else, the houngan became angry. Hurt and rejected, he put a curse on the woman. Within days, she fell ill and died. After her death, two strange things happened. When her body was laid out, the coffin proved to be too short. The woman's head had to be twisted to the side so that she would fit inside. Later, during the wake, a cigarette was dropped on the woman's foot by accident. It left a small but noticeable burn.

14 After the burial, rumors began to arise in the town. A woman with a twisted neck and a burn mark on her foot had been seen in the company of the houngan. These stories were soon forgotten. But years later a woman with a twisted neck and burn mark on her foot again showed up in the town. Many people recognized her as the woman who had been cursed by the voodoo priest.

15 How could this woman have come back to life? Obviously, she had never really died in the first place. Rather, it seems that she had been drugged by the houngan. Experts believe that, like all zombies, she had been so heavily drugged that she appeared to be dead. It was in this state that she was buried. Within hours, however, the houngan dug her up. He then kept her drugged and made her his slave.

16 Houngans are able to get away with this because the native people have great respect for them. No one ever questions a houngan's ability to make a zombie by putting a curse on someone. And so, when the natives see a zombie they do not ask where it came from. It is part of their training not to question the houngan.

17 Partly because of this, most zombies never escape their slavery. The woman with the twisted neck was one who did. The houngan who kept her as a zombie for many years repented at last and released her. However, she never returned to normal. She spent the rest of her life as a speechless idiot.

18 Clairvius Narcisse was luckier. In 1962 Clairvius, who lived in Haiti, suddenly became sick. A few days later, the local doctor pronounced him dead and had him buried. Although he too had been given powerful drugs, he does remember being lowered into the ground. He also recalls hearing the dirt fall onto his coffin. Shortly afterward, two men lifted him from the grave, tied him up and took him to a farm. There Clairvius joined 100 other members of the "walking dead." He became a zombie and was made to work as a field hand.

19 One day, for some reason, he did not receive his drugs and he awoke. Realizing what had happened to him, he fled the farm. But he did not dare go back to his village for fear that the houngan would find him. It was only after 18 years, when the man he suspected of drugging him had died, that Clairvius returned home. The people of the village welcomed him back, and Clairvius even paid a visit to his old grave.

20 Clearly, voodoo is a complex form of magic. Sometimes the drugs used in voodoo cause terrible things, such as zombiism. Sometimes simply a strong belief in the power of voodoo can cause death. This happened to the woman in the Baltimore hospital. And sometimes voodoo seems to work its magic in a mysterious way. The deaths of the girls born on Friday the 13th, for example, cannot be explained by either drugs or strong belief. Whether drugs, faith, or unknown agents are at work, however, voodoo magic has a serious effect on the lives of the people who believe in and practice it.

If you have been timed while reading this article, enter your reading time below. Then turn to the Words-per-Minute Table on page 71 and look up your reading speed (words per minute). Then enter your reading speed on the Reading Speed graph on page 72.

Reading Time: Lesson 2

________ : ________

Minutes *Seconds*

A Finding the Main Idea

One statement below expresses the main idea of the article. One statement is too general, or too broad. The other statement explains only part of the article; it is too narrow. Label the statements using the following key:

M—Main Idea **B—Too Broad** **N—Too Narrow**

_______ 1. Voodoo magic comes from Africa and is now practiced mostly in Haiti.

_______ 2. Voodoo magic is a complex form of magic that can affect people's lives through drugs, strong faith, or unknown agents.

_______ 3. Strong, unexplained forces can have a serious effect on the lives of people who believe in them.

_______ Score 15 points for a correct M answer.

_______ Score 5 points for each correct B or N answer.

_______ **Total Score:** Finding the Main Idea

B Recalling Facts

How well do you remember the facts in the article? Put an X in the box next to the answer that correctly completes each statement about the article.

1. The young woman in Baltimore died
   - ☐ a. in a hospital.
   - ☐ b. in a car accident.
   - ☐ c. on her sixteenth birthday.
2. Voodoo was first practiced in
   - ☐ a. Haiti.
   - ☐ b. Georgia.
   - ☐ c. Africa.
3. The "walking dead" are called
   - ☐ a. houngans.
   - ☐ b. voodoo priests.
   - ☐ c. zombies.
4. The cigarette burn was on the woman's
   - ☐ a. foot.
   - ☐ b. neck.
   - ☐ c. head.
5. Medical experts think that "voodoo death" might be caused by
   - ☐ a. a houngan's spell.
   - ☐ b. extreme terror.
   - ☐ c. drugs.

Score 5 points for each correct answer.

_______ **Total Score:** Recalling Facts

C Making Inferences

When you combine your own experience and information from a text to draw a conclusion that is not directly stated in that text, you are making an inference. Below are five statements that may or may not be inferences based on information in the article. Label the statements using the following key:

C—Correct Inference **F—Faulty Inference**

_______ 1. People born in Haiti on Friday the 13th usually die young.

_______ 2. The doctors in Baltimore did not take proper care of the young woman.

_______ 3. A houngan must dig up a zombie grave soon after burial.

_______ 4. Houngans probably create zombies to save on the cost of labor.

_______ 5. Houngans are very powerful people on the island of Haiti.

Score 5 points for each correct answer.

_______ **Total Score:** Making Inferences

D Using Words Precisely

Each numbered sentence below contains an underlined word or phrase from the article. Following the sentence are three definitions. One definition is closest to the meaning of the underlined word. One definition is opposite or nearly opposite. Label those two definitions using the following key; do not label the remaining definition.

C—Closest **O—Opposite or Nearly Opposite**

1. She said that she was hexed.

_______ a. blessed

_______ b. terrified

_______ c. cursed

2. Vital organs, such as the heart, are affected.

_______ a. large

_______ b. essential

_______ c. unnecessary

3. This belief is so powerful that it dominates the culture of Haiti. People are sure that nothing is beyond the reach of voodoo magic.

_______ a. has great power over

_______ b. does not affect

_______ c. replaces

4. Was it mere coincidence that these two women died when the midwife had declared they would?

_______ a. chance

_______ b. magic

_______ c. a well-laid plan

5. There it thrives on the strong belief that the spirit world is the most important world.

_______ a. fails

_______ b. succeeds

_______ c. depends

_______ Score 3 points for each correct C answer.

_______ Score 2 points for each correct O answer.

_______ **Total Score:** Using Words Precisely

Enter the four total scores in the spaces below, and add them together to find your Reading Comprehension Score. Then record your score on the graph on page 73.

Score	Question Type	Lesson 2
_______	Finding the Main Idea	
_______	Recalling Facts	
_______	Making Inferences	
_______	Using Words Precisely	
_______	**Reading Comprehension Score**	

Author's Approach

Put an X in the box next to the correct answer.

1. The main purpose of the first paragraph is to

☐ a. convince the reader that voodoo magic is powerful.

☐ b. grab the reader's attention.

☐ c. convey a fearful mood.

2. What does the author imply by saying "but he did not dare go back to his village for fear that the houngan would find him"?

☐ a. Clairvius was afraid that the houngan would really kill him.

☐ b. Clairvius was afraid that the houngan would put a hex on him.

☐ c. Clairvius was afraid that the houngan would turn him into a zombie again.

3. Choose the statement below that best describes the author's position in paragraph 15.

☐ a. Drugs, rather than a voodoo curse, creates zombies.

☐ b. The houngan caused the woman to come back to life after she had died.

☐ c. People who take drugs turn into zombies.

4. The author probably wrote this article in order to

☐ a. persuade readers that the spiritual world is the most important world.

☐ b. entertain readers with stories about voodoo magic.

☐ c. encourage readers to question the power of voodoo.

_______ Number of correct answers

Record your personal assessment of your work on the Critical Thinking Chart on page 74.

Summarizing and Paraphrasing

Put an X in the box next to the correct answer for question 2. Follow the directions provided for the other question.

1. Look for the important ideas and events in paragraphs 6 and 7. Summarize those paragraphs in one or two sentences.

____

____

____

____

2. Read the statement about the article below. Then read the paraphrase of that statement. Choose the reason that best tells why the paraphrase does not say the same thing as the statement.

   Statement: The woman in Baltimore who had been placed under a voodoo curse at birth probably died because she believed so strongly in its power.

   Paraphrase: The Baltimore woman died as a result of a voodoo curse.

☐ a. Paraphrase says too much.

☐ b. Paraphrase doesn't say enough.

☐ c. Paraphrase doesn't agree with the statement about the article.

______ Number of correct answers

Record your personal assessment of your work on the Critical Thinking Chart on page 74.

Critical Thinking

Put an X in the box next to the correct answer for questions 1, 2, and 5. Follow the directions provided for the other questions.

1. Which of the following statements from the article is an opinion rather than a fact?

☐ a. "Sometimes a curse is given a little outside help."

☐ b. "The death of the girls born on Friday the 13th, for example, cannot be explained by either drugs or strong belief."

☐ c. "Great stress can cause the blood pressure to drop sharply."

2. From what the article told about voodoo priests, you can predict that

☐ a. they would take a lot of drugs.

☐ b. their actions would never be opposed by the native people.

☐ c. they would stop using drugs to cause zombiism.

3. Choose from the letters below to correctly complete the following statement. Write the letters on the lines.

   On the positive side, ______, but on the negative side ______.

   a. the houngan released the woman with the twisted neck

   b. Clairvius escaped from slavery under the houngan

   c. she never regained her speech or mental abilities

4. Read paragraph 13. Then choose from the letters below to correctly complete the following statement. Write the letters on the lines.

   According to paragraph 13, the ______ because the ______.

   a. woman rejected him

   b. voodoo priest put a hex on a young woman

   c. woman died

CRITICAL THINKING

5. What did you have to do to answer question 3?

- ☐ a. find an opinion (what someone thinks about something)
- ☐ b. find a contrast (how things are different)
- ☐ c. find a cause (why something happened)

_______ Number of correct answers

Record your personal assessment of your work on the Critical Thinking Chart on page 74.

Personal Response

What new question do you have about this topic?

Self-Assessment

I can't really understand how

MYSTERIES OF EASTER ISLAND

These stone faces on Easter Island are the seven Moai monumental heads called Ahu Akivi.

Huge stone faces stare out to sea from the shores of Easter Island. Their vacant eyes and grim smiles seem both to beckon visitors and to warn them away. If these statues could talk, the mysteries of Easter Island would be revealed. But since they can't, many questions still remain unanswered about this South Pacific island.

2 For centuries, the outside world did not even know Easter Island existed. Then in 1722, a Dutch explorer named Jacob Roggeveen stumbled upon it. He named the island "Easter" after the day he first spied it. The local name for the island is Rapa Nui.

3 In describing the island, Roggeveen minced no words. He wrote, "[I]ts wasted appearance could give no other impression than of a singular poverty and barrenness." Indeed, there was not a single tree on the 64-square-mile chunk of land. There was not a bush over 10 feet tall. The island had no animals except the chickens raised by islanders. Aside from the insects that buzzed about, there were no wild creatures at all.

4 The islanders who greeted Roggeveen paddled canoes out to his ship. The

canoes were flimsy and full of holes. It was clear to Roggeveen that these people had no knowledge of shipbuilding. In fact, they had no knowledge of anything beyond their island. Until Roggeveen's arrival, the islanders had assumed they were the only humans in the world.

5 Looking around, Roggeveen could not understand how these forlorn people could have built such stunning statues. The statues stood 30 feet high and weighed up to 82 tons. And there weren't just one or two of them; there were hundreds. Oddly, the statues all had the same shape. They all featured a giant head with long ears, empty eyes, and a sharp nose. Each head rested on a short, thick body.

6 The statues were made of rock found in just one place on the island. That meant the carvings had somehow been transported to their current sites along the shore. But it didn't make sense. The islanders had no timber, no heavy ropes. They had no machines, no motors, not even wheels. What had they used to move the massive statues?

7 Later, as other outsiders came to Easter Island, some facts emerged. But each new piece of information only added to the mystery. Scientists found that all the statues had been built before 1500. Then the work abruptly ceased. Hundreds of half-finished carvings were left lying among the rocks. It was as though the artists had been called away from their work one day and never returned to it. Meanwhile, cannibalism suddenly erupted on the island. Human bones started to turn up in people's garbage heaps. What drastic events could have forced the islanders to begin eating human flesh?

8 Then, too, there is the question of how people got to Easter Island in the first place. The island is a remote spot. Its nearest neighbors are on Pitcairn Island, about 1,400 miles to the west. The nearest continent is South America, 2,000 miles to the east. So how did the islanders' ancestors reach Easter Island? And why did they choose to stay in such a barren place?

9 Many theories have been put forth to explain the findings on Easter Island. Swiss writer Erich Von Daniken claims that its earliest settlers were not humans. He thinks sophisticated aliens from another planet once landed on earth. These aliens, says Von Daniken, built the statues.

10 Other outrageous theories have been proposed. A man named Alan Alford believes ancient gods used the island as a prison for their unfaithful slaves. The slaves built statues to attract the attention of rescuers. Statue building stopped, Alford says, when the slaves were rescued.

11 Most scientists reject such notions. They suggest more likely theories. For instance, they think the island's settlers must have come from one of two places: Polynesia, which is about 2,500 miles to the west, or South America, which lies to the east.

12 Polynesia seems more likely. Polynesians knew how to build boats for

Ahu Tahai, another of the stone faces on Easter Island

long trips. In addition, their crops were the same as the ones grown on the island. And the language spoken on Easter Island is a form of Polynesian.

13 Still, there are problems with this theory. The islanders cut and assembled their statues in a unique way. The only other people who used this technique were South Americans. Also, Polynesians had no written language. But the islanders did. They called it Rongorongo.

14 Experts think the first settlers—whoever they were—had good reasons for staying on Easter Island. At that time—about A.D. 400—Easter Island was not a barren wasteland. It had plenty of trees. It also had ferns, flowers, and other plants. At least 25 kinds of birds made their nests on the island.

15 Old garbage heaps show that the early islanders ate bananas and sweet potatoes. They also ate birds, seals, and chickens. Dolphins were a basic part of their diet. Since dolphins don't live near shore, this fact provides further proof that the islanders knew how to build sturdy boats. Old charcoal pits indicated that meals were cooked over log fires.

16 Apparently, the islanders prospered, and their numbers grew. They needed more homes and more food. This growth, in turn, meant a need for more lumber, firewood, and fishing boats. Every day, trees were cut down to meet these demands.

17 Meanwhile, the statue-carving tradition had begun. No one knows why the islanders built statues. Certainly no one knows why they made the statues so big or why they made them all the same. Many researchers assume the statues served a religious purpose. But what was it? Were the statues built to honor favorite gods? Or to keep evil gods at bay? Or did they serve some other function altogether?

18 Whatever their purpose, the statues presented islanders with a problem. The mammoth blocks of stone had to be moved from the carving pit to the edges of the island. Scientists believe islanders tied the statues to wooden sleds. They then dragged the sleds over wooden rollers. That method would have worked well. But, it, too, would have required cutting down many trees.

19 In the long run, say scientists, it was the destruction of all those trees that doomed Easter Island. By 1500, there were no trees left to cut. Suddenly, there was no way to transport statues. That may explain why so many half-finished statues were left in the carving pit. But by then the islanders had an even bigger problem: they were running out of food.

20 Without tree roots in the ground, the soil eroded and crops failed. Without lumber, fishing boats could not be built, so dolphin meat disappeared from people's diets. Finding no trees for nesting, birds no longer came to the island.

21 For a while, people tried to get by on chickens and small sea snails. They ate every wild creature on the island. Finally, they turned to the only other source of food they could find: each other. This was when cannibalism began on Easter Island.

22 During this terrible period, many of the stone statues were knocked down. People moved into caves and other hiding places. They armed themselves with stone spears and daggers. War raged constantly, with the defeated becoming the victors' next meal. The only carvings people made now were modest statuettes. They showed pathetic souls with sunken cheeks and protruding ribs.

23 After a time, the violence died down. The few survivors struggled to start life anew. However, by then, they had forgotten how to build decent boats. That hardly mattered, though, as they had no wood for shipbuilding. They were lucky just to subsist on the ruined island. It was the inhabitants of this place who greeted Jacob Roggeveen in 1722.

24 Today Easter Island belongs to Chile. It is neither the paradise nor the hell it once was. The people here cherish the island's history. But some of its most intriguing secrets still lay locked in stone. No one has been able to decipher the Rongorongo writings. No one has been able to explain the purpose of the statues. As a result, many truths about the island may remain forever unknown.

If you have been timed while reading this article, enter your reading time below. Then turn to the Words-per-Minute Table on page 71 and look up your reading speed (words per minute). Then enter your reading speed on the Reading Speed graph on page 72.

Reading Time: Lesson 3

_______ : _______

Minutes *Seconds*

A Finding the Main Idea

One statement below expresses the main idea of the article. One statement is too general, or too broad. The other statement explains only part of the article; it is too narrow. Label the statements using the following key:

M—Main Idea **B—Too Broad** **N—Too Narrow**

_______ 1. The destruction of trees doomed Easter Island.

_______ 2. Easter Island is a place of many mysteries.

_______ 3. Many different theories have been proposed to explain the strange statues and other findings on Easter Island.

_______ Score 15 points for a correct M answer.

_______ Score 5 points for each correct B or N answer.

_______ **Total Score:** Finding the Main Idea

B Recalling Facts

How well do you remember the facts in the article? Put an X in the box next to the answer that correctly completes each statement about the article.

1. Jacob Roggeveen stumbled upon Easter Island in
   - ☐ a. A.D. 400.
   - ☐ b. 1722.
   - ☐ c. 1500.
2. When Roggeveen arrived on the island, it was
   - ☐ a. barren and poor.
   - ☐ b. a tropical paradise.
   - ☐ c. inhabited by cannibals.
3. Roggeveen found hundreds of statues that
   - ☐ a. stood 30 feet high and weighed up to 82 tons.
   - ☐ b. resembled the inhabitants of the island.
   - ☐ c. he believed had been built by aliens.
4. Scientists discovered that the statues had been built
   - ☐ a. during the 1700s.
   - ☐ b. before 1500.
   - ☐ c. before A.D. 400.
5. Scientists believe the islanders became cannibals
   - ☐ a. after the destruction of trees led to a lack of food.
   - ☐ b. during a civil war over the statues.
   - ☐ c. to keep evil gods at bay.

Score 5 points for each correct answer.

_______ **Total Score:** Recalling Facts

C Making Inferences

When you combine your own experience and information from a text to draw a conclusion that is not directly stated in that text, you are making an inference. Below are five statements that may or may not be inferences based on information in the article. Label the statements using the following key:

C—Correct Inference **F—Faulty Inference**

_______ 1. The islanders feared Roggeveen.

_______ 2. The construction of the massive statues on Easter Island led to the island's destruction.

_______ 3. Rongorongo is spoken on Easter Island today.

_______ 4. The statuettes built while war raged on the island represented the malnourished islanders.

_______ 5. The inhabitants of Easter Island may have descended from the peoples of Polynesia or South America.

Score 5 points for each correct answer.

_______ **Total Score:** Making Inferences

D Using Words Precisely

Each numbered sentence below contains an underlined word or phrase from the article. Following the sentence are three definitions. One definition is closest to the meaning of the underlined word. One definition is opposite or nearly opposite. Label those two definitions using the following key; do not label the remaining definition.

C—Closest **O—Opposite or Nearly Opposite**

1. Their vacant eyes and <u>grim</u> smiles seem both to beckon visitors and to warn them away.

_______ a. cheerful

_______ b. bleak

_______ c. uncertain

2. Its wasted appearance could give no other impression than of a <u>singular</u> poverty and barrenness.

_______ a. remarkable

_______ b. inherited

_______ c. common

3. Looking around, Roggeveen could not understand how these <u>forlorn</u> people could have built such stunning statues.

_______ a. ignorant

_______ b. desolate

_______ c. overjoyed

4. What had they used to move the <u>massive</u> statues?

_______ a. enormous

_______ b. beautiful

_______ c. insignificant

5. Apparently, the islanders prospered, and their numbers grew.

_______ a. flourished

_______ b. diminished

_______ c. fought constantly

_______ Score 3 points for each correct C answer.

_______ Score 2 points for each correct O answer.

_______ **Total Score:** Using Words Precisely

Enter the four total scores in the spaces below, and add them together to find your Reading Comprehension Score. Then record your score on the graph on page 73.

Score	Question Type	Lesson 3
_______	Finding the Main Idea	
_______	Recalling Facts	
_______	Making Inferences	
_______	Using Words Precisely	
_______	**Reading Comprehension Score**	

Author's Approach

Put an X in the box next to the correct answer.

1. Which of the following statements from the article best describes the islanders who greeted Jacob Roggeveen?

☐ a. "They all featured a giant head with long ears, empty eyes, and a sharp nose."

☐ b. "The islanders knew how to build sturdy boats."

☐ c. "They had no knowledge of anything beyond their island."

2. From the statement "other outrageous theories have been proposed," you can conclude that the author wants the reader to think that

☐ a. most scientists accept these theories.

☐ b. these theories should not be taken seriously.

☐ c. scientists have been unable to disprove these theories.

3. In this article, "they were lucky just to subsist on the ruined island" means the islanders

☐ a. had good reasons for staying on Easter Island.

☐ b. could barely survive on their barren land.

☐ c. thought they were the only humans in the world.

4. How is the author's purpose for writing the article expressed in paragraph 7?

☐ a. The author expresses a negative opinion about cannibalism.

☐ b. The author conveys a dark and frightening mood.

☐ c. The author provides some information about the island but raises new questions about its history.

_______ Number of correct answers

Record your personal assessment of your work on the Critical Thinking Chart on page 74.

Summarizing and Paraphrasing

Put an X in the box next to the correct answer.

1. Below are summaries of the article. Choose the summary that says all the most important things about the article but in the fewest words.

☐ a. The early inhabitants of Easter Island built massive statues. The construction of these statues eventually led to cannibalism and the destruction of the island. However, scientists have been unable to answer many other questions about the island.

☐ b. The inhabitants of Easter Island began to eat human flesh after all the other sources of food on the island had been exhausted.

☐ c. Scientists believe that the construction of the statues on Easter Island led to the island's destruction. However, many questions about the place and its statues remain unanswered.

2. Choose the sentence that correctly restates the following sentence from the article:

"War raged constantly, with the defeated becoming the victors' next meal."

☐ a. The warring islanders ate those who were defeated in battle.

☐ b. After the islanders won the war, they celebrated with a large meal.

☐ c. Those who were defeated in battle were starved to death.

________ Number of correct answers

Record your personal assessment of your work on the Critical Thinking Chart on page 74.

Critical Thinking

Put an X in the box next to the correct answer for questions 2 and 5. Follow the directions provided for the other questions.

1. For each statement below, write O if it expresses an opinion or F if it expresses a fact.

________ a. Ancient gods used Easter Island as a prison for their unfaithful slaves.

________ b. The statues served a religious purpose.

________ c. The early islanders were master shipbuilders.

2. From the information in paragraph 23 you can predict that

☐ a. the islanders probably wanted to eat Roggeveen.

☐ b. the islanders were probably relieved to see Roggeveen.

☐ c. the islanders probably wanted to drive Roggeveen away.

3. Choose from the letters below to correctly complete the following statement. Write the letters on the lines.

In the article the ________ and the ________ are different.

a. massive statues Roggeveen saw in 1722

b. statues made before 1500

c. statues made during the islanders' war

4. Think about cause-effect relationships in the article. Fill in the blanks in the cause-effect chart, drawing from the letters below.

Cause	Effect
Islanders destroyed all the tree roots.	________
________	Cannibalism began on the island.
Fishing boats could no longer be built.	________

a. The inhabitants could find no source of food on the island.

b. Dolphin meat disappeared from the islanders' diets.

c. The soil eroded and crops failed.

5. How are the statues on Easter Island examples of phenomena?

- ☐ a. There is evidence that the statues were built by space aliens.
- ☐ b. The statues all have the same shape and features.
- ☐ c. The function and construction of the statues have never been fully explained.

________ Number of correct answers

Record your personal assessment of your work on the Critical Thinking Chart on page 74.

Personal Response

Would you recommend this article to other students? Explain.

____

____

____

Self-Assessment

The part I found most difficult about the article was

____

____

____

____

I found this difficult because

____

____

____

____

BLACK HOLES

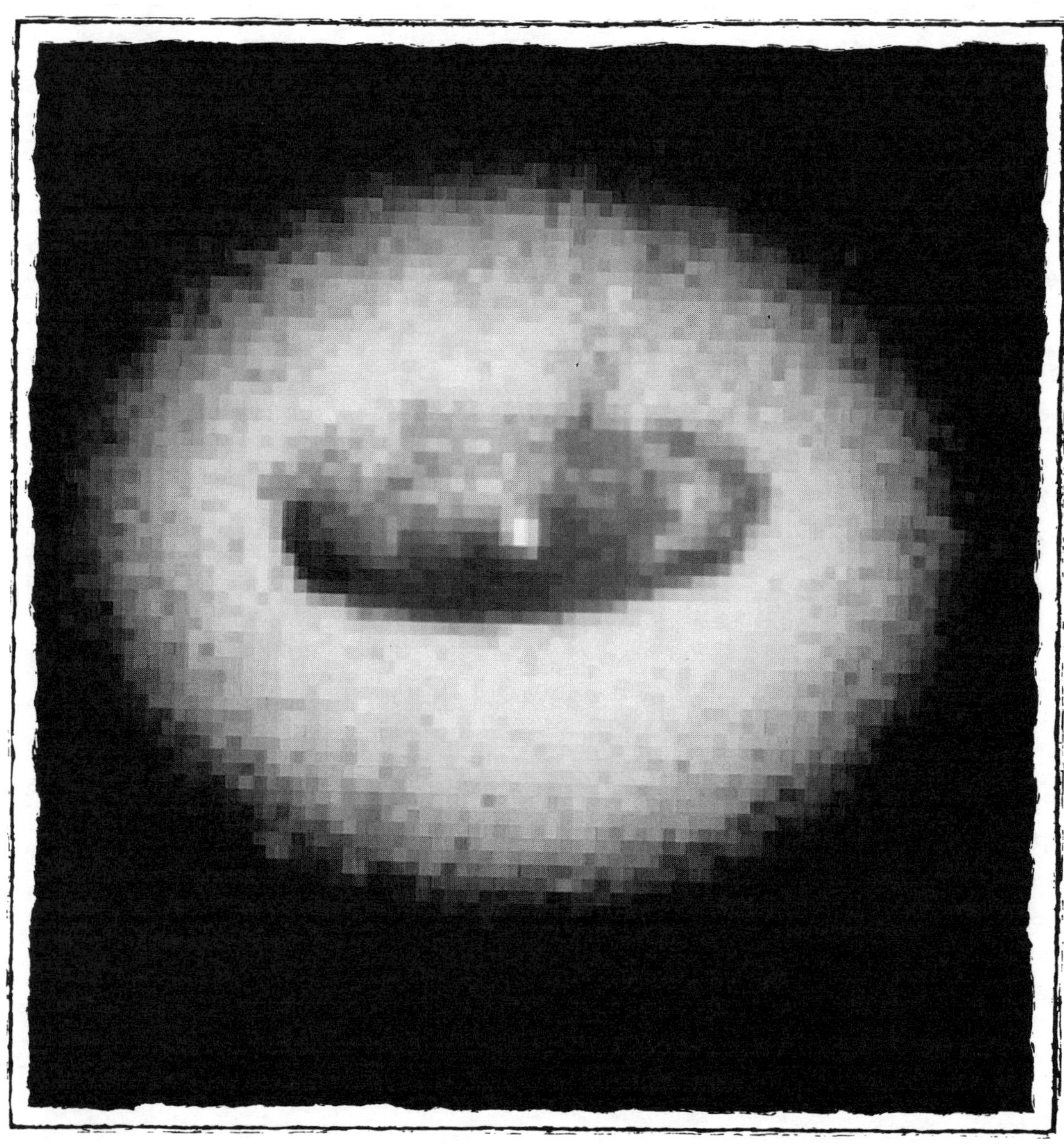

It was a star vastly larger than our own sun. For hundreds of years this giant star burned brightly in its corner of the universe. Then, at the end of its lifespan, a bizarre thing happened. The dying star began to collapse in on itself. While the star was in its death throes, all the matter that made up the star was squeezed together into a smaller and smaller area. Soon the star measured no more than a mile across. Its matter was so tightly packed that a chunk of it the size of a small marble weighed as much as a mountain.

2 As the dead star continued to fall into itself, it brought with it every bit of matter in the area. Every speck of dust, every stray atom, was dragged into it. The star had become a black hole. A black hole is a small area of matter so dense that not even a light beam can escape the pull of its gravity.

3 Since no light can leave black holes, there is no way for us to see them. They are invisible. We know of their existence because of the strange things that happen around them. Light that is traveling

Photo of a black hole provided by the Hubble Space Telescope. The dust disc, the dark oval shape in the center, is about 800 light years across.

through space just vanishes. Very strong x-rays are emitted from invisible objects. These x-rays are thought to be caused by atoms of gas and dust particles bumping into each other as they zoom into the black hole.

4 Just how wild is a black hole? Let's take a look at gravity. A common expression related to gravity is, "What goes up must come down." When someone throws a ball into the air, it must return to Earth. This happens because Earth attracts the ball, or pulls it toward itself. A flowerpot that is knocked off a third-story ledge will always hit the sidewalk. It is only the great thrust of giant rockets that allows the Space Shuttle to escape the pull of Earth's gravity.

5 On a planet with double or triple Earth's gravity, objects would act quite differently, because the pull, or attraction, would be much stronger. A ball thrown into the air would not go very high, and it would plunge quickly back to the surface of the planet. A falling flowerpot would be a lethal weapon. It would kill any luckless pedestrian who might happen to get hit by it. Rockets far more powerful than those used on Earth would be needed to break away from the pull of the planet's gravity.

6 Beams of light, however, would have no trouble at all escaping from this planet. Even if the force of gravity were increased a million times that of Earth, light beams would still not be affected. Humans on such a world, though, would be crushed flatter than their own shadows.

7 Only if the amount of gravity were many billions of times stronger than Earth's would light beams bend back to the surface. That is the case with a black hole. It is hard to imagine just how dense and heavy black hole matter is. A penny made from black hole matter would rip through your pocket and plunge through the earth with the greatest of ease. When it emerged on the other side, it would hover in the air for a moment and then plunge back through the earth.

8 Black holes are the most bizarre objects in the universe. Nothing ever leaves a black hole. No light leaves. No physical objects leave. Once something enters a black hole, it is there forever. Black holes are like permanent detention halls in the sky. If a travel agent were to arrange a flight to a black hole, it would have to be a one-way trip. As the scientist Robert Jastrow said, "It is almost as though the material inside the black hole no longer belongs to our universe."

An artist's impression of a large black hole (lower center) at the center of an active galaxy

9 Suppose, just for the sake of amusement, that you happened to drop into a black hole. What would happen to you? One thing is certain: you would not like it. Whichever part of your body was leading the way would be pulled more strongly by the gravity than the rest of your body.

10 Think of going feet first. Your feet would be pulled down faster than your ears. As a result, you would be drawn into a very thin strand of matter. Then the individual atoms in your body would be pulled apart. The atoms themselves would be torn into neutrons, protons, and electrons. All this would happen within a fraction of one second.

11 Were you to survive the trip, however, some scientists believe that you would emerge in the fourth dimension. You would be in a totally different universe. The point where matter exits from this universe and goes into the next is referred to as a white hole. Some scientists think that black holes might someday serve as time machines of a sort. They would carry people to the remote past or the distant future.

12 To think about black holes means to throw out all our old ideas about time, space, and travel. Scientists believe that there are at least five black holes in our section of the universe. But, then, no one knows for sure. Our knowledge of black holes is based on informed guesswork. Scientists are forced to judge something they cannot see. They will continue investigating these powerful, invisible chunks of matter, hoping to find definite answers. For the rest of us, black holes remain a fantastic mystery whose incredible possibilities lead our minds into dreams and visions of a universe that is far different from what people have always believed it to be.

If you have been timed while reading this article, enter your reading time below. Then turn to the Words-per-Minute Table on page 71 and look up your reading speed (words per minute). Then enter your reading speed on the Reading Speed graph on page 72.

Reading Time: Lesson 4

________ : ________

Minutes *Seconds*

A Finding the Main Idea

One statement below expresses the main idea of the article. One statement is too general, or too broad. The other statement explains only part of the article; it is too narrow. Label the statements using the following key:

M—Main Idea **B—Too Broad** **N—Too Narrow**

_______ 1. Outer space is filled with strange and wonderful phenomena that scientists do not fully understand.

_______ 2. No one has actually seen a black hole because no light can escape from one.

_______ 3. Black holes are strange, extremely dense objects whose existence scientists can only guess about.

_______ Score 15 points for a correct M answer.

_______ Score 5 points for each correct B or N answer.

_______ **Total Score:** Finding the Main Idea

B Recalling Facts

How well do you remember the facts in the article? Put an X in the box next to the answer that correctly completes each statement about the article.

1. A black hole results from the death of a
   - ☐ a. sun like our own.
   - ☐ b. blazing comet.
   - ☐ c. giant star.
2. Gravity in a black hole is
   - ☐ a. twice that of Earth.
   - ☐ b. a hundred times that of Earth.
   - ☐ c. so great that even light can't escape.
3. Black hole matter the size of a marble
   - ☐ a. weighs as much as a mountain.
   - ☐ b. takes two people to lift.
   - ☐ c. would sink several feet into the ground.
4. A trip into a black hole would
   - ☐ a. result in a slow, painful death.
   - ☐ b. take four years to complete.
   - ☐ c. pull a person apart.
5. Some scientists believe that black holes may someday
   - ☐ a. serve as time machines.
   - ☐ b. turn into white holes.
   - ☐ c. be used as relay stations for space travel.

Score 5 points for each correct answer.

_______ **Total Score:** Recalling Facts

C Making Inferences

When you combine your own experience and information from a text to draw a conclusion that is not directly stated in that text, you are making an inference. Below are five statements that may or may not be inferences based on information in the article. Label the statements using the following key:

C—Correct Inference **F—Faulty Inference**

_______ 1. All stars form black holes when they die.

_______ 2. There is no air to breathe in a black hole.

_______ 3. Improved photography will soon allow us to see a black hole.

_______ 4. Light is the last thing to be affected by the pull of gravity.

_______ 5. It is impossible to make a piece of a black hole here on Earth.

Score 5 points for each correct answer.

_______ **Total Score:** Making Inferences

D Using Words Precisely

Each numbered sentence below contains an underlined word or phrase from the article. Following the sentence are three definitions. One definition is closest to the meaning of the underlined word. One definition is opposite or nearly opposite. Label those two definitions using the following key; do not label the remaining definition.

C—Closest **O—Opposite or Nearly Opposite**

1. Then, at the end of its lifespan, a bizarre thing happened.

_______ a. comical

_______ b. weird

_______ c. ordinary

2. Very strong x-rays are emitted from invisible objects.

_______ a. given out

_______ b. studied

_______ c. withheld

3. A falling flowerpot would be a lethal weapon.

_______ a. illegal

_______ b. deadly

_______ c. harmless

4. When it emerged on the other side, it would hover in the air for a moment and then plunge back through Earth.

_______ a. explode

_______ b. sink below

_______ c. float

5. Were you to survive the trip, however, some scientists believe that you would emerge in the fourth dimension.

_______ a. go back

_______ b. die

_______ c. come out

_______ Score 3 points for each correct C answer.

_______ Score 2 points for each correct O answer.

_______ **Total Score:** Using Words Precisely

Enter the four total scores in the spaces below, and add them together to find your Reading Comprehension Score. Then record your score on the graph on page 73.

Score	Question Type	Lesson 4
_______	Finding the Main Idea	
_______	Recalling Facts	
_______	Making Inferences	
_______	Using Words Precisely	
_______	**Reading Comprehension Score**	

Author's Approach

Put an X in the box next to the correct answer.

1. The author uses the first sentence of the article to

☐ a. inform the reader about our own sun.

☐ b. entertain the reader with amazing facts about black holes.

☐ c. compare a star to our own sun.

2. Which of the following statements from the article best describes black holes?

☐ a. "Black holes are the most bizarre objects in the universe."

☐ b. "A black hole is a small area of matter so dense that not even a light beam can escape the pull of its gravity."

☐ c. "To think about black holes means to throw out all our old ideas about time, space, and travel."

3. What does the author imply by saying, "A penny made from black hole matter would rip through your pocket and plunge through the earth with the greatest of ease"?

☐ a. Earth's gravity exerts a very strong pull on black hole matter.

☐ b. Even a small amount of black hole matter is so dense and heavy that no human can hold it.

☐ c. A black hole would destroy Earth in a matter of seconds.

4. How is the author's purpose for writing the article expressed in paragraph 8?

☐ a. The author describes what a trip to a black hole would be like.

☐ b. The author uses facts about black holes to create a frightening mood.

☐ c. The author uses humor, facts, and a quotation to inform the reader about the strange qualities of a black hole.

_______ Number of correct answers

Record your personal assessment of your work on the Critical Thinking Chart on page 74.

Summarizing and Paraphrasing

Put an X in the box next to the correct answer for question 2. Follow the directions provided for the other question.

1. Reread paragraph 1 in the article. Below, write a summary of the paragraph using no more than 25 words.

____

____

____

____

Reread your summary and decide whether it covers the important ideas in the paragraph. Next, decide how to shorten the summary to 15 words or less without leaving out any essential information. Write this summary below.

____

____

____

2. Read the statement about the article below. Then read the paraphrase of that statement. Choose the reason that best tells why the paraphrase does not say the same thing as the statement.

Statement: A person entering a black hole would instantly be drawn into a very thin strand of matter and torn into individual atoms by the object's strong gravitational pull.

Paraphrase: Nothing can escape the pull of a black hole's gravity.

☐ a. Paraphrase says too much.

☐ b. Paraphrase doesn't say enough.

☐ c. Paraphrase doesn't agree with the statement about the article.

_______ Number of correct answers

Record your personal assessment of your work on the Critical Thinking Chart on page 74.

Critical Thinking

Put an X in the box next to the correct answer for questions 1, 2, 4, and 5. Follow the directions provided for the other question.

1. Which of the following statements from the article is an opinion rather than a fact?

☐ a. "Since no light can leave black holes, there is no way for us to see them."

☐ b. "There are at least five black holes in our section of the universe."

☐ c. "It is only the great thrust of giant rockets that allows the Space Shuttle to escape the pull of Earth's gravity."

2. From the article, you can predict that if a spaceship suddenly encountered a black hole in outer space,

☐ a. the passengers onboard the ship would be killed instantly.

☐ b. the passengers would emerge in the fourth dimension.

☐ c. the passengers would enter the distant future.

3. Choose from the letters below to correctly complete the following statement. Write the letters on the lines.

In the article, ________ and ________ are alike.

a. a universe unlike our own

b. black holes

c. the fourth dimension

4. What causes a ball thrown into the air to fall back to the ground?

☐ a. Gravity pulls the object back to Earth.

☐ b. A black hole pulls the object back to Earth.

☐ c. A white hole pulls the object back to Earth.

5. Of the following theme categories, which would this story fit into?

☐ a. the limitations of science

☐ b. humankind's insignificance in the universe

☐ c. Fact is stranger than fiction.

________ Number of correct answers

Record your personal assessment of your work on the Critical Thinking Chart on page 74.

Personal Response

What was most surprising or interesting to you about this article?

____

____

____

Self-Assessment

When reading the article I was having trouble with

____

____

____

____

TRIANGLE OF FEAR

On a calm, clear December afternoon in 1945, Flight 19 took off from the south coast of Florida on a routine Army training mission. The five Avenger planes that made up Flight 19 would never return. Incredibly, a Martin Mariner plane sent to rescue Flight 19 was also lost without a trace. As one Navy officer said at the time, "They vanished as completely as if they'd flown to Mars."

2 Well, Mars was a bit beyond the reach of these airplanes. Yet, whenever planes or ships disappear in the infamous Bermuda Triangle, the wildest stories are heard. Many people think that the waters off the coast of Florida are the deadliest in the world. Legends tell of hundreds of ships and airplanes simply disappearing in the Bermuda Triangle. For this reason, the area is also known as the Hoodoo Sea, or the Limbo of the Lost, or the Triangle of Death.

3 Why is the Bermuda Triangle such a graveyard? Some say that it is a hunting ground for UFOs. According to this theory, UFOs hover above the Bermuda

Five Navy Avenger torpedo bombers disappeared while on a flight from Fort Lauderdale, Florida, on December 5, 1945. This is the best known of all the Bermuda Triangle disappearances.

Triangle waiting to scoop up innocent ships and airplanes. Others say that the lost continent of Atlantis still exists under the sea and is using its magnetic force to pull down ships and planes. Still others claim that the area creates a time warp, causing vessels to vanish into the fourth dimension. Whatever the case, the Bermuda Triangle is made to sound like a place to avoid.

4 In fact, one member of Flight 19 did avoid the Triangle. He claimed he had a premonition about the flight, an unexplainable feeling that something was going to go wrong. So he did not go. The rest of the crew, however, did go. The leader was Lieutenant Charles Taylor, a pilot with over 2,500 hours of flying experience. Flight 19's training mission was to fly 160 miles east, then 40 miles north, then back west to the base at Fort Lauderdale.

5 Not long after the takeoff, trouble developed. Taylor radioed the control tower. "Control tower, this is an emergency. We seem to be off course. We cannot see land. Repeat, we cannot see land."

6 "What is your position?" the tower asked.

7 "We can't be sure of where we are. We seem to be lost."

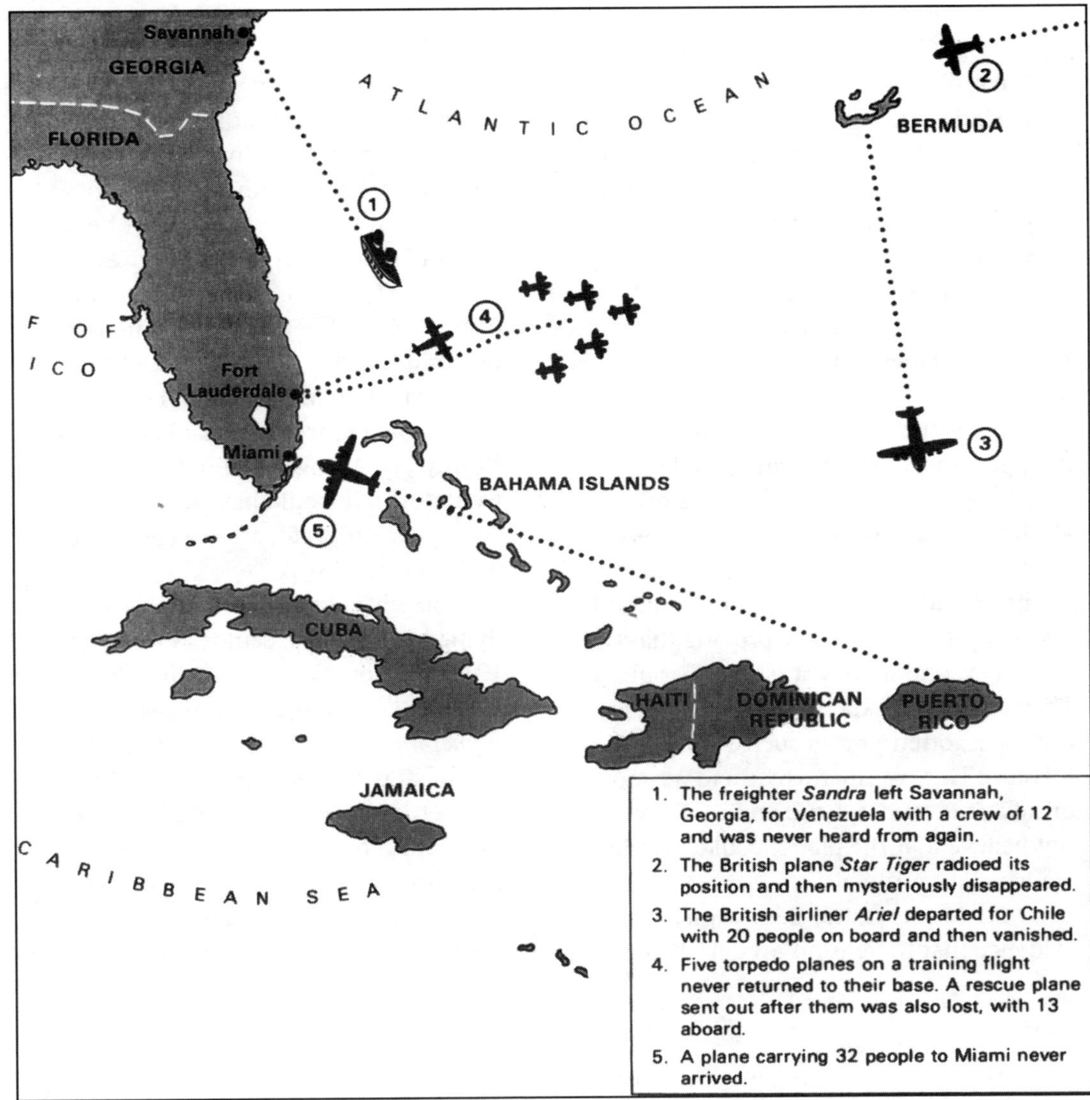

This map shows the area in the Atlantic Ocean known as the Bermuda Triangle.

8 "Head due west," said the tower.

9 "We don't know which way is west. Everything is wrong... strange... we can't be sure of any direction. Even the ocean doesn't look as it should."

10 Later came this message from Flight 19: "We must be about 225 miles northeast of base...it looks like we are..."

11 Then silence.

12 A Martin Mariner flying boat was sent out immediately to rescue the Avengers. But upon entering the Triangle, it too fell silent. The 14 men of Flight 19 were gone. And now 13 more who were involved in the rescue mission were missing too. A massive search of the area by hundreds of boats and planes turned up nothing but water.

13 What is the explanation for these disappearances, which many people regard as the greatest aviation mystery of all time? To true believers in the powers of the Bermuda Triangle, the fate of the five Avengers and the Martin Mariner is just another piece of evidence proving that the Triangle is one spooky stretch of ocean. They argue that experienced pilots could not have gotten lost on such a simple mission. They wonder why there was no oil slick, no wreckage, no bodies. They do not believe that the planes could have just vanished into thin air.

14 On the other hand, there is plenty of evidence that there is no mystery here at all. The Avengers and the Mariner did go down. But skeptics point out that the popular story concerning their disappearance is wrong in almost every way.

15 For example, the pilots were not all experienced airmen. With the exception of Taylor, they were all students. And Taylor was new to the area. The only thing that is really clear from the radio transmissions is that Taylor was completely lost. His compass was not working. At times Taylor thought he was west of Florida, over the Florida Keys in the Gulf of Mexico. But, in fact, he was over the Grand Keys in the Bahamas, east of Florida. Taylor was so confused that he had his men flying in circles. Eventually, at night and in weather that had turned stormy, the Avengers ran out of gas and went down. It would have taken only about 45 seconds for an Avenger to fill with water and sink.

16 And what about the Martin Mariner flying boat that was sent to rescue Flight 19? It did not take off until after dark—at 7:29 P.M. Observers aboard the steamship *Gaines Mills* saw an explosion in midair. The burst of flames occurred exactly where the Martin Mariner was supposed to be. It is not unlikely that the Mariner exploded, for it had a pretty sorry safety record. Gas fumes were always present. Mariners were commonly referred to as "flying gas tanks." A cigarette or a spark could have caused the entire aircraft to burst into a ball of fire.

17 The fate of Flight 19 and the Martin Mariner continues to stir discussion. Since that fateful night in December 1945, several other planes and ships have disappeared in the area of the Bermuda Triangle. This fact has only fueled the fires of debate. But as the U.S. Coast Guard noted in an official communication, "The combined forces of nature and the unpredictability of mankind outdo even the most farfetched science fiction many times each year."

If you have been timed while reading this article, enter your reading time below. Then turn to the Words-per-Minute Table on page 71 and look up your reading speed (words per minute). Then enter your reading speed on the Reading Speed graph on page 72.

Reading Time: Lesson 5

_______ : _______

Minutes *Seconds*

A Finding the Main Idea

One statement below expresses the main idea of the article. One statement is too general, or too broad. The other statement explains only part of the article; it is too narrow. Label the statements using the following key:

M—Main Idea **B—Too Broad** **N—Too Narrow**

______ 1. Both Flight 19 and a Martin Mariner flying boat were lost while flying over the Bermuda Triangle.

______ 2. Because many planes and ships have disappeared in the Bermuda Triangle without a good explanation, many people think the area has strange powers.

______ 3. Many people have been lost at sea under mysterious circumstances.

______ Score 15 points for a correct M answer.

______ Score 5 points for each correct B or N answer.

______ **Total Score:** Finding the Main Idea

B Recalling Facts

How well do you remember the facts in the article? Put an X in the box next to the answer that correctly completes each statement about the article.

1. Flight 19 was
   - ☐ a. a scheduled commercial flight.
   - ☐ b. a routine Army training mission.
   - ☐ c. canceled because of poor weather.
2. Lieutenant Charles Taylor was
   - ☐ a. an experienced pilot.
   - ☐ b. a student pilot.
   - ☐ c. familiar with the Bermuda Triangle.
3. The control tower told Taylor to
   - ☐ a. "head due west."
   - ☐ b. "head due east."
   - ☐ c. "head 225 miles northeast."
4. The Martin Mariner was
   - ☐ a. an island in the Florida Keys.
   - ☐ b. a flying boat.
   - ☐ c. a steamship.
5. The flying boat was known for
   - ☐ a. its excellent safety record.
   - ☐ b. having superior night radar.
   - ☐ c. being a "flying gas tank."

Score 5 points for each correct answer.

______ **Total Score:** Recalling Facts

C Making Inferences

When you combine your own experience and information from a text to draw a conclusion that is not directly stated in that text, you are making an inference. Below are five statements that may or may not be inferences based on information in the article. Label the statements using the following key:

C—Correct Inference **F—Faulty Inference**

_______ 1. The U.S. Army was never uncertain about what had happened to Flight 19 and the Martin Mariner.

_______ 2. Even an experienced pilot can get lost in an unfamiliar area.

_______ 3. The U.S. Army does a poor job of training its pilots.

_______ 4. Many people think that the Bermuda Triangle is governed by forces not found in other parts of the ocean.

_______ 5. When unusual occurrences that cannot be quickly and easily explained take place, people often seek a mysterious cause.

Score 5 points for each correct answer.

_______ **Total Score:** Making Inferences

D Using Words Precisely

Each numbered sentence below contains an underlined word or phrase from the article. Following the sentence are three definitions. One definition is closest to the meaning of the underlined word. One definition is opposite or nearly opposite. Label those two definitions using the following key; do not label the remaining definition.

C—Closest **O—Opposite or Nearly Opposite**

1. On a calm, clear December afternoon in 1945, Flight 19 took off from the south coast of Florida on a routine Army training mission.

_______ a. official

_______ b. regular

_______ c. unusual

2. Yet, whenever planes or ships disappear in the infamous Bermuda Triangle, the wildest stories are heard.

_______ a. celebrated

_______ b. distant

_______ c. having a bad reputation

3. A massive search of the area by hundreds of boats and planes turned up nothing but water.

_______ a. immense

_______ b. well-advertised

_______ c. small

4. But skeptics point out that the popular story concerning their disappearance is wrong in almost every way.

_______ a. believers

_______ b. doubters

_______ c. scientists

5. The combined forces of nature and the unpredictability of mankind outdo even the most farfetched science fiction many times each year.

_______ a. improbable

_______ b. well-written

_______ c. likely

_______ Score 3 points for each correct C answer.

_______ Score 2 points for each correct O answer.

_______ **Total Score:** Using Words Precisely

Enter the four total scores in the spaces below, and add them together to find your Reading Comprehension Score. Then record your score on the graph on page 73.

Score	Question Type	Lesson 5
_______	Finding the Main Idea	
_______	Recalling Facts	
_______	Making Inferences	
_______	Using Words Precisely	
_______	**Reading Comprehension Score**	

Author's Approach

Put an X in the box next to the correct answer.

1. The author's purpose in writing "Triangle of Fear" is to

☐ a. express conflicting opinions about the forces at work within the Bermuda Triangle.

☐ b. persuade the reader to believe that powerful forces are at work within the Bermuda Triangle.

☐ c. entertain the reader with mysterious tales about the Bermuda Triangle.

2. Choose the statement below that is the weakest argument for believing in the powers of the Bermuda Triangle.

☐ a. Experienced pilots have flown over the area and gotten lost.

☐ b. Neither plane wreckage nor bodies have been recovered from the missing flights.

☐ c. The Bermuda Triangle could be a hunting ground for UFOs.

3. In this article the statement that "'the combined forces of nature and the unpredictability of mankind outdo even the most farfetched science fiction many times each year'" means

☐ a. reality is stranger than anything anyone could write.

☐ b. much of science fiction is based on what happens in real life.

☐ c. both people and nature are unpredictable.

_______ Number of correct answers

Record your personal assessment of your work on the Critical Thinking Chart on page 74.

Summarizing and Paraphrasing

Put an X in the box next to the correct answer for questions 2 and 3. Follow the directions provided for the other question.

1. Look for the important ideas and events in paragraphs 15 and 16. Summarize those paragraphs in one or two sentences.

____

____

____

____

2. Below are summaries of the article. Choose the summary that says all the most important things about the article but in the fewest words.

☐ a. In 1945, the planes and crew members of Flight 19 disappeared without a trace over the Bermuda Triangle. The flying boat sent to rescue Flight 19 also vanished.

☐ b. Some people blame the mysterious powers of the Bermuda Triangle for the disappearance in 1945 of Flight 19 and the flying boat sent to rescue it. Others insist that there is a reasonable explanation for the incident.

☐ c. Mystery still surrounds the disappearance in 1945 of Flight 19 over the Bermuda Triangle.

3. Choose the best one-sentence paraphrase for the following sentence from the article:

"To true believers in the powers of the Bermuda Triangle, the fate of the five Avengers and the Martin Mariner is just another piece of evidence proving that the Triangle is one spooky stretch of ocean."

☐ a. Many people believe that ghosts haunt the Bermuda Triangle.

☐ b. Many people believe that the Bermuda Triangle is a powerful, frightening place.

☐ c. For many people, the disappearance of these aircraft helps confirm that the Bermuda Triangle is a frightening place.

_________ Number of correct answers

Record your personal assessment of your work on the Critical Thinking Chart on page 74.

Critical Thinking

Follow the directions provided for questions 1 and 3. Put an X in the box next to the correct answer for the other questions.

1. For each statement below, write O if it expresses an opinion or F if it expresses a fact.

_______ a. Neither wreckage nor bodies were found after Flight 19 and the flying boat disappeared over the Bermuda Triangle.

_______ b. The Bermuda Triangle causes the ships and planes that travel over it to disappear.

_______ c. The lost continent of Atlantis exists beneath the Bermuda Triangle.

2. Based on the events in the article, you can predict that the following will happen next :

☐ a. UFOs will continue to scoop up innocent ships and airplanes.

☐ b. Everyone will agree that the mysterious incidents over the Bermuda Triangle have a logical explanation.

☐ c. Some people will continue to fear and avoid traveling over the Bermuda Triangle.

3. Choose from the letters below to correctly complete the following statement. Write the letters on the lines.

According to the article, the disappearance of Flight 19 caused ________ to ________, and the effect was ________.

a. attempt a rescue

b. a Martin Mariner flying boat

c. the flying boat also disappeared

4. If you were a pilot, how could you use the information in the article to chart a flight plan over the Bermuda Triangle?

☐ a. Like the member of Flight 19 who had a premonition about flying over the Bermuda Triangle, refuse to go.

☐ b. Like the members of the rescue mission, fly over the Bermuda Triangle in a Martin Mariner flying boat.

☐ c. Unlike the crew members of Flight 19, make sure your compass is working and your gas tank is full.

5. In which paragraph did you find the information or details to answer question 3?

____

________ Number of correct answers

Record your personal assessment of your work on the Critical Thinking Chart on page 74.

Personal Response

I can't believe

____

____

____

____

Self-Assessment

One of the things I did best when reading this article was

____

____

____

____

I believe I did this well because

____

____

____

____

SPONTANEOUS HUMAN COMBUSTION

Looking for a hot date? Well, Billy Clifford, a young Englishman, found out that there are hot dates and then there are really hot dates. While he was dancing with his girlfriend in a London disco in the late 1950s, she suddenly burst into flames. Fire spread from her back to her head and hair. Billy and other dancers tried to put out the flames, but it was too late. The girl died on the way to the hospital.

2 The cause of this mysterious fire was never explained. No one had been smoking in the area. There had been no candles on the tables. In short, there had been no source of fire.

3 This case is just one of some 200 such fires that have been reported over the past 400 years. In each case, a human body was consumed by flames when there was no known source of fire present. Often, it was only the person's body that burned. Nearby objects such as curtains, paper, and chairs were left untouched. This strange phenomenon is known as spontaneous human combustion, or SHC for short.

No one knows for sure how spontaneous human combustion occurs. Scientists believe that if cases of SHC are studied closely, they can be explained.

4 Perhaps the most famous case of SHC was the 1951 death of Mrs. Mary Reeser of St. Petersburg, Florida. She was reduced to a small pile of ashes. Yet, her room was left largely undamaged. Many experts on arson were called in to investigate the case. They tried to identify the cause of the fire. None was found. Even the FBI couldn't come up with anything.

5 Dr. Wilton Krogman, an expert on the effects of fire on the human body, finally gave up his search for a cause. The doctor said, "I regard it as the most amazing thing I've ever seen. As I review it, the short hairs on the back of my neck bristle with vague fear. Were I living in the Middle Ages, I'd mutter something about black magic."

6 The facts of the case are scary enough to make the hairs on anyone's neck bristle. Mrs. Mary Reeser was a 67-year-old grandmother and widow. On the evening of July 1, 1951, Mary was prepared for bed by 9 P.M. She was dressed in her nightgown, black satin slippers, and a housecoat. Her landlady, Mrs. Carpenter, had said that she saw Mary briefly around this time and that Mary had been smoking a cigarette while sitting in a chair.

7 Around 5 A.M., Mrs. Carpenter was aroused by the smell of smoke. She

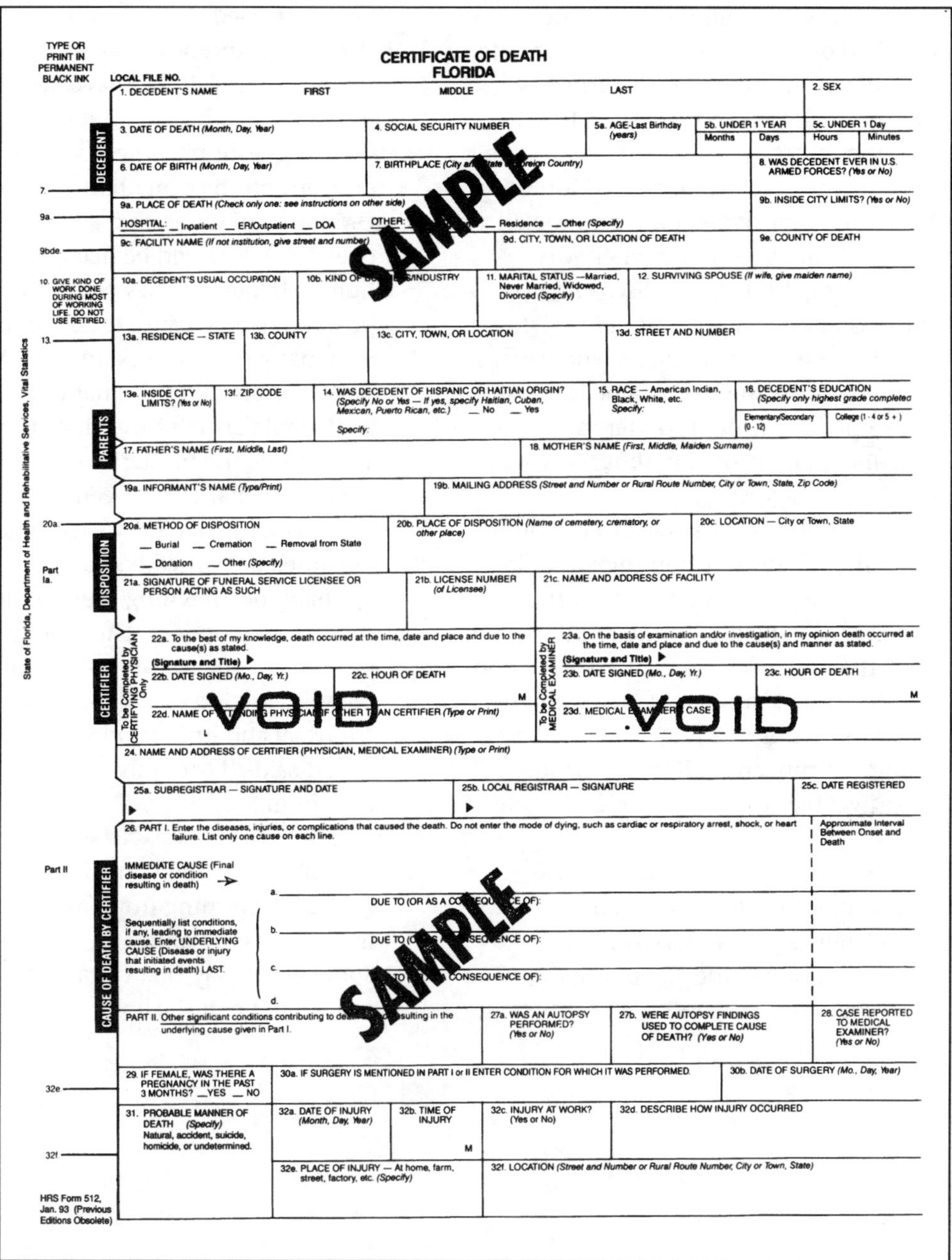
TYPE OR PRINT IN PERMANENT BLACK INK

CERTIFICATE OF DEATH
FLORIDA

LOCAL FILE NO.

DECEDENT

1. DECEDENT'S NAME FIRST MIDDLE LAST | 2. SEX
3. DATE OF DEATH (Month, Day, Year) | 4. SOCIAL SECURITY NUMBER | 5a. AGE-Last Birthday (years) | 5b. UNDER 1 YEAR Months Days | 5c. UNDER 1 Day Hours Minutes
6. DATE OF BIRTH (Month, Day, Year) | 7. BIRTHPLACE (City and State or Foreign Country) | 8. WAS DECEDENT EVER IN U.S. ARMED FORCES? (Yes or No)
9a. PLACE OF DEATH (Check only one: see instructions on other side) HOSPITAL: __ Inpatient __ ER/Outpatient __ DOA OTHER: __ Residence __ Other (Specify) | 9b. INSIDE CITY LIMITS? (Yes or No)
9c. FACILITY NAME (If not institution, give street and number) | 9d. CITY, TOWN, OR LOCATION OF DEATH | 9e. COUNTY OF DEATH
10a. DECEDENT'S USUAL OCCUPATION | 10b. KIND OF BUSINESS/INDUSTRY | 11. MARITAL STATUS —Married, Never Married, Widowed, Divorced (Specify) | 12. SURVIVING SPOUSE (If wife, give maiden name)
13a. RESIDENCE — STATE | 13b. COUNTY | 13c. CITY, TOWN, OR LOCATION | 13d. STREET AND NUMBER
13e. INSIDE CITY LIMITS? (Yes or No) | 13f. ZIP CODE | 14. WAS DECEDENT OF HISPANIC OR HAITIAN ORIGIN? (Specify No or Yes — If yes, specify Haitian, Cuban, Mexican, Puerto Rican, etc.) __ No __ Yes Specify: | 15. RACE — American Indian, Black, White, etc. Specify: | 16. DECEDENT'S EDUCATION (Specify only highest grade completed) Elementary/Secondary (0 - 12) College (1 - 4 or 5 +)

PARENTS

17. FATHER'S NAME (First, Middle, Last) | 18. MOTHER'S NAME (First, Middle, Maiden Surname)
19a. INFORMANT'S NAME (Type/Print) | 19b. MAILING ADDRESS (Street and Number or Rural Route Number, City or Town, State, Zip Code)

DISPOSITION

20a. METHOD OF DISPOSITION __ Burial __ Cremation __ Removal from State __ Donation __ Other (Specify) | 20b. PLACE OF DISPOSITION (Name of cemetery, crematory, or other place) | 20c. LOCATION — City or Town, State
21a. SIGNATURE OF FUNERAL SERVICE LICENSEE OR PERSON ACTING AS SUCH | 21b. LICENSE NUMBER (of Licensee) | 21c. NAME AND ADDRESS OF FACILITY

CERTIFIER

To be Completed by CERTIFYING PHYSICIAN Only
22a. To the best of my knowledge, death occurred at the time, date and place and due to the cause(s) as stated. (Signature and Title)
22b. DATE SIGNED (Mo., Day, Yr.) | 22c. HOUR OF DEATH M
22d. NAME OF ATTENDING PHYSICIAN IF OTHER THAN CERTIFIER (Type or Print)
VOID

To be Completed by MEDICAL EXAMINER
23a. On the basis of examination and/or investigation, in my opinion death occurred at the time, date and place and due to the cause(s) and manner as stated. (Signature and Title)
23b. DATE SIGNED (Mo., Day, Yr.) | 23c. HOUR OF DEATH M
23d. MEDICAL EXAMINER'S CASE
VOID

24. NAME AND ADDRESS OF CERTIFIER (PHYSICIAN, MEDICAL EXAMINER) (Type or Print)
25a. SUBREGISTRAR — SIGNATURE AND DATE | 25b. LOCAL REGISTRAR — SIGNATURE | 25c. DATE REGISTERED

CAUSE OF DEATH BY CERTIFIER

26. PART I. Enter the diseases, injuries, or complications that caused the death. Do not enter the mode of dying, such as cardiac or respiratory arrest, shock, or heart failure. List only one cause on each line. | Approximate Interval Between Onset and Death
IMMEDIATE CAUSE (Final disease or condition resulting in death) a.
DUE TO (OR AS A CONSEQUENCE OF): b.
DUE TO (OR AS A CONSEQUENCE OF): c.
DUE TO (OR AS A CONSEQUENCE OF): d.
Sequentially list conditions, if any, leading to immediate cause. Enter UNDERLYING CAUSE (Disease or injury that initiated events resulting in death) LAST.
PART II. Other significant conditions contributing to death but not resulting in the underlying cause given in Part I. | 27a. WAS AN AUTOPSY PERFORMED? (Yes or No) | 27b. WERE AUTOPSY FINDINGS USED TO COMPLETE CAUSE OF DEATH? (Yes or No) | 28. CASE REPORTED TO MEDICAL EXAMINER? (Yes or No)
29. IF FEMALE, WAS THERE A PREGNANCY IN THE PAST 3 MONTHS? __YES __ NO | 30a. IF SURGERY IS MENTIONED IN PART I or II ENTER CONDITION FOR WHICH IT WAS PERFORMED | 30b. DATE OF SURGERY (Mo., Day, Year)
31. PROBABLE MANNER OF DEATH (Specify) Natural, accident, suicide, homicide, or undetermined. | 32a. DATE OF INJURY (Month, Day, Year) | 32b. TIME OF INJURY M | 32c. INJURY AT WORK? (Yes or No) | 32d. DESCRIBE HOW INJURY OCCURRED
32e. PLACE OF INJURY — At home, farm, street, factory, etc. (Specify) | 32f. LOCATION (Street and Number or Rural Route Number, City or Town, State)

SAMPLE

State of Florida, Department of Health and Rehabilitative Services, Vital Statistics

HRS Form 512, Jan. 93 (Previous Editions Obsolete)

A sample of a Florida death certificate. What would be entered in box 31 for a case of spontaneous human combustion?

thought it was coming from a water pump that had been regularly overheating. She shut down the pump and returned to bed. When she got up an hour later, the smell was gone.

8 At 8 A.M., a telegram arrived for Mary. Mrs. Carpenter signed for it and took it to Mary's apartment. But when Mrs. Carpenter got there, she discovered that the doorknob was hot. Frightened, she called for help. Two painters who were working across the street came running. They opened the door to Mary's apartment and rushed in, but Mary was nowhere in sight.

9 Firefighters soon arrived to put out the small fire. That was when they found Mary. It was a sight that none of them had ever seen before. In the middle of the floor they discovered a charred area about four feet wide. Inside that area were the ghastly remains of a human body. They found a shrunken skull, one foot still wearing a black satin slipper, and a pile of ashes.

10 A thorough study of the remains was conducted. How could a fire so completely consume Mrs. Mary Reeser and yet not affect the rest of the room? How could newspapers on a nearby table be undamaged? Why was the skull shrunken? And how could the one foot in the black satin slipper have been left unburned?

11 The questions came easily. The answers, on the other hand, all fell short. Dr. Krogman stated that a temperature of over 3000° F. would be needed to reduce human bones to ashes. Such intense heat, however, would cause the skull to explode into many small pieces. Instead, Mary's skull had shrunken dramatically. Such heat would also destroy all nearby objects. Yet, outside the mysterious four-foot circle, little harm had been done.

12 It appears that Mary's foot had remained unburned because she was in the habit of stretching it out to relieve some leg discomfort. The foot was found just outside the four-foot-wide circle. The FBI's final report said that the fire was "unusual and improbable." A top arson expert said, "I can only say the victim died from fire."

13 Many theories have been put forward to explain the phenomenon of SHC. They include everything from laser beams to microwaves to flammable human gases. Some people say that certain chemicals can combine in the body and become explosive. Some point out that body oils and fats make good fuels. Some say that static electricity, in rare moments, might do the trick. The list of possible causes goes on and on.

14 The world of science rejects them all. It does not accept the idea of spontaneous human combustion. People do not just burst into flames for no reason at all. Each case, we are told, could be explained if we only studied it more. The case of Mrs. Mary Reeser, however, was studied in great detail, but still investigators were baffled. And so the mystery of SHC remains.

If you have been timed while reading this article, enter your reading time below. Then turn to the Words-per-Minute Table on page 71 and look up your reading speed (words per minute). Then enter your reading speed on the Reading Speed graph on page 72.

Reading Time: Lesson 6

_______ : _______

Minutes *Seconds*

A Finding the Main Idea

One statement below expresses the main idea of the article. One statement is too general, or too broad. The other statement explains only part of the article; it is too narrow. Label the statements using the following key:

M—Main Idea **B—Too Broad** **N—Too Narrow**

_______ 1. Throughout history there have been many fires whose causes are unknown.

_______ 2. Spontaneous human combustion is a phenomenon in which humans are consumed by fire for no apparent reason.

_______ 3. The FBI could not determine the cause of the spontaneous combustion of Mrs. Mary Reeser.

_______ Score 15 points for a correct M answer.

_______ Score 5 points for each correct B or N answer.

_______ **Total Score:** Finding the Main Idea

B Recalling Facts

How well do you remember the facts in the article? Put an X in the box next to the answer that correctly completes each statement about the article.

1. The cause of the fire that killed the girl in the London disco was
   - ☐ a. never explained.
   - ☐ b. a burning cigarette.
   - ☐ c. a candle on a table.
2. Mrs. Mary Reeser was
   - ☐ a. an elderly landlady.
   - ☐ b. a firefighter.
   - ☐ c. a grandmother.
3. At 5 A.M., Mrs. Carpenter
   - ☐ a. put on her housecoat.
   - ☐ b. called for help.
   - ☐ c. shut down the water pump.
4. The one part of Mrs. Reeser's body that wasn't burned was one of her
   - ☐ a. feet.
   - ☐ b. arms.
   - ☐ c. legs.
5. The temperature needed to reduce bones to ashes is
   - ☐ a. 400 degrees Fahrenheit.
   - ☐ b. 3000 degrees Fahrenheit.
   - ☐ c. 2000 degrees Fahrenheit.

Score 5 points for each correct answer.

_______ **Total Score:** Recalling Facts

C Making Inferences

When you combine your own experience and information from a text to draw a conclusion that is not directly stated in that text, you are making an inference. Below are five statements that may or may not be inferences based on information in the article. Label the statements using the following key:

C—Correct Inference **F—Faulty Inference**

_______ 1. Only women are victims of spontaneous human combustion.

_______ 2. Dr. Krogman gave up his search for the cause of the fire that killed Mrs. Reeser because all the logical choices proved to be unsatisfactory.

_______ 3. The smell that Mrs. Carpenter detected at 5 A.M. was probably not from the water pump, but from Mrs. Reeser.

_______ 4. The FBI and the arson experts simply did not look hard enough to find the cause of the fire.

_______ 5. Although we don't know what they are, there must be many causes for spontaneous human combustion.

Score 5 points for each correct answer.

_______ **Total Score:** Making Inferences

D Using Words Precisely

Each numbered sentence below contains an underlined word or phrase from the article. Following the sentence are three definitions. One definition is closest to the meaning of the underlined word. One definition is opposite or nearly opposite. Label those two definitions using the following key; do not label the remaining definition.

C—Closest **O—Opposite or Nearly Opposite**

1. In each case, a human body was <u>consumed</u> by flames when there was no known source of fire present.

_______ a. preserved

_______ b. surrounded

_______ c. destroyed

2. This strange phenomenon is known as <u>spontaneous</u> human combustion, or SHC for short.

_______ a. natural

_______ b. unusual

_______ c. planned

3. The facts of the case are scary enough to make the hairs on anyone's neck <u>bristle</u>.

_______ a. stand on end

_______ b. lie down

_______ c. itch

4. Inside that area were the ghastly remains of a human body.

_______ a. attractive

_______ b. scarce

_______ c. horrible

5. They include everything from laser beams to microwaves to flammable human gases.

_______ a. fire-resistant

_______ b. burnable

_______ c. liquid

_______ Score 3 points for each correct C answer.

_______ Score 2 points for each correct O answer.

_______ **Total Score:** Using Words Precisely

Enter the four total scores in the spaces below, and add them together to find your Reading Comprehension Score. Then record your score on the graph on page 73.

Score	Question Type	Lesson 6
_______	Finding the Main Idea	
_______	Recalling Facts	
_______	Making Inferences	
_______	Using Words Precisely	
_______	**Reading Comprehension Score**	

Author's Approach

Put an X in the box next to the correct answer.

1. The author uses the first sentence of the article to

☐ a. entertain the reader with a humorous question.

☐ b. inform the reader about spontaneous human combustion.

☐ c. describe the phenomenon of spontaneous human combustion.

2. From the statement "the answers, on the other hand, all fell short," you can conclude that the author wants the reader to think that no one

☐ a. took the time to look for satisfactory answers.

☐ b. can satisfactorily explain why fire consumed Mary Reeser.

☐ c. accepted the answers the experts came up with.

3. In this article, the statement "'were I living in the Middle Ages, I'd mutter something about black magic'" means that

☐ a. a magician caused Mary Reeser to burn to death.

☐ b. witchcraft, rather than natural causes, is responsible for SHC.

☐ c. people living in the Middle Ages understood the causes of SHC.

4. Choose the statement below that best explains how the author addresses the opposing point of view in the article.

☐ a. To scientists who do not accept the idea of SHC, the author suggests that laser beams cause the phenomenon.

☐ b. To those skeptical about the causes of SHC, the author points out that body oils and fats could cause the phenomenon.

☐ c. To those who claim that each case of SHC has a logical explanation, the author quotes experts who were completely bewildered by the cases they had investigated.

_______ Number of correct answers

Record your personal assessment of your work on the Critical Thinking Chart on page 74.

Summarizing and Paraphrasing

Put an X in the box next to the correct answer for question 3. Follow the directions provided for the other questions.

1. Complete the following one-sentence summary of the article using the lettered phrases from the phrase bank below. Write the letters on the lines.

Phrase Bank:

a. a description of the phenomenon

b. a summary of the theories about the phenomenon

c. the circumstances of Mary Reeser's death

The article about spontaneous human combustion begins with ________, goes on to explain ________, and ends with ________.

2. Reread paragraph 8 in the article. Below, write a summary of the paragraph in no more than 25 words.

____

____

____

____

Reread your summary and decide whether it covers the important ideas in the paragraph. Next, decide how to shorten the summary to 15 words or less without leaving out any essential information. Write this summary below.

____

____

3. Read the statement about the article below. Then read the paraphrase of that statement. Choose the reason that best tells why the paraphrase does not say the same thing as the statement.

   Statement: Even though Mrs. Mary Reeser had been smoking a cigarette when Mrs. Carpenter last saw her, arson experts doubt that the cigarette could have caused the fire that consumed Mary.

   Paraphrase: Arson experts doubt that Mary was smoking a cigarette when she burst into flames.

☐ a. Paraphrase says too much.

☐ b. Paraphrase doesn't say enough.

☐ c. Paraphrase doesn't agree with the statement about the article.

________ Number of correct answers

Record your personal assessment of your work on the Critical Thinking Chart on page 74.

Critical Thinking

Put an X in the box next to the correct answer for questions 1 and 4. Follow the directions provided for the other questions.

1. From what Dr. Wilton Krogman said, you can predict that other experts in his field would

☐ a. not be mystified by Mary's case.

☐ b. use black magic to solve Mary's case.

☐ c. be equally puzzled by Mary's case.

2. Using what you know about a normal fire and what is told about spontaneous human combustion in the article, name three ways a normal fire is similar to and three ways it is different from spontaneous human combustion. Cite the paragraph number(s) where you found details in the article to support your conclusions.

Similarities

___

___

___

Differences

___

___

___

3. Read paragraph 12. Then choose from the letters below to correctly complete the following statement. Write the letters on the lines.

   According to paragraph 12, ________ because ________.

   a. she stretched it out to relieve discomfort in her leg
   b. her foot was outside the four-foot circle
   c. Mary's foot remained

4. What did you have to do to answer question 3?

☐ a. find an effect (something that happened)
☐ b. find a cause (why something happened)
☐ c. find a comparison (how things are the same)

________ Number of correct answers

Record your personal assessment of your work on the Critical Thinking Chart on page 74.

Personal Response

How do you think the firefighters felt when they arrived to put out the fire in Mary Reeser's apartment?

___

___

___

___

Self-Assessment

One good question about this article that was not asked would be

___

___

___

___

and the answer is

___

___

___

___

MOON MADNESS

Can a full moon drive people crazy? Does it make dogs howl more often at night or cause fish to jump? Does it inspire criminals to rob and kill more? Does the full moon make weird individuals act even weirder? And does it make emergency rooms fill up because there are more injuries and accidents?

2 Moon madness isn't a new idea. Throughout history people have believed that a full moon really does cause unusual behavior. In fact, the word *lunatic* comes from the Latin word *luna*, which means "moon." Today this belief is still shared by many workers in emergency rooms and crisis centers. Police and 911 operators, too, say they get more calls during a full moon.

3 These operators also say that they get more strange calls. "We get weirder calls, stupid stuff," said Connie Kelson, a police dispatcher from Salt Lake City. One caller kept yelling, "I'm having lizards! I'm having lizards!" Another caller screamed, "The golf balls are coming! The golf balls are coming!"

4 A few studies support these claims. One 1983 study showed that calls from

Farmers have names for full moons in different months of the year. A common belief in the past was that certain crops would grow better if planted under the light of a full moon.

people who took poison by mistake went up during a full moon. But far more studies suggest that there is no link between the phases of the moon and how we behave. A 1993 study, for example, looked at more than 82,000 police calls. These calls all dealt with domestic violence. This study showed no link between the frequency of calls and full moons.

5 Some nurses report that more women give birth during a full moon. The theory is that the moon's gravity tugs on the fluid in the womb, which helps to speed up the birth process. Other nurses say they see more births after a big storm than during a full moon. It's not clear which group is right. Perhaps they're both wrong. In any case, reports show that many people believe the full moon can and does make odd things happen.

6 Some skeptics suggest that those who believe in moon madness look for evidence that supports their beliefs and ignore facts that don't. Scientist Lynn Lyon thinks that people may simply be more aware of what happens during a full moon. Many times people recall something that occurred during a full moon. But Lyon says, "they never compare that back with the times when it wasn't a full moon."

7 Farmers, too, have always been aware of full moons. They have even given names to those that appear at the beginning of seasons. The full moon in March, for example, is called the sugar moon. In June, the full moon is the strawberry moon. And in September, it is the harvest moon.

8 Legend says that it is better to plant certain crops under a full moon. *The Old Farmer's Almanac* still advises people to "plant flowers and vegetables which bear crops above the ground during the light of the moon." Even so, many farmers plant their crops whenever the ground is ready without giving the moon a second thought.

9 What is it about the moon that makes claims about its power so plausible? We already know that the moon's gravity causes ocean tides. Anyone who has been to the seashore can see how dramatic this pull can be. Can the moon also influence smaller bodies of water? A few people say yes. They embrace the concept of "biological tides." One such believer is Dr. Arnold Lieber. In 1996, he wrote a book called *How the Moon Affects You.* Doctor Lieber notes that the human body is 80 percent liquid. The moon, he claims, can cause tides in a person's body. When bodily fluids become unbalanced—as can occur during a full moon—people may act in bizarre ways.

10 Lieber is not the only one who feels that the moon can influence our behavior. Nobel Prize winner Robert Millikan once said, "If man is not affected in some way by the planets, sun, and moon, he is the

We know the moon controls the oceans' tides. Does it control "biological tides" in the human body too?

only thing on earth that isn't." In addition to tides, the moon does seem to affect how animals behave. In some species, for instance, mating patterns seem to change with the moon.

11 Does the moon affect humans? Most scientists scoff at the notion of biological tides. The pull of the moon's gravity is much too small, they say. Astronomer George Abell says that the moon's pull on the human body is less than the weight of a mosquito! Such a pull, Abell and others claim, couldn't have much impact on people's behavior.

12 What about the light from a full moon? A full moon, after all, can be quite bright. Is that what drives us nuts? Is all that reflected sunlight somehow affecting our minds? Maybe the extra brightness disturbs people's sleep. Or maybe the full moon's glow makes it easier for criminals to see their way around at night. But what if it is a cloud-covered full moon? Does that make a difference? There is no evidence either way.

13 Maybe the moon doesn't affect our bodies, but it does affect our minds. After all, the moon has always been a powerful symbol. Many past societies worshipped the moon. For some, the moon inspired their first concept of a god. Today the calendar is based on the sun, but almost all ancient calendars were based on the moon. Even today Christians celebrate Easter on the first Sunday after the full moon following the first day of spring.

14 When people walk outside under a full moon, they almost always notice it. We are drawn to the moon. A full moon seems to cast a spell over people. It's romantic. If you call someone "moony," it means that he or she is dreamy, or moonstruck. So it's no wonder that the moon is evoked in hundreds of love songs and poems.

15 Some people feel that the moon will keep them safe. They wear moon-shaped charms around their necks. For those who believe in moon madness, though, a full moon can be scary. That's when all the crazy people are on the loose.

16 Clearly, the moon can influence how we act. But is the cause of our behavior the moon itself or our beliefs about the moon? There seems to be just enough evidence to keep the debate going. No final answer will ever please everyone. True believers, such as Lieber, will always say, "Yes, the moon does affect us in ways we can't control." Skeptics will always counter with the question, "Where's the proof?"

If you have been timed while reading this article, enter your reading time below. Then turn to the Words-per-Minute Table on page 71 and look up your reading speed (words per minute). Then enter your reading speed on the Reading Speed graph on page 72.

Reading Time: Lesson 7

_______ : _______

Minutes *Seconds*

A Finding the Main Idea

One statement below expresses the main idea of the article. One statement is too general, or too broad. The other statement explains only part of the article; it is too narrow. Label the statements using the following key:

M—Main Idea **B—Too Broad** **N—Too Narrow**

_______ 1. Many people believe that the full moon causes strange behavior.

_______ 2. The moon's gravity affects bodies of water.

_______ 3. The moon is a powerful symbol.

_______ Score 15 points for a correct M answer.

_______ Score 5 points for each correct B or N answer.

_______ **Total Score:** Finding the Main Idea

B Recalling Facts

How well do you remember the facts in the article? Put an X in the box next to the answer that correctly completes each statement about the article.

1. The notion that a full moon causes unusual behavior
   - ☐ a. was introduced by 911 operators.
   - ☐ b. has persisted throughout history.
   - ☐ c. dates back to the 1800s.
2. The assertion that delivery rooms are busier during a full moon
   - ☐ a. is well documented with proof.
   - ☐ b. has not been proven or disproved.
   - ☐ c. is an old wives' tale.
3. According to the concept of biological tides,
   - ☐ a. the water in human bodies is affected by the moon's gravity.
   - ☐ b. people act strangely during low tides.
   - ☐ c. farmers should plant certain crops under a full moon.
4. Almost all ancient calendars were based on the
   - ☐ a. moon.
   - ☐ b. sun.
   - ☐ c. seasons.
5. Most people agree that the moon
   - ☐ a. affects our bodies more than our minds.
   - ☐ b. has a strong gravitational pull on our bodies.
   - ☐ c. affects our minds more than our bodies.

Score 5 points for each correct answer.

_______ **Total Score:** Recalling Facts

C Making Inferences

When you combine your own experience and information from a text to draw a conclusion that is not directly stated in that text, you are making an inference. Below are five statements that may or may not be inferences based on information in the article. Label the statements using the following key:

C—Correct Inference **F—Faulty Inference**

_______ 1. Some people believe a full moon has mystical powers.

_______ 2. All farmers schedule their planting seasons according to the phases of the moon.

_______ 3. Everyone should stay indoors when the moon is full because crazy people are on the loose.

_______ 4. Scientists disagree about the moon's effect on people's behavior.

_______ 5. All emergency rooms are busier during full moons.

Score 5 points for each correct answer.

_______ **Total Score:** Making Inferences

D Using Words Precisely

Each numbered sentence below contains an underlined word or phrase from the article. Following the sentence are three definitions. One definition is closest to the meaning of the underlined word. One definition is opposite or nearly opposite. Label those two definitions using the following key; do not label the remaining definition.

C—Closest **O—Opposite or Nearly Opposite**

1. Does it <u>inspire</u> criminals to rob and kill more?

_______ a. encourage

_______ b. force

_______ c. prevent

2. These calls all dealt with <u>domestic</u> violence.

_______ a. foreign

_______ b. household

_______ c. brutal

3. This study showed no link between the <u>frequency</u> of calls and full moons.

_______ a. regularity

_______ b. length

_______ c. scarcity

4. <u>Skeptics</u> will always counter with the question, "Where's the proof?"

_______ a. doubters

_______ b. hecklers

_______ c. supporters

5. What is it about the moon that makes claims about its power so plausible?

_______ a. outrageous

_______ b. believable

_______ c. original

_______ Score 3 points for each correct C answer.

_______ Score 2 points for each correct O answer.

_______ **Total Score:** Using Words Precisely

Enter the four total scores in the spaces below, and add them together to find your Reading Comprehension Score. Then record your score on the graph on page 73.

Score	Question Type	Lesson 7
_______	Finding the Main Idea	
_______	Recalling Facts	
_______	Making Inferences	
_______	Using Words Precisely	
_______	**Reading Comprehension Score**	

Author's Approach

Put an X in the box next to the correct answer.

1. The main purpose of the first paragraph is to

☐ a. encourage the reader to consider whether a full moon can affect behavior.

☐ b. entertain the reader with stories about moon madness.

☐ c. persuade the reader to believe that a full moon causes strange behavior.

2. From the statements below, choose those that you believe the author would agree with.

☐ a. Some people have strong opinions about the power of the moon to affect human behavior.

☐ b. The studies that show no link between unusual behavior and full moons are unreliable.

☐ c. The moon can influence how people act.

3. Choose the statement below that is the weakest argument for moon madness.

☐ a. Many workers in emergency rooms and crisis centers claim they receive more calls during a full moon.

☐ b. People tend to remember what happened to them during a full moon.

☐ c. The moon has always been a powerful symbol in many ancient societies.

4. In this article the statement, "a full moon seems to cast a spell over people" means that a full moon

☐ a. scares many people.

☐ b. can make people feel dreamy or romantic.

☐ c. causes some people to commit crimes.

_______ Number of correct answers

Record your personal assessment of your work on the Critical Thinking Chart on page 74.

Summarizing and Paraphrasing

Put an X in the box next to the correct answer for question 3. Follow the directions provided for the other questions.

1. Look for the important ideas and events in paragraphs 2 and 3. Summarize those paragraphs in one or two sentences.

____

____

____

2. Complete the following one-sentence summary of the article using the lettered phrases from the phrase bank below. Write the letters on the lines.

Phrase Bank:

a. several theories about the moon's effect on humans

b. a review of the studies on the relationship between a full moon and behavior

c. the idea that people's beliefs about the moon may affect their behavior

The article about moon madness begins with _______, goes on to explain _______, and ends with _______.

3. Choose the sentence that correctly restates the following sentence from the article:

"Some skeptics suggest that those who believe in moon madness look for evidence that supports their beliefs and ignore facts that don't."

☐ a. People who believe in moon madness use many facts to support their theory.

☐ b. Those who doubt the power of a full moon to affect human behavior suggest that believers provide more proof.

☐ c. Those who believe in moon madness tend to pay little attention to facts that don't reinforce their ideas.

_______ Number of correct answers

Record your personal assessment of your work on the Critical Thinking Chart on page 74.

CRITICAL THINKING

Critical Thinking

Put an X in the box next to the correct answer for questions 1 and 2. Follow the directions provided for the other questions.

1. Which of the following statements from the article is an opinion rather than a fact?

☐ a. "Far more studies suggest that there is no link between the phases of the moon and how we behave."

☐ b. "The moon can cause tides in a person's body."

☐ c. "Many past societies worshipped the moon."

2. From what the article told about moon madness, you can predict that

☐ a. some people will continue to draw a connection between a full moon and bizarre activity.

☐ b. *The Old Farmer's Almanac* will stop advising people to plant certain crops under a full moon.

☐ c. people will stop referring to the moon in love songs and poems.

3. Choose from the letters below to correctly complete the following statement. Write the letters on the lines.

   On the positive side, a full moon ________, but on the negative side, a full moon ________.

   a. can make people feel more romantic
   b. can inspire weird behavior
   c. in September is called the harvest moon

4. In which paragraph did you find the information or details to answer question 1? __________

________ Number of correct answers

Record your personal assessment of your work on the Critical Thinking Chart on page 74.

Personal Response

Describe a time when you or someone you know or heard about was affected by moon madness.

____

____

____

____

Self-Assessment

Before reading this article, I already knew

____

____

____

Compare and Contrast

Think about the articles you have read in Unit One. Pick the four phenomena you most enjoyed reading about or were most intrigued by. Describe the phenomena in the first column of the chart below. Use information you learned from the articles to fill in the empty boxes in the chart.

Phenomenon	What made this so interesting?	Whom or what does this affect?	What do scientists say about this?

The phenomenon that seemed to have a logical explanation is ______________________. I think this because ______________

____

____

Words-per-Minute Table

Unit One

Directions: If you were timed while reading an article, refer to the Reading Time you recorded in the box at the end of the article. Use this words-per-minute table to determine your reading speed for that article. Then plot your reading speed on the graph on page 72.

Lesson	Sample	1	2	3	4	5	6	7	
No. of Words	570	1318	1331	1361	937	947	897	1081	
Minutes and Seconds									*Seconds*
1:30	380	879	887	907	625	631	598	721	**90**
1:40	342	791	799	817	562	568	538	649	**100**
1:50	311	719	726	742	511	517	489	590	**110**
2:00	285	659	666	681	469	474	449	541	**120**
2:10	263	608	614	628	432	437	414	499	**130**
2:20	244	565	570	583	402	406	384	463	**140**
2:30	228	527	532	544	375	379	359	432	**150**
2:40	214	494	499	510	351	355	336	405	**160**
2:50	201	465	470	480	331	334	317	382	**170**
3:00	190	439	444	454	312	316	299	360	**180**
3:10	180	416	420	430	296	299	283	341	**190**
3:20	171	395	399	408	281	284	269	324	**200**
3:30	163	377	380	389	268	271	256	309	**210**
3:40	155	359	363	371	256	258	245	295	**220**
3:50	149	344	347	355	244	247	234	282	**230**
4:00	143	330	333	340	234	237	224	270	**240**
4:10	137	316	319	327	225	227	215	259	**250**
4:20	132	304	307	314	216	219	207	249	**260**
4:30	127	293	296	302	208	210	199	240	**270**
4:40	122	282	285	292	201	203	192	232	**280**
4:50	118	273	275	282	194	196	186	224	**290**
5:00	114	264	266	272	187	189	179	216	**300**
5:10	110	255	258	263	181	183	174	209	**310**
5:20	107	247	250	255	176	178	168	203	**320**
5:30	104	240	242	247	170	172	163	197	**330**
5:40	101	233	235	240	165	167	158	191	**340**
5:50	98	226	228	233	161	162	154	185	**350**
6:00	95	220	222	227	156	158	150	180	**360**
6:10	92	214	216	221	152	154	145	175	**370**
6:20	90	208	210	215	148	150	142	171	**380**
6:30	88	203	205	209	144	146	138	166	**390**
6:40	86	198	200	204	141	142	135	162	**400**
6:50	83	193	195	199	137	139	131	158	**410**
7:00	81	188	190	194	134	135	128	154	**420**
7:10	80	184	186	190	131	132	125	151	**430**
7:20	78	180	182	186	128	129	122	147	**440**
7:30	76	176	177	181	125	126	120	144	**450**
7:40	74	172	174	178	122	124	117	141	**460**
7:50	73	168	170	174	120	121	115	138	**470**
8:00	71	165	166	170	117	118	112	135	**480**

Plotting Your Progress: Reading Speed

Unit One

Directions: If you were timed while reading an article, write your words-per-minute rate for that article in the box under the number of the lesson. Then plot your reading speed on the graph by putting a small X on the line directly above the number of the lesson, across from the number of words per minute you read. As you mark your speed for each lesson, graph your progress by drawing a line to connect the X's.

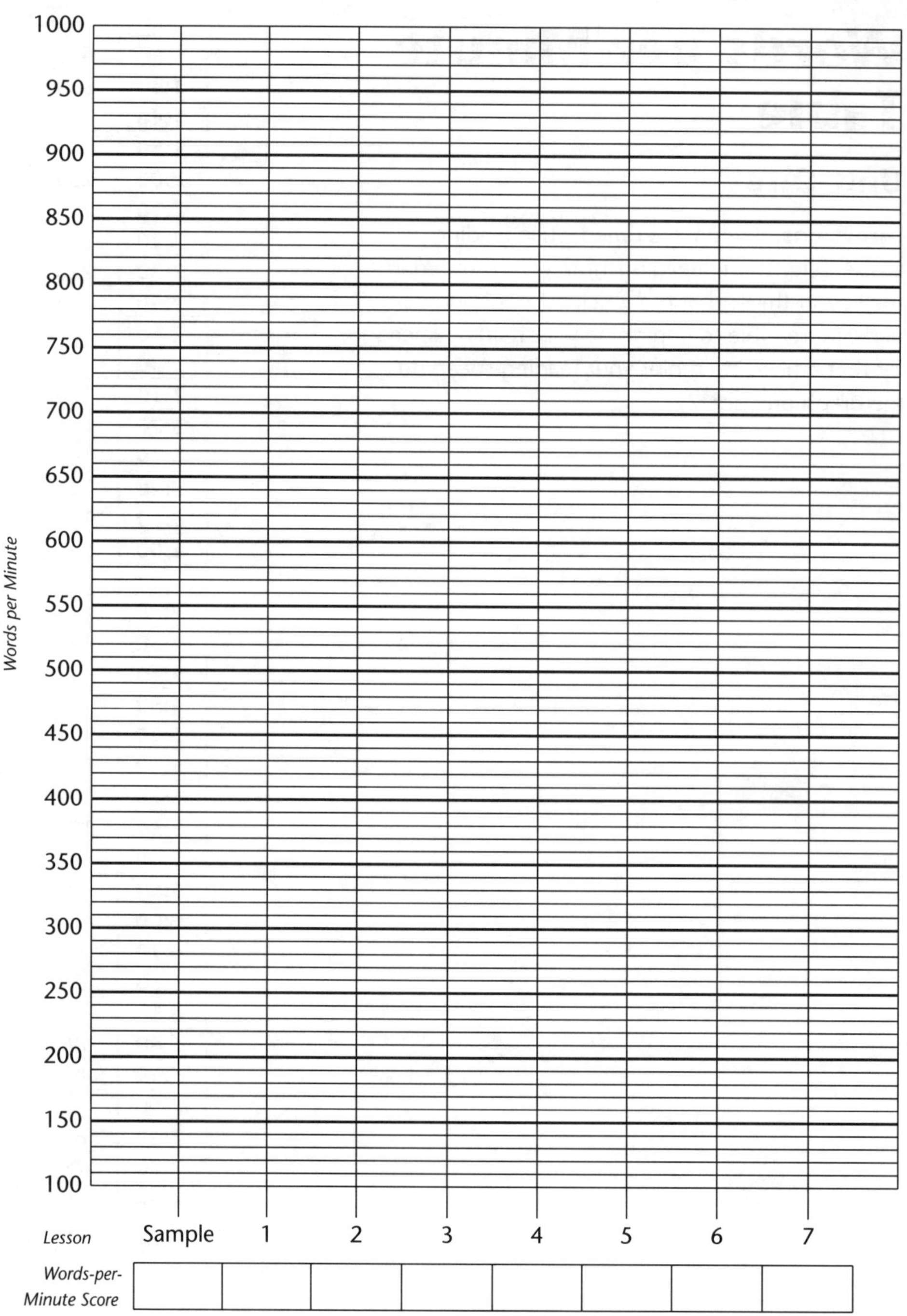

Plotting Your Progress: Reading Comprehension

Unit One

Directions: Write your Reading Comprehension score for each lesson in the box under the number of the lesson. Then plot your score on the graph by putting a small X on the line directly above the number of the lesson and across from the score you earned. As you mark your score for each lesson, graph your progress by drawing a line to connect the X's.

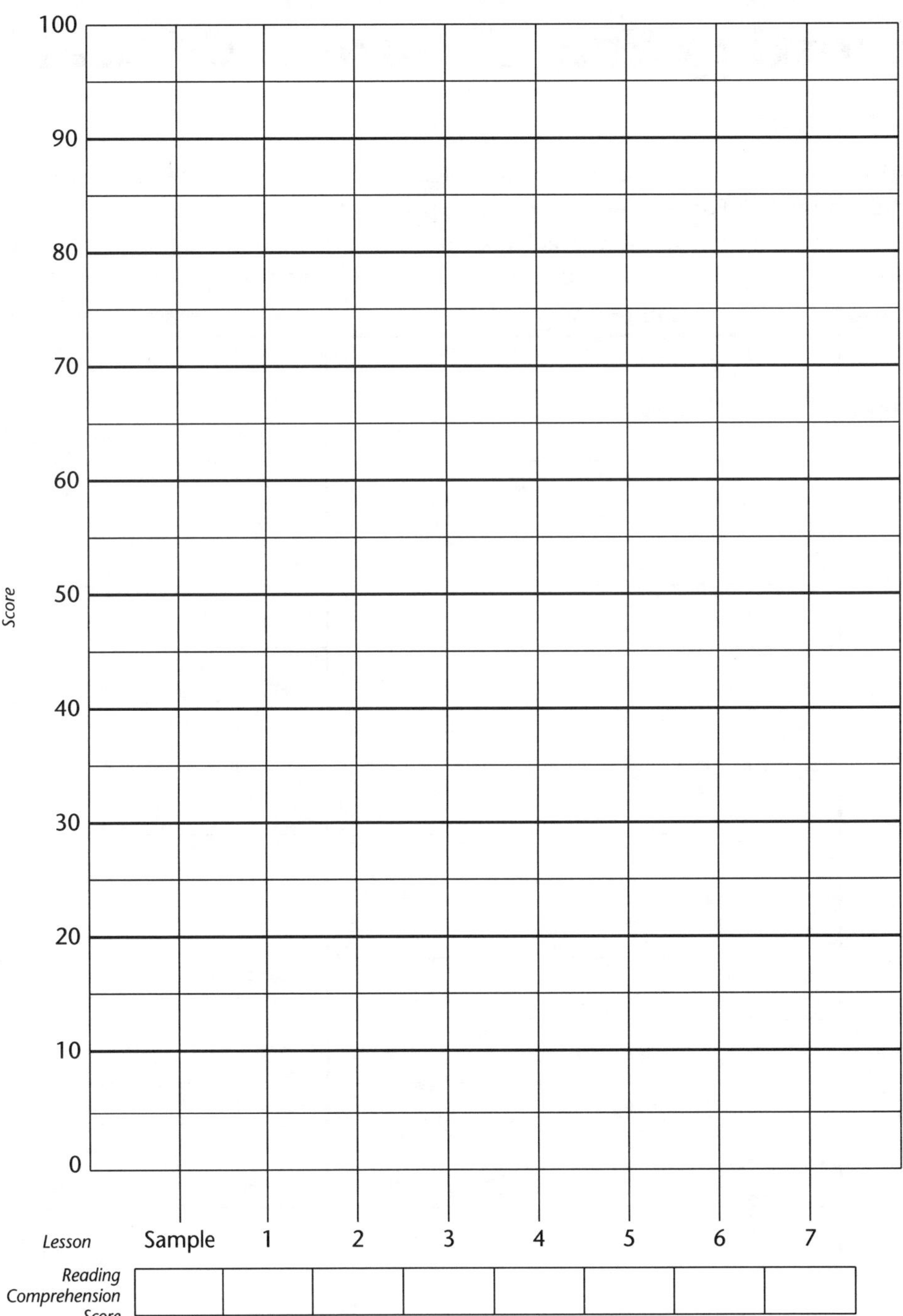

Plotting Your Progress: Critical Thinking

Unit One

Directions: Work with your teacher to evaluate your responses to the Critical Thinking questions for each lesson. Then fill in the appropriate spaces in the chart below. For each lesson and each type of Critical Thinking question, do the following: Mark a minus sign (–) in the box to indicate areas in which you feel you could improve. Mark a plus sign (+) to indicate areas in which you feel you did well. Mark a minus-slash-plus sign (–/+) to indicate areas in which you had mixed success. Then write any comments you have about your performance, including ideas for improvement.

Lesson	Author's Approach	Summarizing and Paraphrasing	Critical Thinking
Sample			
1			
2			
3			
4			
5			
6			
7			

UNIT TWO

SUNSPOTS
Solar Blemishes

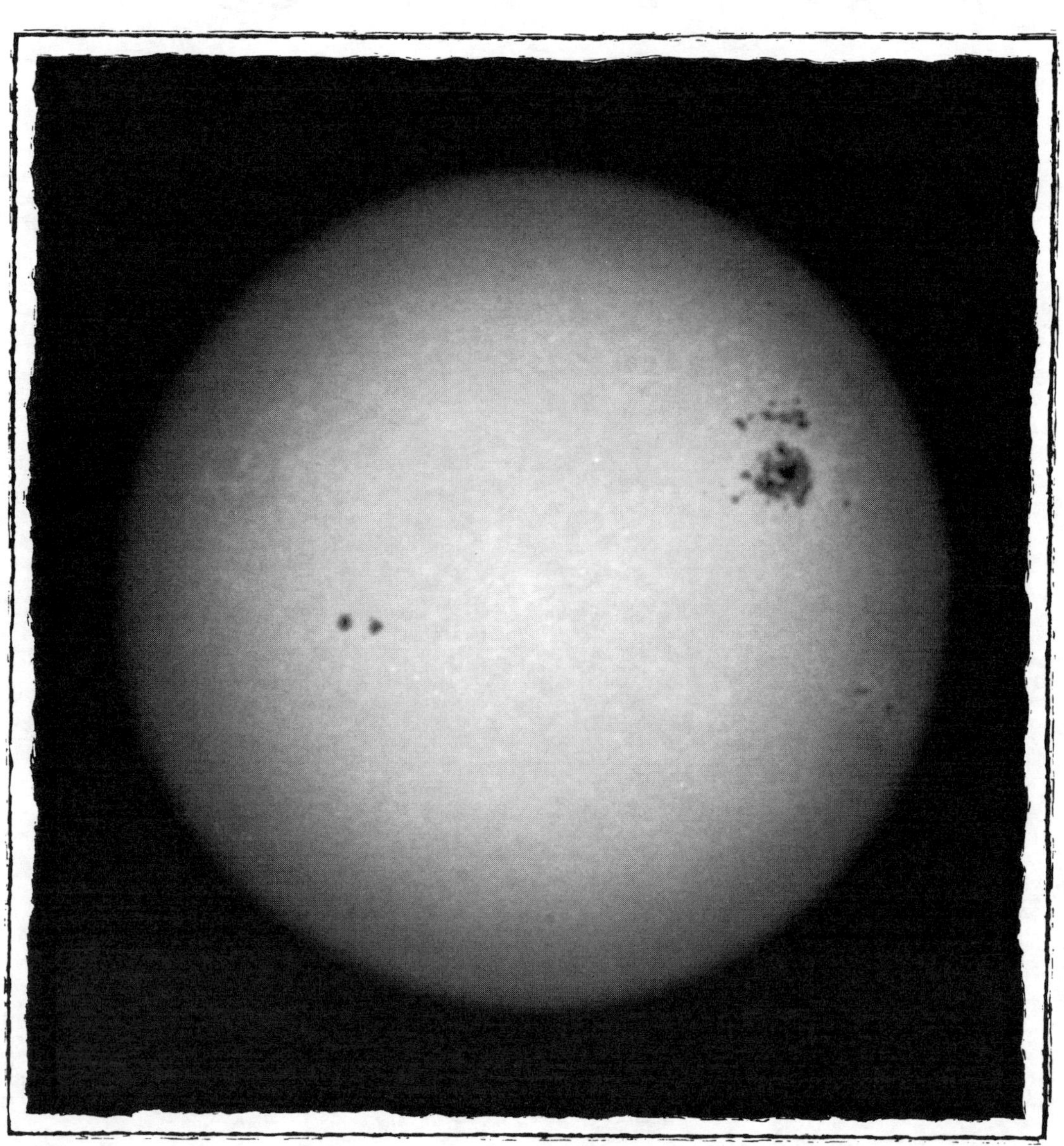

We usually think of the Sun as a constant, predictable heavenly body, a great power that can be counted on not to change. That is because the Sun goes about its business in a very routine way. We know that this giant ball of burning gas always rises in the east and sets in the west. It turns on a daily 24-hour cycle and a yearly 365-day cycle. We plant our gardens and set our clocks by it. And we know that the Sun is out there shining away even on a cloudy day. Few things in life are as perfect and as predictable as the Sun seems to be.

2 But is the Sun, in fact, perfect and constant? Can we predict accurately its every move? The Italian scientist Galileo, in the 16th century, was the first person to train a telescope on the Sun. What he saw smashed forever the idea that the Sun is just a simple ball of light. He noticed several dark specks on the surface of the Sun. These solar blemishes are called sunspots.

3 Today scientists are studying these sunspots very closely. They want to know just what sunspots are and what impact

This visible light image of the Sun shows large sunspots. Sunspots are dark in color because their temperature is lower than the surrounding surface of the Sun.

they may have on life on Earth. It seems that for every answer they get, however, two new questions arise.

4 Seen through a telescope, a sunspot looks like a great swirl of iron filings around a magnet. Sunspots look dark because they are cooler than the rest of the Sun. They may appear small on the surface of the Sun, but they are huge by Earth's standards. Some sunspots are 50,000 miles wide, which makes them far larger than Earth itself. But they are not permanent. Sunspots arise and then disappear. A single sunspot can last a few days or several months. The average lifespan of a sunspot is about one week.

5 No one can explain why some sunspots last longer than others. In fact, no one can explain for sure how sunspots are created in the first place. Scientists, however, do have some ideas, which are based on some things they know for sure about the Sun. They know that the hydrogen and helium gases that make up the Sun are in constant motion. This motion is caused in part by the vast temperature differences between the interior of the Sun and the Sun's surface. Temperatures in the hidden interior are about 40 million degrees Farenheit. Temperatures on the surface range between 6,000 and 10,000 degrees. The hotter gases inside the Sun are constantly moving toward the surface, while the colder surface gases sink toward the interior.

6 In 1908, George Ellery Hale, an American scientist, discovered that the Sun also has a strong magnetic field. But unlike the magnetic field of Earth, which is generated by the solid, stable mass of the planet, the magnetic field of the Sun is generated by gases. These gases flow up and down and side to side. This movement causes the Sun's magnetic field to change and move around.

7 Yet, even the flow of these gases is not constant. Sometimes the magnetic field becomes relatively stable. Scientists don't know why this happens, but they do know that when the field is stable, the number of sunspots is low. When the field is active, however, the hotter gases from inside the Sun can force their way to the surface. This causes the surface of the Sun to expand and buckle. The result is anywhere from a few to a hundred sunspots.

8 Sunspot activity slowly increases until it reaches a peak about every 11 years. This peak is called a solar maximum. After a solar maximum, the sunspots begin to fade again. The time of lowest activity is called a solar minimum. Scientists are not sure what causes this 11-year cycle.

9 In any event, the rise and fall of sunspot activity means that the Sun does not send a constant amount of heat to Earth. During a solar maximum, the Sun as a whole gets slightly hotter. Even though the sunspots themselves are

The colorful aurora borealis, also called the northern lights, is sometimes visible in the night skies in northern regions.

relatively cool, the rest of the Sun's surface heats up. No one knows why this happens, but scientists have been able to measure an increase in the Sun's heat during a solar maximum.

10 Most of the time this additional heat has little impact on Earth because the solar maximum does not last a long time. Likewise, the solar minimum doesn't last long enough to cool the Earth. But what would happen if, for some reason, there were only a few sunspots for a long period of time? Would Earth then cool down?

11 It seems that it would. In fact, in the 17th century it did. The normal 11-year sunspot cycle had one major gap. From 1645 to 1715 there were almost no sunspots. No one knows what caused this 70-year break in the normal pattern, but scientists do think that it had a clear effect on Earth's weather.

12 Scientists believe that this long solar minimum caused a "little ice age." The Sun was putting out less heat and Earth was growing steadily colder. Rivers which never freeze now, like the Rio Grande in the United States and the Thames in England, froze during that period. Winters were colder and the growing season was shorter. Food was scarce and many people faced a "starving time." No one can predict if or when another long break in the normal sunspot cycle might occur.

13 Sunspots can also affect Earth in more immediate ways. The aurora borealis, or northern lights, has been linked to sunspots. Wherever there is sunspot activity, immense plumes of hot gas particles are driven out from the Sun. These are even greater during a solar maximum. When these particles collide with Earth's air particles, they give off a bright electrical charge. The result is a stunning display of northern lights. These northern lights glow like a fluorescent tube in the evening sky of the arctic regions. Some look like long thin rays that combine to form sheets of light.

14 Free light shows are not the only effect of sunspots. Electrical storms are more common during a solar maximum. Also, radio waves, which bounce off the upper atmosphere, are often disrupted, and TV signals from satellites can be interrupted.

15 One other effect was suggested by the late science writer Isaac Asimov. Sunspots could cause a country's defensive radar to break down. The radar screens could simply go blank. What would happen if one country could accurately predict when a sunspot would interfere with the radar of an enemy nation? That country could launch a surprise attack. The country whose radar was not working would not know about the incoming planes and rockets. Luckily no one is close to making such accurate forecasts about sunspots.

16 Isaac Asimov also commented on the great effect that the Sun has on Earth. He wrote, "If the Sun were to as much as hiccup, life on Earth might be baked out, or frozen out." So far, the Sun has been able to hold its breath. Still, this great fireball is not as predictable and constant as we once thought it was. Sunspots can interfere with communication systems and radar. They can also influence our weather, causing prolonged cold spells and crop failures. We can no longer take the Sun for granted. Its impact on our lives might be greater than anyone ever realized.

If you have been timed while reading this article, enter your reading time below. Then turn to the Words-per-Minute Table on page 133 and look up your reading speed (words per minute). Then enter your reading speed on the Reading Speed graph on page 134.

Reading Time: Lesson 8

________ : ________

Minutes *Seconds*

A Finding the Main Idea

One statement below expresses the main idea of the article. One statement is too general, or too broad. The other statement explains only part of the article; it is too narrow. Label the statements using the following key:

M—Main Idea **B—Too Broad** **N—Too Narrow**

_______ 1. The Sun has been shown to be less stable than people believed it to be.

_______ 2. Sunspots, which are evidence of the Sun's instability, can affect Earth's weather and communications systems.

_______ 3. Sunspot activity increases and decreases in a regular cycle.

_______ Score 15 points for a correct M answer.

_______ Score 5 points for each correct B or N answer.

_______ **Total Score:** Finding the Main Idea

B Recalling Facts

How well do you remember the facts in the article? Put an X in the box next to the answer that correctly completes each statement about the article.

1. Sunspots look like
- ☐ a. dark swirls of iron filings.
- ☐ b. exploding volcanoes.
- ☐ c. brilliant flashes of light.

2. When the Sun's magnetic field is stable, the number of sunspots is
- ☐ a. high.
- ☐ b. steadily increasing.
- ☐ c. low.

3. The normal sunspot cycle takes
- ☐ a. 70 years.
- ☐ b. 8 years.
- ☐ c. 11 years.

4. The one major break in the normal sunspot cycle lasted
- ☐ a. 11 years.
- ☐ b. 22 years.
- ☐ c. 70 years.

5. During a solar maximum, the Sun
- ☐ a. becomes hotter.
- ☐ b. cools down.
- ☐ c. gets larger.

Score 5 points for each correct answer.

_______ **Total Score:** Recalling Facts

C Making Inferences

When you combine your own experience and information from a text to draw a conclusion that is not directly stated in that text, you are making an inference. Below are five statements that may or may not be inferences based on information in the article. Label the statements using the following key:

C—Correct Inference **F—Faulty Inference**

_______ 1. There is still much to learn about how sunspots affect Earth.

_______ 2. The magnetic field of the Sun is less stable than the magnetic fields of other stars.

_______ 3. Another 70-year break in the sunspot cycle would bring cooler temperatures around the world.

_______ 4. During a solar minimum there are no sunspots at all.

_______ 5. Most problems with radio and TV signals are caused by sunspots.

Score 5 points for each correct answer.

_______ **Total Score:** Making Inferences

D Using Words Precisely

Each numbered sentence below contains an underlined word or phrase from the article. Following the sentence are three definitions. One definition is closest to the meaning of the underlined word. One definition is opposite or nearly opposite. Label those two definitions using the following key; do not label the remaining definition.

C—Closest **O—Opposite or Nearly Opposite**

1. These solar <u>blemishes</u> are called sunspots.

_______ a. beauty spots

_______ b. gases

_______ c. blotches

2. During a solar <u>maximum</u>, the Sun as a whole gets slightly hotter.

_______ a. highest point

_______ b. magnetic field

_______ c. lowest point

3. We usually think of the Sun as a constant, <u>predictable</u> heavenly body, a great power that can be counted on not to change.

_______ a. expected and prepared for

_______ b. confusing and constantly changing

_______ c. large and hot

4. Wherever there is sunspot activity, <u>immense plumes</u> of hot gas particles are driven out from the Sun.

_______ a. small sparks

_______ b. large drops

_______ c. huge jets

5. The result is a stunning display of northern lights.

_______ a. dull performance

_______ b. lovely exhibition

_______ c. sudden appearance

_______ Score 3 points for each correct C answer.

_______ Score 2 points for each correct O answer.

_______ **Total Score:** Using Words Precisely

Enter the four total scores in the spaces below, and add them together to find your Reading Comprehension Score. Then record your score on the graph on page 135.

Score	Question Type	Lesson 8
_______	Finding the Main Idea	
_______	Recalling Facts	
_______	Making Inferences	
_______	Using Words Precisely	
_______	**Reading Comprehension Score**	

Author's Approach

Put an X in the box next to the correct answer.

1. What does the author mean by the statement "so far, the Sun has been able to hold its breath"?

☐ a. The atmosphere on the Sun is unlike that on Earth.

☐ b. So far, the Sun has not undergone a sudden change in its cycle, which would have a negative effect on Earth.

☐ c. So far, scientists have been unable to make accurate forecasts about sunspots.

2. From the statement "it seems that for every answer they get, however, two new questions arise," you can conclude that the author wants the reader to think that

☐ a. scientists cannot agree on the information they've gathered on sunspots.

☐ b. it is difficult to understand the nature of sunspots.

☐ c. scientists know less about sunspots now than they did 50 years ago.

3. What does the author imply by saying, "No one can predict if or when another long break in the normal sunspot cycle might occur"?

☐ a. A long break in the sunspot cycle might mean the death of our Sun.

☐ b. Scientists will never understand the sunspot cycle.

☐ c. An ice age or another "starving time" can occur at any time, without warning.

4. The author probably wrote this article in order to
- ☐ a. inform the reader about the existence of sunspots.
- ☐ b. emphasize the similarities between Earth and the Sun.
- ☐ c. convey to the reader how little scientists know about sunspots.

_________ Number of correct answers

Record your personal assessment of your work on the Critical Thinking Chart on page 136.

Summarizing and Paraphrasing

Put an X in the box next to the correct answer.

1. Below are summaries of the article. Choose the summary that says all the most important things about the article but in the fewest words.
- ☐ a. Unpredictable sunspot activity can interfere with our communication systems and influence our weather.
- ☐ b. Activity on the Sun can affect Earth in many ways.
- ☐ c. Scientists study sunspots to determine the impact of their activity on Earth, but many questions remain unanswered.

2. Choose the sentence that correctly restates the following sentence from the article:

   "The hotter gases inside the Sun are constantly moving toward the surface, while the cooler surface gases sink toward the interior."
- ☐ a. As the Sun's hot, interior gases rise, the cooler gases on the surface of the Sun descend toward its core.
- ☐ b. As the Sun's hot, interior gases fall, the cooler gases on the surface of the Sun rise.
- ☐ c. The hotter gases within the Sun's core heat the cooler gases on the Sun's surface.

_________ Number of correct answers

Record your personal assessment of your work on the Critical Thinking Chart on page 136.

Critical Thinking

Put an X in the box next to the correct answer for questions 1, 3, and 4. Follow the directions provided for the other questions.

1. From what Isaac Asimov said, you can predict that
- ☐ a. the gases from a large sunspot could fall to Earth and burn up the planet.
- ☐ b. unusual sunspot activity could so affect our weather that all life on Earth would be destroyed.
- ☐ c. unusual sunspot activity could result in a world war.

2. Choose from the letters below to correctly complete the following statement. Write the letters on the lines.

   In the article, __________ and __________ are different.

   a. the aurora borealis

   b. a solar maximum

   c. the northern lights

3. What was the effect of the long solar minimum between 1645 and 1715?

☐ a. There was an increase in electrical storms.

☐ b. Radar screens went blank.

☐ c. Winters were colder and rivers in mild climates froze.

4. What causes the Sun's surface to expand and buckle?

☐ a. a solar maximum

☐ b. the movement of hotter gases to the Sun's surface

☐ c. the eruption of anywhere from a few to a hundred sunspots

5. Which paragraphs from the article provide evidence that supports your answer to question 3?

____

________ Number of correct answers

Record your personal assessment of your work on the Critical Thinking Chart on page 136.

Personal Response

If you could ask the author of the article one question, what would it be?

____

____

____

____

Self-Assessment

From reading this article, I have learned

____

____

____

____

CAN SOME PEOPLE SEE THE FUTURE?

For 10 nights in a row, David Booth had the same nightmare. In his dream he saw an American Airlines airplane plunging to earth. Every night he saw the plane explode in a ball of red flames. David's vision was so clear he said it was "like watching television."

2 David called the airline and federal officials to tell them of his dream. Not wanting to take chances, they listened. But there was not enough detail to David's dream for any action to be taken. David did not know when or where the accident in his dream was taking place. Four days later, on May 25, 1979, an American Airlines jet crashed at Chicago's O'Hare International Airport. Two hundred seventy-five people were killed. It was the worst air disaster in the history of the United States.

3 One day in 1485, a young English farmhand named Robert Nixon started to shout while plowing a field. He cried, "No Dick, now Harry! Oh, ill done, Dick; oh well done, Harry; Harry has gained the day!"

4 The other farm workers were surprised to hear Robert speak so clearly. Before this outburst, he had rarely spoken. In fact, because he almost never talked, many people thought that Robert was mentally retarded. Although his coworkers were startled by Robert's cry, they didn't think it meant anything. It was only the next day that Robert's words began to make sense. At the very moment that Robert had been uttering his strange cries, Henry Tudor (Harry) had been defeating King Richard III (Dick) at the Battle of Bosworth Field. Since the battle had taken place many miles away, there was no way that Robert could have known about the outcome.

5 Henry Tudor, who became King Henry VII of England, was told of Robert's unusual experience on the day of the battle, and he asked Robert to come and see him. Robert was not thrilled by the request. In fact, he was thrown into a fit, because he had seen a vision of himself starving to death in the king's castle.

6 When he at last presented himself to the king, Robert's powers were tested. The king hid a precious stone. Pretending to be upset over the loss of the stone, the king asked Robert to help him find it. Robert calmly replied, "He who hides can find." The king was so impressed by this that Robert became a court favorite. The king ordered every word Robert said to be written down.

7 But Robert's vision of starving to death in the castle still lingered. When he explained his fears to the king, Henry

Chicago firefighters probe through the wreckage of an American Airlines flight which crashed on takeoff from O'Hare International Airport.

A bust of Henry VII, King of England

reassured him that he would always be able to eat all he wanted. Unfortunately, this made other members of the royal staff jealous.

8 One day King Henry went on a journey, and Robert was left in the care of one of the king's officers. To protect Robert, the officer locked him in one of the king's closets. But soon after, the officer was called away from the castle on urgent business. He forgot to tell anyone where Robert was, and he left no key to the closet. When the officer returned, it was too late. Robert had starved to death.

9 Then there was Kenneth MacKenzie, a Scot who lived in the 17th century. He was known as the "Brahan Seer." MacKenzie could foretell the future with astonishing clarity by looking through a small stone with a hole in it. Many people went to consult with him about their futures. But he is best known for his prophecy of the Doom of the Seaforths.

10 One day the Seer was called to the Countess of Seaforth. She asked to know why her husband had not come back from Paris. His return was long overdue. The Seer looked through his stone and saw the husband in the company of a beautiful woman. When he told this to the countess, she became livid. She had the Seer killed by forcing him headfirst into a barrel of hot tar.

11 Before the Seer died, though, he proclaimed the Doom of the Seaforths. He said, "I see into the far future and I read the doom of the race of my oppressor. The long line of the Seaforths will end in extinction and sorrow."

12 But the Seer did not stop there. He continued, giving exact details of the demise of the Seaforth Dynasty. The last Seaforth, he prophesied, would be deaf and dumb. This man would have four fair-haired sons, but every one of them would die before his father. Their hour of death would come when the Seaforths had four neighbors with the following features: one would be buck-toothed, one half-witted, one harelipped, and the fourth a stammerer. The Seer even specified the names of these four neighbors.

13 It took more than 100 years for the Doom of the Seaforths to be fulfilled. But it was. The last Seaforth was deaf and dumb. He had four fair-haired sons, but not one outlived him. At the time of his sons' deaths, there were four neighbors who matched precisely the description given by the Brahan Seer so many years earlier. The long line of the Seaforths did indeed end in "extinction and sorrow."

14 Did Robert Nixon and the Brahan Seer really see into the future? Did David Booth somehow know of the Chicago airplane crash days before it took place? Or were these merely cases of freak coincidence?

15 Do some people have a "sixth sense" that goes beyond our ordinary grasp of time and space? Perhaps. The evidence strongly suggests that this is so. It may even be that we all have this extra sense, but only a few of us ever learn how to use it.

If you have been timed while reading this article, enter your reading time below. Then turn to the Words-per-Minute Table on page 133 and look up your reading speed (words per minute). Then enter your reading speed on the Reading Speed graph on page 134.

Reading Time: Lesson 9

_______ : _______

Minutes *Seconds*

A Finding the Main Idea

One statement below expresses the main idea of the article. One statement is too general, or too broad. The other statement explains only part of the article; it is too narrow. Label the statements using the following key:

M—Main Idea **B—Too Broad** **N—Too Narrow**

_______ 1. David Booth had a vision that an American Airlines jet would crash.

_______ 2. Some individuals have powers that most people do not possess.

_______ 3. Some people seem to have the ability to see what will take place in the future.

_______ Score 15 points for a correct M answer.

_______ Score 5 points for each correct B or N answer.

_______ **Total Score:** Finding the Main Idea

B Recalling Facts

How well do you remember the facts in the article? Put an X in the box next to the answer that correctly completes each statement about the article.

1. David Booth's dream showed the
   - ☐ a. name of the airport.
   - ☐ b. name of the airline.
   - ☐ c. time of the accident.
2. Henry Tudor
   - ☐ a. lost his battle against Richard III.
   - ☐ b. was angry over Robert's vision.
   - ☐ c. became king of England.
3. Robert's second vision was that he would
   - ☐ a. be killed by the king's guards.
   - ☐ b. starve to death in the king's castle.
   - ☐ c. become a court favorite.
4. The "Brahan Seer" told the future by
   - ☐ a. gazing into a crystal ball.
   - ☐ b. consulting the position of the stars.
   - ☐ c. looking through a small stone with a hole in it.
5. The Doom of the Seaforths
   - ☐ a. was immediately fulfilled.
   - ☐ b. took more than 100 years to be fulfilled.
   - ☐ c. was foretold by Robert Nixon.

Score 5 points for each correct answer.

_______ **Total Score:** Recalling Facts

Making Inferences

When you combine your own experience and information from a text to draw a conclusion that is not directly stated in that text, you are making an inference. Below are five statements that may or may not be inferences based on information in the article. Label the statements using the following key:

C—Correct Inference **F—Faulty Inference**

_______ 1. David Booth has the ability to predict all airline crashes.

_______ 2. King Henry VII believed that some people really do have a "sixth sense."

_______ 3. The Countess of Seaforth had the Brahan Seer killed because she was angry about what he told her about her husband.

_______ 4. Prophecies always foretell something evil.

_______ 5. If everyone would try equally hard, we would all have the ability to foretell the future.

Score 5 points for each correct answer.

_______ **Total Score:** Making Inferences

D Using Words Precisely

Each numbered sentence below contains an underlined word or phrase from the article. Following the sentence are three definitions. One definition is closest to the meaning of the underlined word. One definition is opposite or nearly opposite. Label those two definitions using the following key; do not label the remaining definition.

C—Closest **O—Opposite or Nearly Opposite**

1. Before this <u>outburst</u>, he had rarely spoken.

_______ a. sudden shout

_______ b. long period of silence

_______ c. accident

2. But Robert's vision of starving to death in the castle still <u>lingered</u>.

_______ a. hurried away

_______ b. angered

_______ c. remained

3. When he explained his fears to the king, Henry <u>reassured</u> him that he would always be able to eat all he wanted.

_______ a. made uncertain and fearful

_______ b. set someone's mind at ease

_______ c. reminded

4. When he told this to the countess, she became <u>livid</u>.

_______ a. very angry

_______ b. calm

_______ c. frightened

5. He continued, giving exact details of the demise of the Seaforth dynasty.

_______ a. destruction

_______ b. history

_______ c. birth

_______ Score 3 points for each correct C answer.

_______ Score 2 points for each correct O answer.

_______ **Total Score:** Using Words Precisely

Enter the four total scores in the spaces below, and add them together to find your Reading Comprehension Score. Then record your score on the graph on page 135.

Score	Question Type	Lesson 9
_______	Finding the Main Idea	
_______	Recalling Facts	
_______	Making Inferences	
_______	Using Words Precisely	
_______	**Reading Comprehension Score**	

Author's Approach

Put an X in the box next to the correct answer.

1. The main purpose of the first paragraph is to

☐ a. inform the reader about people who can see the future.

☐ b. describe David's vision.

☐ c. persuade the reader that some people can see the future.

2. Choose the statement below that best describes the author's position in paragraph 15.

☐ a. Everyone has a sixth sense and can see into the future.

☐ b. No one can really predict the future.

☐ c. Some people probably can use their sixth sense and see into the future.

3. The author tells this story mainly by

☐ a. retelling personal experiences.

☐ b. using his or her imagination and creativity.

☐ c. telling different stories about the same topic.

_______ Number of correct answers

Record your personal assessment of your work on the Critical Thinking Chart on page 136.

Summarizing and Paraphrasing

Put an X in the box next to the correct answer for question 3. Follow the directions provided for the other questions.

1. Look for the important ideas and events in paragraphs 1 and 2. Summarize those paragraphs in one or two sentences.

____

____

____

2. Reread paragraph 8 in the article. Below, write a summary of the paragraph in no more than 25 words.

____

____

____

____

Reread your summary and decide whether it covers the important ideas in the paragraph. Next, decide how to shorten the summary to 15 words or less without leaving out any essential information. Write this summary below.

____

____

____

3. Choose the best one-sentence paraphrase for the following sentence from the article:

   "Henry Tudor, who became King Henry VII of England, was told of Robert's unusual experience on the day of the battle, and he asked Robert to come and see him."

☐ a. After King Henry VII heard about Robert's vision of the battle, he invited the young farmhand to his castle.

☐ b. On the day of the battle, Henry Tudor asked Robert to come and see him.

☐ c. After hearing about Robert's vision, King Henry VII of England went to see the young farmhand.

_______ Number of correct answers

Record your personal assessment of your work on the Critical Thinking Chart on page 136.

Critical Thinking

Put an X in the box next to the correct answer for questions 2 and 5. Follow the directions provided for the other questions.

1. For each statement below, write O if it expresses an opinion and write F if it expresses a fact.

_______ a. Henry Tudor defeated King Richard III at the Battle of Bosworth Field.

_______ b. The plane David Booth saw in his vision was the one that crashed at O'Hare International Airport.

_______ c. The Seaforth dynasty died out just as the Brahan Seer predicted that it would.

2. Based on King Henry VII's actions as told in this article, you can predict that he would have been

☐ a. amused that Robert had foretold his own death.

☐ b. afraid to replace Robert with someone else who could foretell the future.

☐ c. greatly upset by Robert's death.

3. Choose from the letters below to correctly complete the following statement. Write the letters on the lines.

In the article, _________ and _________ are alike.

a. Kenneth MacKenzie

b. Henry Tudor

c. Robert Nixon

4. Read paragraph 10. Then choose from the letters below to correctly complete the following statement. Write the letters on the lines.

According to paragraph 10, the Brahan Seer _________ because the Brahan Seer _________.

a. told the Countess of Seaforth that her husband had been unfaithful

b. was put to death

c. foretold the Doom of the Seaforths

5. What did you have to do to answer question 2?

☐ a. find a comparison (how things are the same)

☐ b. find a fact (something that you can prove is true)

☐ c. draw a conclusion (a sensible statement based on the text and your experience)

_________ Number of correct answers

Record your personal assessment of your work on the Critical Thinking Chart on page 136.

Personal Response

A question I would like answered by David Booth is

____

____

____

____

Self-Assessment

When reading the article, I was having trouble with

____

____

____

THE SPECIAL GIFTS OF AUTISTIC SAVANTS

Nadia was six years old when her mother called the Child Development Clinic in Nottingham, England. Nadia's mother was worried. Her daughter had not yet learned how to talk. Although the girl had been attending a special school for severely subnormal children, she seemed to be making no progress. A psychologist at the clinic agreed to see Nadia. But even the experts at the clinic were not prepared for the special child they were about to meet.

2 Nadia was a large girl for her age. Her movements were slow and clumsy. She knew only 10 words. She did not respond to the psychologist who took her into the playroom, and she gave no clues to what she was thinking. Did she understand the words that were being spoken to her? Was she simply being stubborn and uncooperative? Or could she really not understand the speech of others?

3 While one psychologist tried to work with the girl, Nadia's mother talked to the woman who ran the clinic. During their talk, Nadia's mother mentioned her daughter's drawings. In fact, she had

Nadia drew this horse and rider when she was five years old. Note the details she included in the horse's bridle and the rider's tunic, trumpet, and hand. Can you find a squirrel on the side of the horse?

brought some with her, and she pulled them out of her purse to show the woman. As the clinic director looked at the pictures, she was amazed. The drawings were absolutely superb!

4 Within a few weeks it became clear to the staff at the clinic that Nadia was a most unusual girl. In almost every way she seemed severely retarded. On many tests for development she did no better than an 18-month-old baby. She could understand simple commands, such as "Put your coat on," but she could not speak more than 10 words. Usually she could only echo what other people said. If someone said "Hello, Nadia," she might repeat, "Hello, Nadia." She could not tie her shoes or fasten a buckle. She could not skip or hop on one foot.

5 The only exception to her low level of performance was her drawing, which was phenomenal. She could draw better than most adults, and she had mastered the basic skills needed to produce impressive works of art. Unlike many children, Nadia had not shown much interest in drawing people or houses. Her favorite subject was horses. She could draw horses running, turning, standing, and prancing. She drew minute details of bridles, saddles, and facial features. And these drawings were always done without looking at pictures of her subjects. She did not trace her drawings, she created them. They were originals.

6 The most remarkable fact was that Nadia had been drawing like this since she was three years old. Her talent had not developed slowly; instead, it had simply appeared. She could draw as well when she was three as she could at the age of six.

7 Nadia, it seemed, was an "autistic savant." The word *savant* is a French word meaning "learned or well-informed." A savant is usually thought of as a person with detailed knowledge in some specialized field. The term *autistic savant* is used to describe someone who possesses one highly developed skill but might be deficient in other skills. Nadia's special skill was drawing.

8 Other autistic savants have been known to have a special flair for music or a great mechanical ability. One man had an IQ of 40, which meant his mental age was about six and a half. Yet he could rewire stereo equipment, repair clocks, fix bicycles, and build lamps. He could take a dishwasher apart, clean it, and then put it back together again.

9 Another autistic savant had an IQ of only 20. Still, this woman could play the piano beautifully, even though she could not read music. She did not need to practice in order to master a piece. If she heard it sung or even hummed once, she could play it flawlessly—and in the same key in which she had heard it.

10 The most common ability of autistic savants, however, is calendar counting. This is the ability to immediately name

When an average six-year-old draws a horse, it looks like this. Compare this to five-year-old Nadia's drawing.

the day of the week for any given date in a 20- or 30-year period. One autistic savant who had this ability was a man with an IQ of 8 and a mental age of one and a half years. He was so severely handicapped that he had to be cared for in a hospital. He could not feed or dress himself, and he had almost no language skills. Yet, when he was asked what day of the week November 27, 1930 had been, he correctly identified Thursday. When he was tested further, he could do the same for almost every date from 1915 to 1945.

11 How did Nadia and the other autistic savants acquire their special talents? No one is quite sure. One theory is that autistic savants have photographic memories. When they see or hear something, they are able to remember it exactly. They can then reproduce it on their own at a later date. This may in fact be true for some autistic savants, but it does not explain Nadia's case. Sometimes Nadia's drawings did resemble pictures from her storybooks, but she would usually alter these images, and she often created her own unique pictures.

12 Other experts have argued that the talents of autistic savants are the result of practice. These experts believe that autistic savants receive a great deal of praise for their skill. This encourages them to develop it more highly. Again, this may help to explain some cases, but it does not explain Nadia. Nadia did not practice, and her talent did not develop slowly.

13 A final theory is that these people's lack of language skills causes their special talents to emerge. Those who put this theory forward argue that because autistic savants cannot talk, their minds try to make up for this by moving in another direction. Unlike other children, their minds are not working on building basic language skills. They can, therefore, concentrate on just their one special skill.

14 This last theory does seem to relate to Nadia. As the staff at the clinic in Nottingham worked with her, Nadia's speech slowly developed. By the time she was nine she was learning to talk. She could also add and subtract simple numbers, and she could read and write basic sentences. As Nadia's speech developed, her drawing ability faded. She stopped drawing pictures on her own. Soon, she would only draw when asked to do so. Her pictures became less detailed and less complex. While her drawing skill was still unusual for such a young child, it was no longer incredible.

If you have been timed while reading this article, enter your reading time below. Then turn to the Words-per-Minute Table on page 133 and look up your reading speed (words per minute). Then enter your reading speed on the Reading Speed graph on page 134.

Reading Time: Lesson 10

________ : ________

Minutes *Seconds*

A Finding the Main Idea

One statement below expresses the main idea of the article. One statement is too general, or too broad. The other statement explains only part of the article; it is too narrow. Label the statements using the following key:

M—Main Idea **B—Too Broad** **N—Too Narrow**

_____ 1. Some people, known as autistic savants, might have a very low level of general intelligence but one special, highly developed skill.

_____ 2. Some mentally retarded people have special talents.

_____ 3. Though Nadia could hardly speak or understand what was said to her, she could draw exceptionally well.

_____ Score 15 points for a correct M answer.

_____ Score 5 points for each correct B or N answer.

_____ **Total Score:** Finding the Main Idea

B Recalling Facts

How well do you remember the facts in the article? Put an X in the box next to the answer that correctly completes each statement about the article.

1. When Nadia was first taken to the clinic she was
   - ☐ a. six years old.
   - ☐ b. three years old.
   - ☐ c. nine years old.
2. The experts at the clinic found Nadia's mental age to be about
   - ☐ a. three years.
   - ☐ b. six years.
   - ☐ c. 18 months.
3. Nadia's favorite subject to draw was
   - ☐ a. people.
   - ☐ b. houses.
   - ☐ c. horses.
4. A savant is someone who is
   - ☐ a. an idiot.
   - ☐ b. an artist.
   - ☐ c. knowledgeable.
5. The most common ability of autistic savants is
   - ☐ a. drawing.
   - ☐ b. calendar counting.
   - ☐ c. playing the piano.

Score 5 points for each correct answer.

_____ **Total Score:** Recalling Facts

C Making Inferences

When you combine your own experience and information from a text to draw a conclusion that is not directly stated in that text, you are making an inference. Below are five statements that may or may not be inferences based on information in the article. Label the statements using the following key:

C—Correct Inference **F—Faulty Inference**

_______ 1. Nadia's mother knew that her daughter's drawings were special or unusual.

_______ 2. The experts at the clinic had seen many cases just like Nadia's.

_______ 3. Nadia's drawing ability could have been even better if she could only have read books about drawing.

_______ 4. Only female autistic savants develop an interest in art or music.

_______ 5. When Nadia's ability to draw began to fade, it was probably because her mind had begun working on language skills.

Score 5 points for each correct answer.

_______ **Total Score:** Making Inferences

D Using Words Precisely

Each numbered sentence below contains an underlined word or phrase from the article. Following the sentence are three definitions. One definition is closest to the meaning of the underlined word. One definition is opposite or nearly opposite. Label those two definitions using the following key; do not label the remaining definition.

C—Closest **O—Opposite or Nearly Opposite**

1. Although the girl had been attending a special school for severely subnormal children, she seemed to be making no progress.

_______ a. very retarded

_______ b. highly artistic

_______ c. highly intelligent

2. The drawings were absolutely superb!

_______ a. excellent

_______ b. poor

_______ c. unusual

3. Other autistic savants have been known to have a special flair for music or a great mechanical ability.

_______ a. inability

_______ b. attraction

_______ c. talent

4. Sometimes Nadia's drawings did resemble pictures from her storybooks, but she would usually alter these images, and she often created her own unique pictures.

_____ a. like no other

_____ b. not original

_____ c. pretty

5. A final theory is that these people's lack of language skills causes their special talents to emerge.

_____ a. hold back

_____ b. come forward

_____ c. be recognized

_____ Score 3 points for each correct C answer.

_____ Score 2 points for each correct O answer.

_____ **Total Score:** Using Words Precisely

Enter the four total scores in the spaces below, and add them together to find your Reading Comprehension Score. Then record your score on the graph on page 135.

Score	Question Type	Lesson 10
_____	Finding the Main Idea	
_____	Recalling Facts	
_____	Making Inferences	
_____	Using Words Precisely	
_____	**Reading Comprehension Score**	

Author's Approach

Put an X in the box next to the correct answer.

1. What does the author mean by the statement "she did not respond to the psychologist who took her into the playroom, and she gave no clues to what she was thinking"?

☐ a. Nadia played by herself but ignored the psychologist.

☐ b. Nadia did not talk or communicate with the psychologist in any way.

☐ c. Nadia was angry that she had been brought to see the psychologist and so refused to speak.

2. Which of the following statements from the article best describes Nadia?

☐ a. "Nadia was a large girl for her age."

☐ b. "She could not skip or hop on one foot."

☐ c. "She could draw better than most adults, and she had mastered the basic skills needed to produce impressive works of art."

3. From the statements below, choose those that you believe the author would agree with.

☐ a. Autistic savants become expert at one special skill because most basic skills remain undeveloped.

☐ b. Nadia preferred to express herself visually rather than verbally.

☐ c. The staff at the clinic shouldn't have taught Nadia how to read and write because that caused her drawing ability to fade.

4. The author probably wrote this article in order to

☐ a. tell the reader about the remarkable talents of autistic savants.

☐ b. describe the lives of autistic savants.

☐ c. compare autistic savants with people of average intelligence.

_____ Number of correct answers

Record your personal assessment of your work on the Critical Thinking Chart on page 136.

Summarizing and Paraphrasing

Put an X in the box next to the correct answer for questions 2 and 3. Follow the directions provided for the other question.

1. Complete the following one-sentence summary of the article using the lettered phrases from the phrase bank below. Write the letters on the lines.

Phrase Bank:

a. a discussion of theories that might explain Nadia's special talent

b. a description of Nadia

c. Nadia's phenomenal drawing ability

The article about autistic savants begins with ________, goes on to explain ________, and ends with ________.

2. Below are summaries of the article. Choose the summary that says all the most important things about the article but in the fewest words.

☐ a. Autistic savants cannot read, write, or speak on a basic level, but they do learn how to do one thing exceptionally well. Some become excellent artists or musicians, while others become skilled at calendar counting.

☐ b. Although Nadia only had the developmental skills of an 18-month-old baby, her talent for drawing far exceeded that of most adults.

☐ c. Although severely retarded in basic language skills, Nadia and other autistic savants develop exceptional skills in one specialized field.

3. Read the statement about the article below. Then read the paraphrase of that statement. Choose the reason that best tells why the paraphrase does not say the same thing as the statement.

Statement: Some people believe that autistic savants have photographic memories, which allow them to recall with great precision something they have seen or heard.

Paraphrase: People with photographic memories can remember quite clearly the things they have seen or heard.

☐ a. Paraphrase says too much.

☐ b. Paraphrase doesn't say enough.

☐ c. Paraphrase doesn't agree with the statement about the article.

________ Number of correct answers

Record your personal assessment of your work on the Critical Thinking Chart on page 136.

CRITICAL THINKING

Critical Thinking

Put an X in the box next to the correct answer for questions 1 and 4. Follow the directions provided for the other questions.

1. Based on the information in paragraph 14, you can predict that Nadia would

☐ a. continue to draw less and less as her verbal skills improved.

☐ b. become a drawing instructor.

☐ c. stop working on developing her language skills so that she could draw more complex pictures.

2. Choose from the letters below to correctly complete the following statement. Write the letters on the lines.

   On the positive side, autistic savants __________, but on the negative side, autistic savants __________.

   a. can have a special flair for music or a great mechanical ability

   b. are severely retarded

   c. excel in one particular area

3. Choose from the letters below to correctly complete the following statement. Write the letters on the lines.

   According to the article, learning to talk caused ________ to ________, and the effect was ________.

   a. her drawings became less complex

   b. Nadia

   c. lose interest in drawing

4. Of the following theme categories, which would this story fit into?

☐ a. Practice makes perfect.

☐ b. Everyone has a unique talent.

☐ c. Life is unfair.

_________ Number of correct answers

Record your personal assessment of your work on the Critical Thinking Chart on page 136.

Personal Response

If I were the author, I would add

____

____

because

____

____

Self-Assessment

While reading the article, the easiest thing for me was

____

____

____

____

TSUNAMIS
Killer Waves

This illustration shows a tsunami engulfing buildings. Note the erupting volcano in the background.

"Tsunami!" came the cry in the distance.

2 At first, 18-year-old Mieko Browne thought it was an April Fool's joke. Then she looked up and saw that it wasn't. A massive wall of water was headed straight for her house in Hilo, Hawaii. Mieko's mother saw it, too. She pushed Mieko inside the house, slamming the door shut just as the wave ripped the house off its foundation.

3 A series of waves then sucked the house in and out of Hilo Bay. As the two women looked helplessly out a window, they saw dead bodies floating by, surrounded by dead fish and other debris. They saw one boy clinging desperately to a piece of lumber. On the third wild rush back to the shore, Mieko and her mother got lucky. Their house crashed into the side of a factory that hadn't been uprooted. Somehow, Mieko and her mother managed to scramble out of the house and into the safety of the factory.

4 Many other Hawaiians were not so lucky. It was April 1, 1946, and the city of Hilo had just been hit by a series of giant

waves called a *tsunami*. (A tsunami may be just one wave. More often, however, it is a series of waves.) The tsunami in 1946 was the most deadly in Hawaiian history. The waves killed 170 people and injured more than 160 others. The people had no warning at all. It is said that if you can see a tsunami, it is too late to get out of its way. A tsunami moves that fast. One moment the people of Hilo were enjoying a fine day; the next moment they were face to face with a deadly tower of water.

5 What causes these monster waves? First, it is important to know what doesn't cause them. Tsunamis have nothing to do with tides. They can hit at high tide or low tide or at any time in between. Tides are caused by the pull of gravity between the earth and the moon. So it is wrong to refer to a tsunami as a tidal wave. Also, ordinary waves are created when wind passes over the water. Wind, no matter how wild, cannot create a tsunami. Even a hurricane cannot produce a tsunami.

6 Most tsunamis are caused by unseen forces on the floor of the ocean. Often the cause is a large earthquake under the sea. Tsunamis can also be started by underwater volcanoes. They can even be caused by volcanoes near the sea. The key factor is a sudden rise or drop in the ocean floor. That triggers the water above the floor to start moving. And it moves extremely fast. A tsunami travels about 500 miles an hour—about the speed of a jet plane. The tsunami that struck Hilo was started by an earthquake off the coast of Alaska more than 2,200 miles away. It only took the killer waves about five hours to reach Hilo.

7 On the open ocean, a sailor wouldn't even notice a tsunami. It might be 100 miles long but only about two or three feet high. A wave that size can't generate enough power to spill a cup of coffee on board a ship. But when a tsunami nears land, all its vast energy becomes concentrated and the wave can rise up 100 feet or more.

8 As a tsunami approaches land, it sucks the water out of a harbor or beach in an

An earthquake, followed by a tsunami, caused massive destruction on Okushiri Island in 1993.

instant. (*Tsunami* comes from the Japanese words *tsu*, meaning "harbor," and *nami*, meaning "wave.") The sucking action leaves fish flopping on the sand and probably wondering where all the water went. But then, the water curls up like some mythical monster and comes roaring back to the shore.

9 Most tsunamis occur in the Pacific Ocean. That's because that region has a large number of earthquakes and volcanoes. Tsunamis have also struck in the Indian Ocean and in the eastern Atlantic. They can even hit smaller bodies of water, such as the Black Sea.

10 Tsunamis have cut a deadly path through human history. The first recorded case occurred in A.D. 365 on July 21. The tsunami was triggered by a huge earthquake on the ocean floor. The terrible waves struck Alexandria, Egypt, and killed thousands of people.

11 The worst tsunami ever occurred on an island in Indonesia. It was caused by a volcano called Krakatoa. In late August 1883, Krakatoa erupted. Soon after, a 100-foot wave hit the islands of Sumatra and Java. The crushing water destroyed thousands of homes and boats. The wave wiped nearly 300 towns off the map. Worse, it took the lives of more than 36,000 people.

12 On June 15, 1896, another tsunami struck Japan. This one was caused by an underwater earthquake. It took just an hour for the wave to reach Sanriku Beach. There, thousands of people had gathered to celebrate a religious festival. They had no chance to escape. A 75-foot wave caught them completely by surprise. More than 26,000 people drowned.

13 Imagine the shock of local fishermen, who had been fishing a couple of miles offshore when the tsunami struck. The wave had rolled harmlessly under their boats. The men hadn't felt a thing. But when they returned to the beach, they saw the vast wreckage and piles of dead bodies on the beach. To them, it must have seemed as if the world had come to an end.

14 Today, scientists are learning how to predict tsunamis. Since the Hilo disaster, early warning systems have been developed. Large earthquakes and volcanoes are closely monitored. Scientists can now plot how long it will take for a tsunami to reach vulnerable places.

15 Still, the system is not perfect. Tsunamis still kill. In 1992, one struck Indonesia, taking more than 1,000 lives. In 1993, a tsunami in Japan killed 330 people. A tsunami in the Philippines took the lives of 62 people in 1994.

16 The biggest problem with forecasting tsunamis is predicting whether the waves will be killers or harmless ripples. The power of a tsunami depends on many factors. One is the contour of the land. The shape of the land can funnel a wave into a small area with disastrous results. Or it can spread the wave out over a wide area, greatly reducing the damage.

17 Differences in land shape make it nearly impossible to provide precise warnings. In October 1995, there was a strong earthquake off the coast of Japan. A full-scale tsunami warning was issued for all of southern Japan. Thousands of people fled from the shore. Three hours later, the warning was lifted. The biggest wave to hit the mainland had been 4½ inches high. One small island reported a six-foot wave. And that was it!

18 False alarms are dangerous. Katsuyuki Abe, a top tsunami expert, explains why. He says that the current warnings are "too rough, the area too wide. There is a fear that [such false alarms] will create a boy-who-cried-wolf effect, that people will stop listening."

19 They better not, though. Tsunami warnings should never be taken lightly. Just ask anyone who has seen a tsunami up close. Mieko Browne won't take any more chances. When she got married, she told her husband: "We're not living at the beach. We're going to live in the mountains!"

If you have been timed while reading this article, enter your reading time below. Then turn to the Words-per-Minute Table on page 133 and look up your reading speed (words per minute). Then enter your reading speed on the Reading Speed graph on page 134.

Reading Time: Lesson 11

______ : ______

Minutes *Seconds*

A Finding the Main Idea

One statement below expresses the main idea of the article. One statement is too general, or too broad. The other statement explains only part of the article; it is too narrow. Label the statements using the following key:

M—Main Idea **B—Too Broad** **N—Too Narrow**

_______ 1. A tsunami is a series of fast-moving, deadly waves that are most often triggered by underwater earthquakes or volcanoes.

_______ 2. The tsunami that struck Hilo, Hawaii, in 1946 killed 170 people.

_______ 3. Most tsunamis occur in the Pacific Ocean.

_______ Score 15 points for a correct M answer.

_______ Score 5 points for each correct B or N answer.

_______ **Total Score:** Finding the Main Idea

B Recalling Facts

How well do you remember the facts in the article? Put an X in the box next to the answer that correctly completes each statement about the article.

1. Most tsunamis are caused by
- ☐ a. movements on the ocean floor.
- ☐ b. tidal changes.
- ☐ c. very strong winds or hurricanes.

2. A tsunami travels about
- ☐ a. 200 miles per hour.
- ☐ b. 500 miles per hour.
- ☐ c. 100 miles per hour.

3. As a tsunami approaches land, it
- ☐ a. sucks the water out of a harbor in an instant.
- ☐ b. loses power.
- ☐ c. triggers an earthquake.

4. The first recorded case of a tsunami occurred in
- ☐ a. 1883.
- ☐ b. 1896.
- ☐ c. A.D. 365.

5. The biggest problem with forecasting tsunamis is
- ☐ a. predicting when they will strike.
- ☐ b. predicting where they will strike.
- ☐ c. determining how large the waves will be.

Score 5 points for each correct answer.

_______ **Total Score:** Recalling Facts

C Making Inferences

When you combine your own experience and information from a text to draw a conclusion that is not directly stated in that text, you are making an inference. Below are five statements that may or may not be inferences based on information in the article. Label the statements using the following key:

C—Correct Inference **F—Faulty Inference**

_______ 1. A tsunami moves so quickly that people in its path cannot escape from it.

_______ 2. Early warning systems can help protect people from tsunamis.

_______ 3. False alarms increase people's awareness of tsunamis.

_______ 4. People on a boat in the middle of the ocean would not be aware of an approaching tsunami.

_______ 5. When a volcano or earthquake is detected in an area, its residents should be on the alert for a tsunami warning.

Score 5 points for each correct answer.

_______ **Total Score:** Making Inferences

D Using Words Precisely

Each numbered sentence below contains an underlined word or phrase from the article. Following the sentence are three definitions. One definition is closest to the meaning of the underlined word. One definition is opposite or nearly opposite. Label those two definitions using the following key; do not label the remaining definition.

C—Closest **O—Opposite or Nearly Opposite**

1. Large earthquakes and volcanoes are closely monitored.

_______ a. disregarded

_______ b. felt

_______ c. observed closely

2. But when a tsunami nears land, all its vast energy becomes concentrated and the wave can rise up 100 feet or more.

_______ a. limited

_______ b. immense

_______ c. recycled

3. But then, the water curls up like some mythical monster and comes roaring back to the shore.

_______ a. historical

_______ b. imaginary

_______ c. hideous

4. Differences in land shape make it nearly impossible to provide precise warnings.

_______ a. annual

_______ b. exact

_______ c. inaccurate

5. Scientists can now plot how long it will take for a tsunami to reach vulnerable places.

_______ a. unprotected

_______ b. faraway

_______ c. well defended

_______ Score 3 points for each correct C answer.

_______ Score 2 points for each correct O answer.

_______ **Total Score:** Using Words Precisely

Enter the four total scores in the spaces below, and add them together to find your Reading Comprehension Score. Then record your score on the graph on page 135.

Score	Question Type	Lesson 11
_______	Finding the Main Idea	
_______	Recalling Facts	
_______	Making Inferences	
_______	Using Words Precisely	
_______	**Reading Comprehension Score**	

Author's Approach

Put an X in the box next to the correct answer.

1. The author uses the first sentence of the article to

☐ a. inform the reader about tsunamis.

☐ b. describe the qualities of a tsunami.

☐ c. encourage the reader to find out about tsunamis.

2. The author's purpose in writing "Tsunamis: Killer Waves" is to

☐ a. express an opinion about tsunami warning systems.

☐ b. inform the reader about tsunamis.

☐ c. describe the devastation caused by tsunamis.

3. What does the author imply by saying "There is a fear that [such false alarms] will create a boy-who-cried wolf effect"?

☐ a. Too many false alarms may cause people to panic.

☐ b. Too many false alarms may prevent people from taking any warnings seriously.

☐ c. Some people fear that the false alarms are the result of childish pranks.

4. How is the author's purpose for writing the article expressed in paragraph 5?

☐ a. The author describes the effect of the wind on tsunamis.

☐ b. The author emphasizes the similarities between tidal waves and tsunamis.

☐ c. The author explains the difference between tidal waves and tsunamis.

_______ Number of correct answers

Record your personal assessment of your work on the Critical Thinking Chart on page 136.

Summarizing and Paraphrasing

Follow the directions provided for question 1. Put an X in the box next to the correct answer for question 2.

1. Look for the important ideas and events in paragraphs 12 and 13. Summarize those paragraphs in one or two sentences.

____

____

____

2. Choose the sentence that correctly restates the following sentence from the article:

"The shape of the land can funnel a wave into a small area with disastrous results."

☐ a. The force of a tsunami wave concentrated in a small, narrow area can have devastating results.

☐ b. A tsunami wave can destroy the shape of the land in a small area.

☐ c. Small areas are more likely to be struck by tsunamis.

_______ Number of correct answers

Record your personal assessment of your work on the Critical Thinking Chart on page 136.

Critical Thinking

Put an X in the box next to the correct answer for questions 1, 2, and 5. Follow the directions provided for the other questions.

1. Which of the following statements from the article is an opinion rather than a fact?

☐ a. "Wind, no matter how wild, cannot create a tsunami."

☐ b. "Tsunami warnings should never be taken lightly."

☐ c. "Tsunamis have cut a deadly path through human history."

2. From what the article told about tsunamis, you can predict that

☐ a. scientists will stop issuing tsunami warnings in Japan.

☐ b. scientists will be able to prevent tsunamis from occurring.

☐ c. tsunamis will continue to strike coastal areas of the Pacific Ocean.

3. Choose from the letters below to correctly complete the following statement. Write the letters on the lines.

In the article, _______ and _______ are different.

a. tidal waves

b. a series of waves triggered by an underwater volcano

c. tsunamis

CRITICAL THINKING

4. Think about cause-effect relationships in the article. Fill in the blanks in the cause-effect chart, drawing from the letters below.

Cause	Effect
The ocean floor rises or drops sharply.	__________
__________	A 100-foot wave hit Sumatra and Java.
__________	Thousands fled the Japanese shore in 1995.

a. Krakatoa erupted.
b. A full-scale tsunami warning was issued for all of southern Japan.
c. The water above the floor starts moving.

5. Of the following theme categories, which would this story fit into?

☐ a. No man is an island.
☐ b. Life is unpredictable.
☐ c. People are powerless before the force of nature.

________ Number of correct answers

Record your personal assessment of your work on the Critical Thinking Chart on page 136.

Personal Response

I know how Mieko Browne feels because

____

____

____

____

Self-Assessment

I'm proud of how I answered question _______ in section __________ because

____

____

____

____

MULTIPLE PERSONALITIES

Juanita Maxwell was 25 years old when she was put on trial. She was charged with the beating death of 73-year-old Inez Kelly. Juanita, a married mother of two, had been working as a maid at a hotel in Fort Myers, Florida, when the murder occurred. The state of Florida charged that Juanita had killed Inez Kelly, a guest at the hotel, in a dispute over a fountain pen.

2 When Juanita took the stand in August of 1981, she was somber and subdued. Alan Klein, who, as Juanita's social worker, had helped her with her problems, was on hand at the trial. Because of his close relationship with Juanita, he was allowed to question her as part of her defense. When Klein asked her if she smoked or drank, Juanita replied quietly, "No, sir." In response to questions about the murder of Inez Kelly, Juanita maintained that she remembered little about the night.

3 Then, in a dramatic gesture, Klein asked to speak to "Wanda." Juanita closed her eyes and lowered her head. When she looked up again a few seconds later, she was a different person. Giggling now, and

True multiple personalities are rare, but they can result from a childhood trauma or shock. In these cases, the personality fragments and acquires its own identity.

speaking in a boisterous voice, she identified herself as Wanda Weston. She said that she was a childhood friend of Juanita Maxwell.

4 To the observers in the courtroom, the change was both baffling and convincing. Speaking as Wanda, the defendant now freely admitted to the habits of smoking and drinking. She even confessed to the use of marijuana. In sharp contrast to Juanita, Wanda Weston seemed boastful and brash. While Juanita had said that she loved her husband very much, Wanda said that she wished he was dead. In fact, she announced that she had tried to kill him herself.

5 Feeling sure of herself, Wanda then began to tell the story of Inez Kelly's murder. According to Wanda, Juanita had lent Ms. Kelly the pen, and it was Juanita who went to Ms. Kelly's room to retrieve it. But when Inez Kelly denied borrowing the pen and slammed the door in Juanita's face, Wanda Weston took over.

6 Wanda stormed into Ms. Kelly's room and demanded the pen. "She told me to get out of the room," Wanda said, "so I picked up the lamp and beat her with it." By the time Wanda stopped the beating, Inez Kelly was dead.

7 In relating her tale, Wanda showed no signs of guilt or shame. When asked if she thought she had overreacted, Wanda declared that she did not think so. "People these days—you can't trust them. You got to let them know where you're coming from," she said.

8 At this point, Klein called Juanita back. Again the defendant closed her eyes and lowered her head. When she looked up, the smile and the confident manner had been replaced by a frightened look. The defendant rubbed her forehead as though in pain. Juanita Maxwell had returned.

9 Before leaving the stand, Juanita was asked two questions: Did she kill Inez

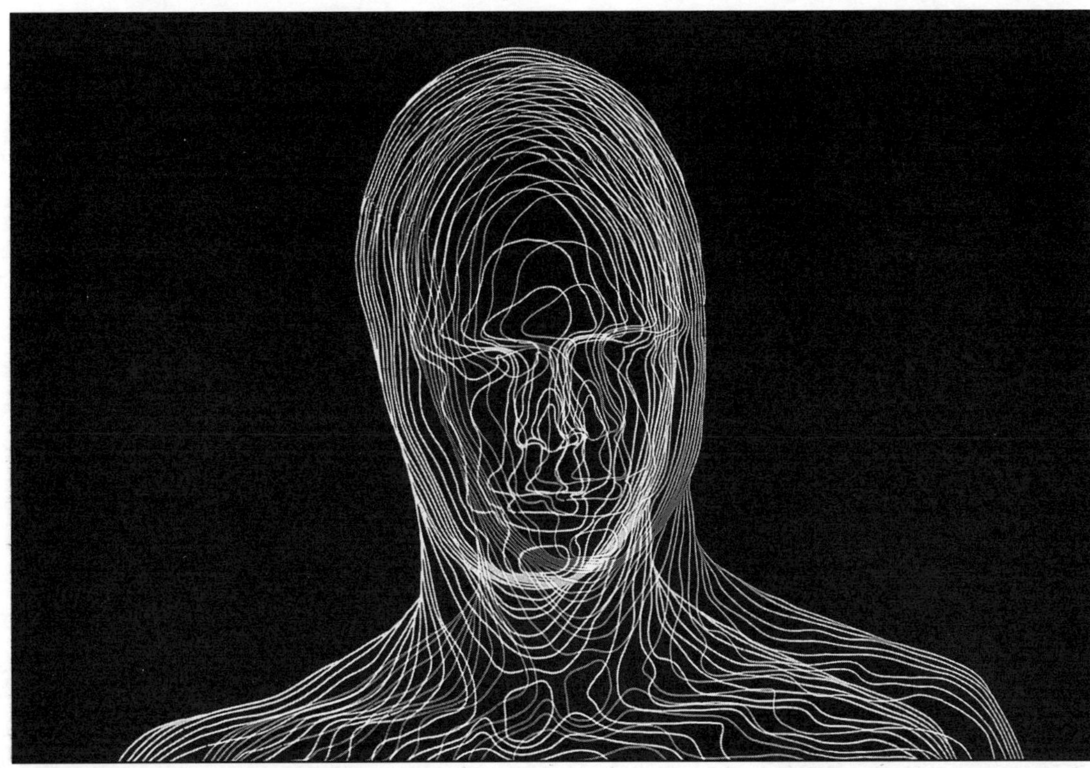

Using NASA technology, a "Bodygram" uses two superimposed images to show multiple personalities.

Kelly? "Well, they say I did, so I have to take their word for it," she said quietly. Did she know Wanda? "Yeah," she replied, "she causes me a lot of trouble."

10 No one who witnessed this scene was surprised when Juanita Maxwell was declared "not guilty by reason of insanity." As the verdict was read, Juanita fell into her husband's arms crying, "I love you, I love you."

11 Was it all a trick? Was Juanita Maxwell playing a clever game to get away with murder? Some people thought so. Some thought that she was pretending to be sick and to have a second personality so she could escape a prison sentence. If the judge was convinced that she was insane when the murder occurred, then she would not be held responsible for her crime.

12 But the judge did not think Juanita was trying to fool him. He believed that she really was the victim of a character named Wanda, whom she could not control. He said that Juanita, a woman without even a high school diploma, was not clever enough to trick both the social worker and the psychiatrist who testified to her dual identity. He felt that she could not possibly have put on an act that would have fooled these highly trained people.

13 In fact, most experts feel that while true multiple personalities are rare, they do exist. A person may develop a separate and distinct personality as a result of a severe trauma or shock. Most often this happens in childhood. If an event or situation is too stressful for a child to cope with, he or she may try very hard to forget that it ever happened. When this effort to forget is violent enough, a strange thing happens. An entire part of the personality splits off from the child's awareness. This fragment acquires its own identity, and thus a multiple personality is born.

14 We will never know whether Juanita Maxwell did indeed suffer from this frightening disease. What we do know is that Inez Kelly is dead, and that the person who admitted killing her was found not guilty. But the woman who sometimes calls herself Juanita, sometimes Wanda, is now in a Florida psychiatric hospital.

If you have been timed while reading this article, enter your reading time below. Then turn to the Words-per-Minute Table on page 133 and look up your reading speed (words per minute). Then enter your reading speed on the Reading Speed graph on page 134.

Reading Time: Lesson 12

________ : ________

Minutes *Seconds*

A Finding the Main Idea

One statement below expresses the main idea of the article. One statement is too general, or too broad. The other statement explains only part of the article; it is too narrow. Label the statements using the following key:

M—Main Idea **B—Too Broad** **N—Too Narrow**

_______ 1. Multiple personalities can be so complete that more than one person can exist in one body.

_______ 2. Juanita was a quiet, shy person, while Wanda was a loud, aggressive person.

_______ 3. A bad childhood experience can have a powerful impact on a person.

_______ Score 15 points for a correct M answer.

_______ Score 5 points for each correct B or N answer.

_______ **Total Score:** Finding the Main Idea

B Recalling Facts

How well do you remember the facts in the article? Put an X in the box next to the answer that correctly completes each statement about the article.

1. Inez Kelly was a
- ☐ a. social worker.
- ☐ b. murder victim.
- ☐ c. part of Juanita's personality.

2. Wanda Weston did not
- ☐ a. smoke.
- ☐ b. try to kill her husband.
- ☐ c. love her husband.

3. The murder weapon used was a
- ☐ a. lamp.
- ☐ b. hammer.
- ☐ c. fountain pen.

4. The court found Juanita Maxwell
- ☐ a. guilty.
- ☐ b. not guilty.
- ☐ c. not guilty by reason of insanity.

5. Multiple personalities are
- ☐ a. rare.
- ☐ b. unknown.
- ☐ c. quite common.

Score 5 points for each correct answer.

_______ **Total Score:** Recalling Facts

C Making Inferences

When you combine your own experience and information from a text to draw a conclusion that is not directly stated in that text, you are making an inference. Below are five statements that may or may not be inferences based on information in the article. Label the statements using the following key:

C—Correct Inference **F—Faulty Inference**

_______ 1. When a person has multiple personalities, one of the personalities is likely to be a murderer.

_______ 2. Inez Kelly was not aware that Juanita had multiple personalities.

_______ 3. Alan Klein was aware of the dual identity of Juanita and Wanda before the trial began.

_______ 4. It is impossible for anyone to fool a social worker or a judge.

_______ 5. Most children who have a difficult childhood do not develop true multiple personalities.

Score 5 points for each correct answer.

_______ **Total Score:** Making Inferences

D Using Words Precisely

Each numbered sentence below contains an underlined word or phrase from the article. Following the sentence are three definitions. One definition is closest to the meaning of the underlined word. One definition is opposite or nearly opposite. Label those two definitions using the following key; do not label the remaining definition.

C—Closest **O—Opposite or Nearly Opposite**

1. Giggling now, and speaking in a boisterous voice, she identified herself as Wanda Weston.

_______ a. quiet and calm

_______ b. loud and spirited

_______ c. angry

2. To the observers in the courtroom, the change was both baffling and convincing.

_______ a. puzzling

_______ b. understandable

_______ c. complete

3. In sharp contrast to Juanita, Wanda Weston seemed boastful and brash.

_______ a. dishonest

_______ b. bold

_______ c. shy

4. A person may develop a separate and distinct personality as a result of a severe trauma or shock.

_______ a. clearly defined

_______ b. unpleasant

_______ c. fuzzy

5. An entire part of the personality splits off from the child's awareness. This fragment acquires its own identity, and thus a multiple personality is born.

_______ a. section

_______ b. memory

_______ c. whole

_______ Score 3 points for each correct C answer.

_______ Score 2 points for each correct O answer.

_______ **Total Score:** Using Words Precisely

Enter the four total scores in the spaces below, and add them together to find your Reading Comprehension Score. Then record your score on the graph on page 135.

Score	Question Type	Lesson 12
_______	Finding the Main Idea	
_______	Recalling Facts	
_______	Making Inferences	
_______	Using Words Precisely	
_______	**Reading Comprehension Score**	

Author's Approach

Put an X in the box next to the correct answer.

1. The author uses the first sentence of the article to

☐ a. introduce Juanita Maxwell and her situation to the reader.

☐ b. describe the qualities of someone with multiple personalities.

☐ c. compare Juanita Maxwell and Wanda Weston.

2. What does the author mean by the statement "when she looked up again a few seconds later, she was a different person"?

☐ a. When Juanita raised her head, she felt much better.

☐ b. When Juanita raised her head, another personality had taken over her mind and body.

☐ c. When Juanita raised her head, another person had taken her place on the witness stand.

3. Choose the statement below that is the weakest argument for believing that Juanita Maxwell suffered from multiple personalities.

☐ a. She remembered little about what happened when Wanda took over.

☐ b. Her personality completely changed when Wanda took over.

☐ c. She was not clever enough to fool people because she did not have a high school diploma.

4. The author tells this story mainly by

☐ a. telling different stories about the same topic.

☐ b. telling one story about the topic.

☐ c. comparing different topics.

_______ Number of correct answers

Record your personal assessment of your work on the Critical Thinking Chart on page 136.

Summarizing and Paraphrasing

Put an X in the box next to the correct answer for question 2. Follow the directions provided for the other question.

1. Complete the following one-sentence summary of the article using the lettered phrases from the phrase bank below. Write the letters on the lines.

Phrase Bank:

a. Juanita's murder trial

b. Juanita's treatment in a mental hospital

c. Juanita's relationship to Wanda

The article about multiple personalities begins with ________, goes on to explain ________, and ends with ________.

2. Choose the best one-sentence paraphrase for the following sentence from the article:

"If the judge was convinced that she was insane when the murder occurred, then she would not be held responsible for her crime."

- ☐ a. The judge was insane when he ruled that Juanita was not guilty of murder.
- ☐ b. Juanita would not be found guilty if the judge thought she was crazy when the murder was committed.
- ☐ c. If the judge believed that Juanita had not committed murder, she would not be found guilty.

________ Number of correct answers

Record your personal assessment of your work on the Critical Thinking Chart on page 136.

Critical Thinking

Put an X in the box next to the correct answer for questions 1, 3, and 4. Follow the directions provided for the other questions.

1. From Wanda Weston's actions as told in this article, you can predict that

- ☐ a. Wanda would kill Juanita in the mental hospital.
- ☐ b. Wanda would escape from the mental hospital.
- ☐ c. Juanita would not be released from the mental hospital until her other personality had been conquered.

2. Using what you know about Juanita Maxwell and what is told about Wanda Weston in the article, name three ways Juanita is similar to and three ways she is different from Wanda. Cite the paragraph number(s) where you found details in the article to support your conclusions.

Similarities

____

____

____

Differences

____

____

____

3. What was the effect of Inez Kelly's slamming the door in Juanita's face?

☐ a. Ms. Kelly denied borrowing a pen.

☐ b. Wanda Weston took over and killed Ms. Kelly.

☐ c. Juanita demanded the pen back.

4. If you were a judge, how could you use the information in the article to determine whether someone is suffering from a multiple personality?

☐ a. Find out what the person's social worker and psychiatrist think about the case

☐ b. Find out whether the person suffered a severe trauma in childhood

☐ c. Find out whether the person smokes, drinks, or uses marijuana

5. Which paragraphs from the article provide evidence that supports your answer to question 3?

____

______ Number of correct answers

Record your personal assessment of your work on the Critical Thinking Chart on page 136.

Personal Response

What would you have done when Wanda Weston addressed the courtroom?

____

____

____

____

Self-Assessment

A word or phrase in the article that I do not understand is

____

____

____

____

SECRETS OF THE BOG PEOPLE

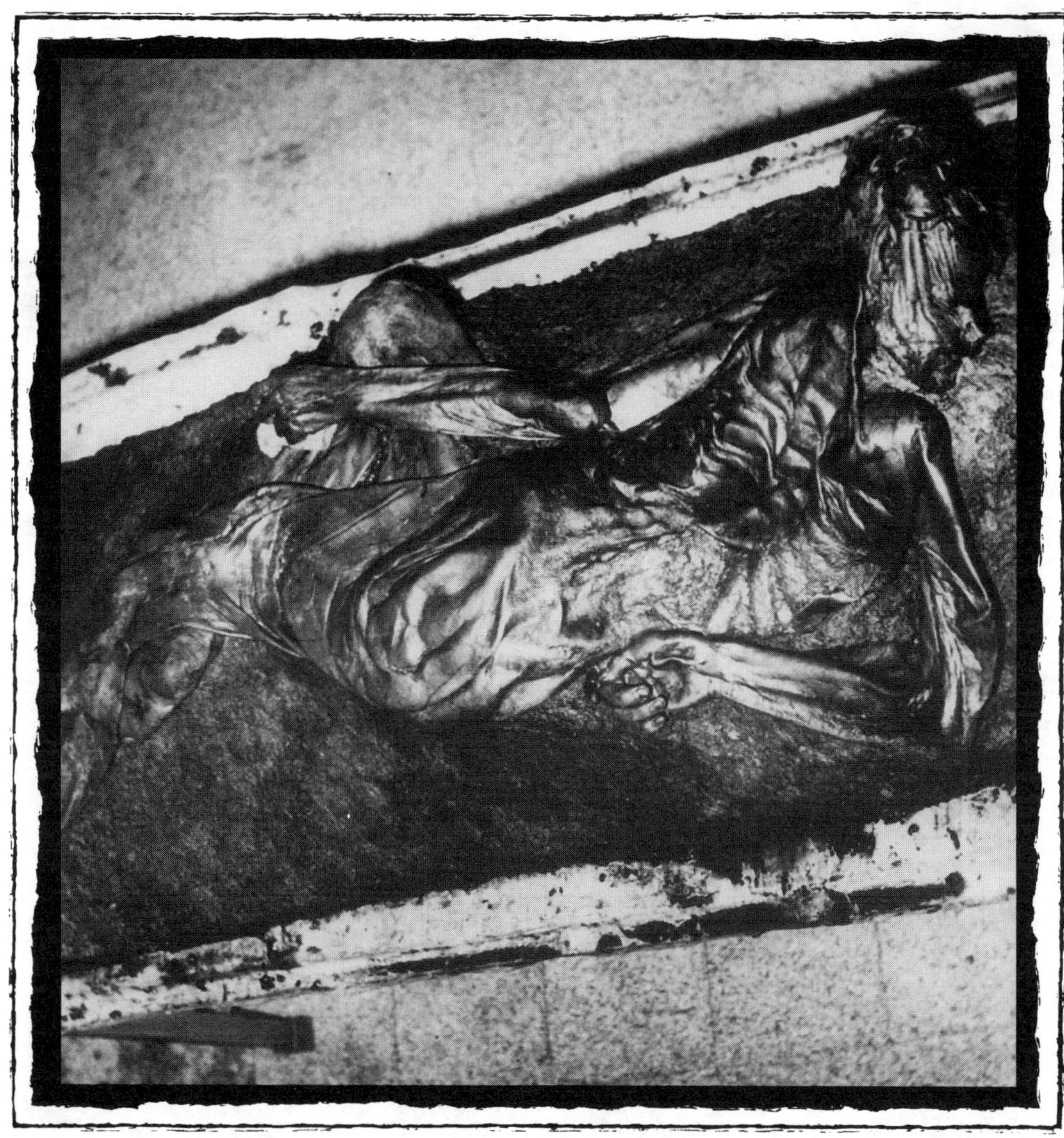

One of the bog people, discovered in 1952, was hanged 2000 years earlier, probably as a sacrifice to Nerthus, the goddess of fertility. It would have been an honor to be selected for this sacrifice.

When workers in a Danish peat bog stumbled upon a dead body in 1950, they knew right away they had found a murder victim. The murder weapon—a rope used for hanging—was still around the corpse's neck.

2 As the workers dug the body out of the peat, it seemed clear to them that the murder had taken place quite recently. The victim's flesh, skin, and hair were still intact. A wool-lined sheepskin cap and animal-skin belt showed no signs of disintegration. Staring grimly at the small body, the workers concluded they had found the Danish schoolboy who had disappeared on a class trip a year earlier.

3 It turned out the workers were wrong. The body was that of a man, not of a little boy. The stubble on his chin indicated he was old enough to shave. Still, nobody knew who the victim was. For 30 years, nobody knew much of anything about the corpse found that day in 1950. Other bodies were found in nearby bogs and they, too, were assumed to be victims of recent violence. The method of killing

varied. One man had been killed with arrows, another had been stabbed, and one girl had been strangled. It was unnerving to find these corpses, but few people thought they had historical value. None of them seemed to be particularly old.

4 That belief was shattered by a discovery made in Lindow Moss, England, in 1984. In a peat bog there, workers found a body they later dubbed Lindow Man. He, too, had been killed—strangled by a cord that left deep marks around his neck. In addition, he had been hit several times on the head and once from behind with such force that one of his ribs cracked.

5 What set Lindow Man apart from the other bog people was that he had been unearthed in the 1980s, not the 1950s. By the 1980s, researchers had precise ways of dating dead bodies. Tests done on Lindow Man revealed that he had been dead for an astonishingly long time. His corpse was estimated to be 2,000 years old.

6 That news sent scientists back to check the age of previously discovered bog people. They tested the corpse mistakenly thought to be the Danish schoolboy. That body—now called Tollund Man—also proved to be 2,000 years old. Case after case revealed the same results: each bog person had been killed between 2,000 and 2,500 years ago.

7 Many people wondered how such old corpses could be in such good shape. Scientists had the answer. It all had to do with the conditions in a peat bog. A peat bog forms when moss begins growing in a low-lying area. The moss causes the land to become soggy and extremely acidic. Under those conditions, bacteria cannot survive. Dead plants that are washed into this low-lying area do not rot away because no bacteria can live long enough to do the job. In fact, peat is nothing more than compressed layers of dead vegetation.

8 The conditions that prevent dead plants from rotting will do the same thing for a human body. The body won't rot because no bacteria can get at it. At the same time, the body won't dry out because it is surrounded by moisture. As a result, bodies deposited in peat bogs can be preserved for centuries.

9 As researchers began to add up the number of ancient corpses dug out of the bogs of northwest Europe, they were amazed. Nearly 2,000 had been found. Most of the bodies had already been destroyed. Many had been reburied in cemeteries by well-meaning people. Once in regular soil, the bodies quickly decomposed. Other corpses had been put in storage where they shriveled up and dried to dust. Still, enough bodies had been preserved for scientists to study. The results of their studies are both intriguing and perplexing.

10 Few of the bog people died peaceful deaths; in fact, most appear to have been

A peat bog in Ireland. Peat is used as fuel to heat homes.

murder victims. Some had their skulls crushed. Several had been strangled. Two people known as the Weerdingen Couple had been stabbed to death. Dätgen Man's head had been cut off, and Elling Woman had been hanged.

11 The corpse called Grauballe Man met a particularly gruesome end. Shortly before his death, he had eaten a deadly fungus. There is no way of telling whether he ate it accidentally, on purpose, or under duress. In any case, the fungus would have caused him to suffer convulsions and hallucinations. He would have felt as though his feet, hands, and mouth were on fire. While suffering through this, Grauballe Man was stripped naked. His shin was fractured, his skull was cracked, and his neck was slit from ear to ear.

12 Although scientists can figure out how various bog people were killed, no one knows why they were killed. Some experts think the bog people were criminals who were executed and thrown in bogs as punishment for their crimes. There is some evidence to support that view. Huldremose Woman's arms and legs were hacked with sharp blades and an arm cut off while she was still alive. Says Danish archaeologist Christian Fischer, "The overkill tells me that [she was] really disliked by the community...." Windeby Girl had half of her head shaved before she was strangled. Researchers report that head shaving was once a common punishment for disgraced women.

13 The ancient Roman writer Tacitus confirmed that bogs were burial places for undesirables. In A.D. 98, he wrote a passage on the subject. He stated: "The coward, the unwarlike, the man stained with abominable vices, is plunged into the mire or the morass."

14 A second theory is that the bog people were not criminals at all. Rather, they were respected members of society whose death was a kind of honor. According to this theory, the bog people were killed as sacrifices to the gods. Once again, some evidence supports this idea. Many bog people went to their deaths well dressed and carefully groomed. Some wore lambskin capes. Huldremose Woman wore a beautiful checked wool skirt. Elling Woman's hair was braided in three elaborate patterns. The soft hands of the Grauballe Man show he was unaccustomed to manual labor.

15 As further proof, Christian Fischer points out that many victims were placed in their graves with care. Their bodies were nicely arranged. Their eyelids were pulled down over their eyes. Finally, Tacitus, the same writer who told how criminals were thrown into bogs, also wrote about human sacrifices. According to him, rituals honoring Mother Earth sometimes ended with drowning several people in the bogs.

16 One other fact adds to the mystery of the bog people. Most were in poor health at the time of their death. No one can say how their health compared with that of others in their society, but most who ended up in the bogs suffered from intestinal worms. Many had suffered broken bones earlier in their lives. Many also had arthritis, inflamed muscles, and other ailments. Is it possible that murder in the bogs was a way of ending these people's misery?

17 Scientists are still trying to learn more about the bog people, but they may never uncover all their secrets. It is likely that we will never know for sure what led so many people to perish in the cold, wet bogs of Europe.

If you have been timed while reading this article, enter your reading time below. Then turn to the Words-per-Minute Table on page 133 and look up your reading speed (words per minute). Then enter your reading speed on the Reading Speed graph on page 134.

Reading Time: Lesson 13

________ : ________

Minutes *Seconds*

Finding the Main Idea

One statement below expresses the main idea of the article. One statement is too general, or too broad. The other statement explains only part of the article; it is too narrow. Label the statements using the following key:

M—Main Idea **B—Too Broad** **N—Too Narrow**

______ 1. The bodies of people who were killed between 2,000 and 2,500 years ago were preserved in bogs in northwest Europe.

______ 2. The acidic conditions in a peat bog prevent dead plants and animals from rotting.

______ 3. Scientists were amazed by the number of bodies dug out of the bogs.

______ Score 15 points for a correct M answer.

______ Score 5 points for each correct B or N answer.

______ **Total Score:** Finding the Main Idea

B Recalling Facts

How well do you remember the facts in the article? Put an X in the box next to the answer that correctly completes each statement about the article.

1. The body found in a Danish peat bog in 1950 proved to be that of
   - ☐ a. Tollund Man.
   - ☐ b. a Danish schoolboy.
   - ☐ c. Lindow Man.
2. Scientists determined the true age of the bog people in the
   - ☐ a. 1950s.
   - ☐ b. 1980s.
   - ☐ c. 1990s.
3. The conditions in the peat bogs
   - ☐ a. led to the deaths of the bog people.
   - ☐ b. caused the corpses of the bog people to decompose quickly.
   - ☐ c. helped preserve the corpses of the bog people.
4. Most of the bog people died
   - ☐ a. in their sleep.
   - ☐ b. extremely violent deaths.
   - ☐ c. due to natural causes.
5. Some experts believe that the bog people were killed as sacrifices to the gods, because many
   - ☐ a. were tortured before they died.
   - ☐ b. went to their deaths well dressed and carefully groomed.
   - ☐ c. suffered particularly gruesome deaths.

Score 5 points for each correct answer.

______ **Total Score:** Recalling Facts

C Making Inferences

When you combine your own experience and information from a text to draw a conclusion that is not directly stated in that text, you are making an inference. Below are five statements that may or may not be inferences based on information in the article. Label the statements using the following key:

C—Correct Inference **F—Faulty Inference**

_______ 1. People would not have buried the bodies found in the bogs if they had known how old the bodies were.

_______ 2. Bacteria are necessary for decomposition to take place.

_______ 3. The bodies of all the people who died 2,000 years ago in northwest Europe were thrown into peat bogs.

_______ 4. People who lived 2,000 years ago were smaller than people today.

_______ 5. Those who murdered Grauballe Man and the others and buried them in the peat bogs knew that the victims' bodies would be preserved for centuries.

Score 5 points for each correct answer.

_______ **Total Score:** Making Inferences

D Using Words Precisely

Each numbered sentence below contains an underlined word or phrase from the article. Following the sentence are three definitions. One definition is closest to the meaning of the underlined word. One definition is opposite or nearly opposite. Label those two definitions using the following key; do not label the remaining definition.

C—Closest **O—Opposite or Nearly Opposite**

1. It was <u>unnerving</u> to find these corpses, but few people thought they had historical value.

_______ a. unsettling

_______ b. inconvenient

_______ c. comforting

2. In fact, peat is nothing more than <u>compressed</u> layers of dead vegetation.

_______ a. condensed

_______ b. evaporated

_______ c. loose

3. There is no way of telling whether he ate it accidentally, on purpose, or under <u>duress</u>.

_______ a. force

_______ b. voluntary conditions

_______ c. unconsciousness

4. The results of their studies are both <u>intriguing</u> and perplexing.

_______ a. fascinating

_______ b. uninteresting

_______ c. inconclusive

5. The soft hands of the Grauballe Man show he was unaccustomed to <u>manual</u> labor.

_______ a. automated

_______ b. forced

_______ c. by hand

_______ Score 3 points for each correct C answer.

_______ Score 2 points for each correct O answer.

_______ **Total Score:** Using Words Precisely

Enter the four total scores in the spaces below, and add them together to find your Reading Comprehension Score. Then record your score on the graph on page 135.

Score	Question Type	Lesson 13
_______	Finding the Main Idea	
_______	Recalling Facts	
_______	Making Inferences	
_______	Using Words Precisely	
_______	**Reading Comprehension Score**	

Author's Approach

Put an X in the box next to the correct answer.

1. The main purpose of the first paragraph is to

☐ a. hook the reader's attention with the description of a murder mystery.

☐ b. inform the reader about the bog people.

☐ c. express an opinion about why the bog people were killed.

2. From the statements below, choose those that you believe the author would agree with.

☐ a. The bodies of the bog people should never have been disturbed.

☐ b. The bodies of the bog people provide clues about the ancient cultures and practices of northwest Europe.

☐ c. The people who reburied the bodies in cemeteries should not be criticized for their actions.

3. Some experts claim the bog people were criminals. The author addresses the opposing point of view in the article by describing the

☐ a. care with which the bodies were handled.

☐ b. effect of the fungus eaten by Grauballe Man.

☐ c. violence of their deaths.

_______ Number of correct answers

Record your personal assessment of your work on the Critical Thinking Chart on page 136.

Summarizing and Paraphrasing

Put an X in the box next to the correct answer for questions 1 and 3. Follow the directions provided for the other question.

1. Below are summaries of the article. Choose the summary that says all the most important things about the article but in the fewest words.

☐ a. The bog people died between 2,000 and 2,500 years ago. Many of the bog people, including the Weerdingen Couple and Windeby Girl, died violent deaths. Although scientists know how some of the bog people died, they do not know why the people were killed.

☐ b. The bog people died at least 2,000 years ago. Scientists have been able to determine how the bog people died but not why they were killed.

☐ c. Nearly 2,000 people were found buried in the bogs of northwest Europe. These people had died between 2,000 and 2,500 years ago.

2. Reread paragraph 11 in the article. Below, write a summary of the paragraph in no more than 25 words.

____

____

____

____

Reread your summary and decide whether it covers the important ideas in the paragraph. Next, decide how to shorten the summary to 15 words or less without leaving out any essential information. Write this summary below.

____

____

____

3. Choose the sentence that correctly restates the following sentence from the article:

"'The coward, the unwarlike, the man stained with abominable vices, is plunged into the mire or the morass."

☐ a. Those who could not defend themselves were murdered and thrown into the bogs.

☐ b. The bog people jumped into the bogs because they feared their terrible tormentors.

☐ c. Cowards, deserters, and criminals were buried in the bogs.

______ Number of correct answers

Record your personal assessment of your work on the Critical Thinking Chart on page 136.

Critical Thinking

Put an X in the box next to the correct answer for questions 1 and 4. Follow the directions provided for the other questions.

1. From the article, you can predict that if another body is found in a bog, it will be

☐ a. left in the bog.

☐ b. stored so it won't disintegrate.

☐ c. buried in a cemetery.

CRITICAL THINKING

2. Using what you know about Grauballe Man and what is told about Huldremose Woman in the article, name three ways Grauballe Man is similar to and different from Huldremose Woman. Cite the paragraph number(s) where you found details in the article to support your conclusions.

   Similarities

   ____

   ____

   ____

   Differences

   ____

   ____

   ____

3. Choose from the letters below to correctly complete the following statement. Write the letters on the lines.

   According to the article, the moss in a peat bog caused _________ to _________, and the effect was _________.

   a. die

   b. the bacteria in the bog

   c. the bodies in the bog were preserved

4. If you were a scientist, how could you use the information in the article to study a bog person?

   - ☐ a. Like other experts, braid the person's hair in three elaborate patterns.
   - ☐ b. Like Tacitus, write about the rituals honoring Mother Earth.
   - ☐ c. Like Christian Fischer, study the person's clothing, appearance, and manner of death.

5. Which paragraphs from the article provide evidence that supports your answer to question 3?

   ____

_________ Number of correct answers

Record your personal assessment of your work on the Critical Thinking Chart on page 136.

Personal Response

I wonder why

____

____

____

Self-Assessment

I was confused about question _______ in section ___________ because

____

____

____

____

KILLERS IN PAJAMAS

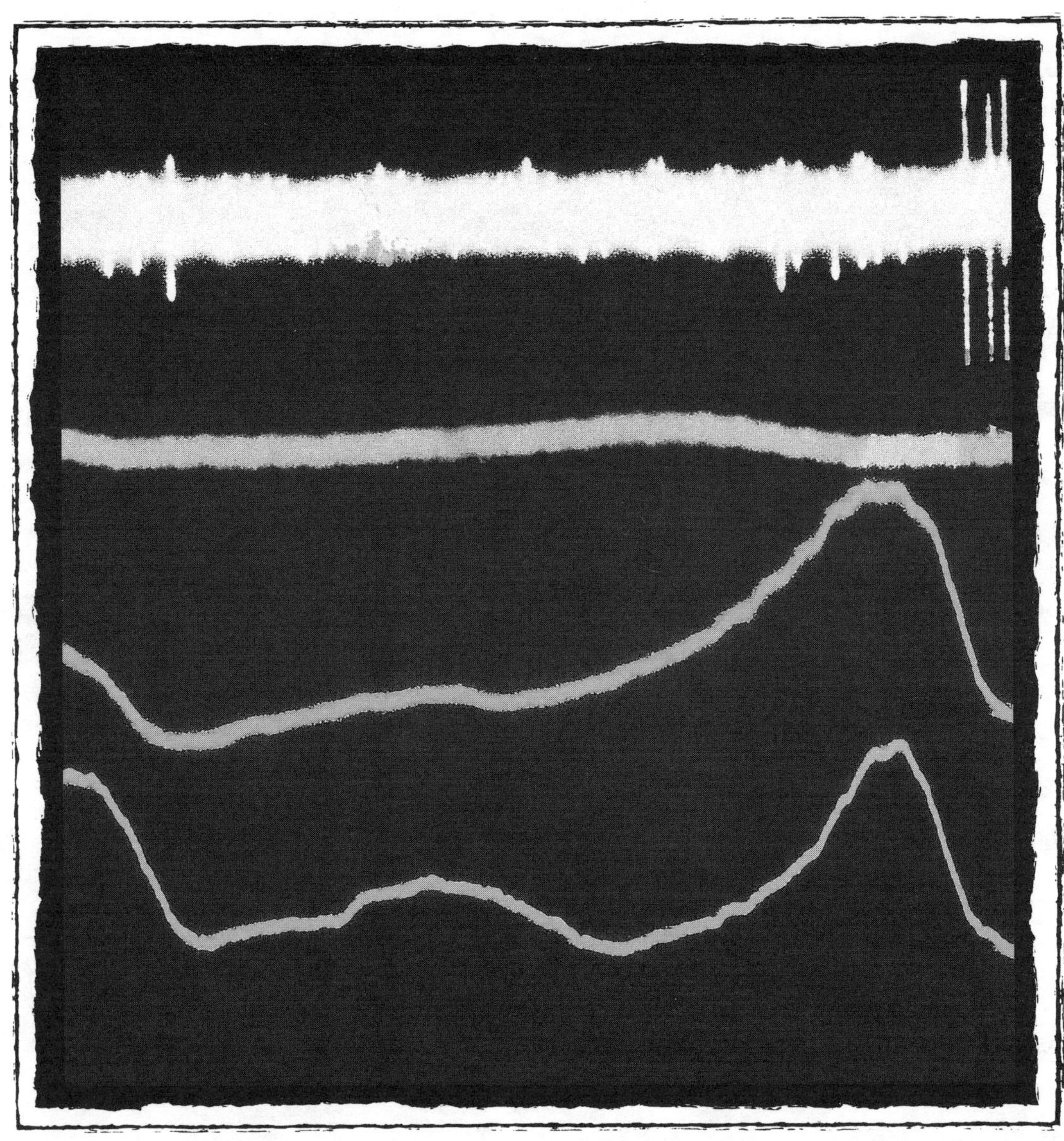

The brain waves of a sleeping person. The top line shows the Dream Brain Cell, the second shows REM activity, and the last two show visual waves.

Sometimes people toss and turn in their sleep. Sometimes they fall out of bed. But is it possible for a person to get up, drive to another location, and commit a crime while remaining sound asleep? According to Ken Parks, the answer is yes.

2 In 1987, Parks was living in Ontario, Canada. The 23-year-old man needed money; he had no job and his gambling debts were piling up. Still, his life had its bright spots. His wife had recently given birth to a baby daughter. And he enjoyed a particularly good relationship with his in-laws. His mother-in-law referred to him lovingly as a "gentle giant."

3 Early on the morning of May 14, Parks got out of bed. He slipped into his car and drove the 15 miles to his in-laws' house. After entering the house, he attacked the couple with a kitchen knife. He badly wounded his father-in-law and stabbed his mother-in-law to death. Afterwards, Parks drove to the police station and turned himself in, murmuring, "I think I have killed some people...."

4 In court, Parks's attorneys argued that their client was an innocent man. He

could not be convicted of murder, they said, because he had been asleep throughout the attack.

5 Parks is not the only one who has claimed sleep as a defense in a murder case. One devoted husband chased his wife out into the street one night. Neighbors tried to save the woman, but the man pushed them aside. He killed his wife by stabbing her and smashing her head on the pavement. Then he got into his car and sat there peacefully, his eyes closed and his body relaxed. He later said he had slept through the whole thing.

6 In Kentucky, a 16-year-old girl picked up two revolvers late one evening. She fired several times, killing her father and six-year-old brother and wounding her mother. She later told police she had been dreaming of burglars breaking into the house. In her dream, the burglars were trying to kill her family. She said she must have fired the guns while she was in the middle of this dream.

7 To many people, the idea of sleeping killers seems ridiculous. But doctors say it can happen. In fact, there are two different ways a person can sleep his or her way through a crime. One way is through REM sleep disorder. The other is as a result of *somnambulism*, or good old-fashioned sleepwalking.

8 According to his doctors, Ken Parks was a sleepwalker. That meant his trouble started when he was in the deepest kind of sleep, a sleep so intense that no dreams can occur. Somehow, during this stage of sleep, a small part of Parks's brain suddenly roused itself. While the rest of his brain remained deep in slumber, that one part woke up enough to direct body movement.

9 The roused section of Parks's brain was confused; it sent bizarre messages to the rest of his body. But no other part of his brain was alert enough to counteract the messages. Everything Parks did that terrible morning was controlled by just one small, befuddled portion of his brain. The rest of his mind had no idea what was happening. Parks had no intent to kill and no awareness that he was becoming violent. By the time the rest of his brain woke up, the damage was done.

10 What could cause an isolated part of a person's brain to wake up like that? Doctors say severe stress can do it. (Remember, Parks had a new baby, was in debt, and couldn't find work.) Consuming too much caffeine can do it. So can drinking too much alcohol. Similarly, changes in sleep schedules—such as switching from a day job to a night job—can put someone at risk. And finally, a condition called sleep apnea can rouse a small section of the brain.

11 A person with sleep apnea stops breathing for short periods of time during sleep. When breathing starts again, it

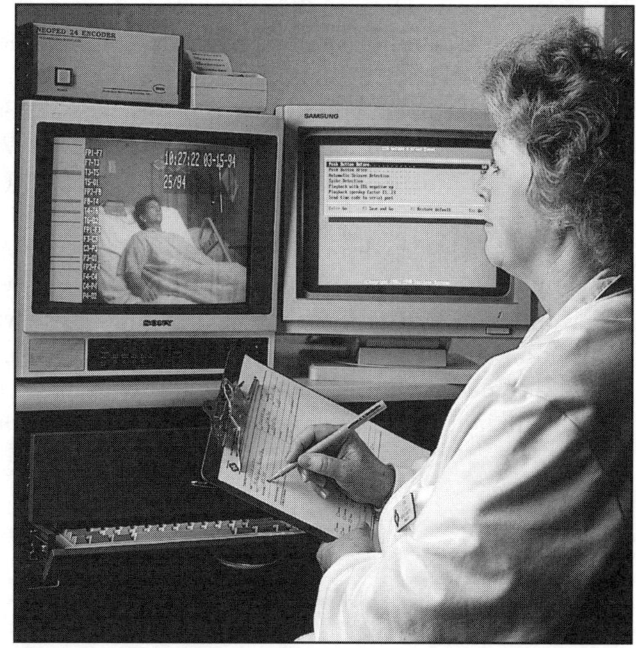

A researcher exploring sleep disorders observes a subject.

often does so with a roar—or more accurately, with a snore. The snore can actually startle a small part of the brain into a more alert state. Doctors believe this is what happened to the man who killed his wife in the street. He had a long history of severe sleep apnea.

12 The second way someone can sleep through a murder is as a result of REM sleep disorder. This is a rare condition with no known cause. The condition formed the basis of the defense for the Kentucky girl who shot her family. She was not in the deep dreamless state that Ken Parks experienced. Rather, she was in the middle of REM sleep. REM stands for rapid eye movement and occurs only when a person is dreaming.

13 Normally, a person in REM sleep does not move. All motor functions are suspended. The heart still pumps, the lungs still take in air, and the eye muscles are free to make their rapid motions. But beyond that, the body is temporarily paralyzed.

14 With REM sleep disorder, however, no such paralysis occurs. The dreaming person is able to thrash around, acting out his or her dream in a near-panic state. This disorder has caused mothers to throw their children out of windows to "save" them from nonexistent fires. It has caused men to beat their wives to death because they dreamt an intruder was in their homes.

15 When Ken Parks's case went to court, he was found innocent. Likewise, the man who killed his wife in the street and the Kentucky girl were eventually cleared of all charges. But some observers worry that the so-called "sleeping defense" may be overused. For instance, a man in Butler, Pennsylvania, claimed he had been sleeping when he shot and killed his wife. But the man had a history of abusing his wife even when he was awake. Furthermore, he showed no remorse when he discussed what he had done with police.

16 Then there was the case of the "sleepwalking burglar." This man broke into an apartment in Calgary, Canada, at 4:30 one Saturday morning. He picked up a VCR and was about to carry it off when the owners surprised him. The man apologized to the owners, telling them he was sleepwalking. As proof, he pointed to the pajamas and robe he was wearing. The owners took back their VCR, let the man go, and went back to bed. The man then went on to steal $4,200 worth of goods from neighboring apartments.

17 While no one can predict who will suffer from REM sleep disorder, researchers say sleepwalking runs in families. Many children have episodes of sleepwalking, but most people outgrow it by the time they are fully grown.

18 In 1 to 6 percent of the population, however, sleepwalking continues into adulthood. And if one of your parents was an adult sleepwalker, you are six times more likely to be one yourself. So if you ever find you've been wandering asleep through the house some night, be sure all the sharp knives are locked away.

If you have been timed while reading this article, enter your reading time below. Then turn to the Words-per-Minute Table on page 133 and look up your reading speed (words per minute). Then enter your reading speed on the Reading Speed graph on page 134.

Reading Time: Lesson 14

________ : ________

Minutes *Seconds*

A Finding the Main Idea

One statement below expresses the main idea of the article. One statement is too general, or too broad. The other statement explains only part of the article; it is too narrow. Label the statements using the following key:

M—Main Idea **B—Too Broad** **N—Too Narrow**

______ 1. Stress, too much caffeine or alcohol, or changes in sleep schedules can cause sleepwalking.

______ 2. Sleep disorders can have tragic consequences.

______ 3. Some people claim that they should not be convicted of murder or other crimes because they were actually asleep during the attacks.

______ Score 15 points for a correct M answer.

______ Score 5 points for each correct B or N answer.

______ **Total Score:** Finding the Main Idea

B Recalling Facts

How well do you remember the facts in the article? Put an X in the box next to the answer that correctly completes each statement about the article.

1. A person can sleep through a crime as a result of
   - ☐ a. extreme stress or lack of sleep.
   - ☐ b. somnambulism or REM sleep disorder.
   - ☐ c. drinking too much alcohol or changes in sleep schedules.
2. A person with sleep apnea
   - ☐ a. stops breathing briefly during sleep.
   - ☐ b. never snores during sleep.
   - ☐ c. is more likely to murder someone.
3. During REM sleep disorder,
   - ☐ a. the eyes move rapidly while a person dreams.
   - ☐ b. all motor functions are suspended.
   - ☐ c. a person can act out his or her dream.
4. After the "sleepwalking burglar" was let go, he
   - ☐ a. went on to steal more goods.
   - ☐ b. went back to sleep.
   - ☐ c. killed his wife.
5. Most people who were sleepwalkers as children
   - ☐ a. continue to sleepwalk when they grow up.
   - ☐ b. outgrow it as adults.
   - ☐ c. commit crimes in their sleep.

Score 5 points for each correct answer.

______ **Total Score:** Recalling Facts

C Making Inferences

When you combine your own experience and information from a text to draw a conclusion that is not directly stated in that text, you are making an inference. Below are five statements that may or may not be inferences based on information in the article. Label the statements using the following key:

C—Correct Inference **F—Faulty Inference**

_______ 1. In some cases, sleepwalking can be a credible defense against a murder charge.

_______ 2. Only people with sleep apnea snore in their sleep.

_______ 3. When Ken Parks went to his in-laws' house, he was acting out a dream.

_______ 4. Some people may try to pose as sleepwalkers in order to get away with crimes.

_______ 5. Adults who tend to sleepwalk should be locked in their bedrooms every night.

Score 5 points for each correct answer.

_______ **Total Score:** Making Inferences

D Using Words Precisely

Each numbered sentence below contains an underlined word or phrase from the article. Following the sentence are three definitions. One definition is closest to the meaning of the underlined word. One definition is opposite or nearly opposite. Label those two definitions using the following key; do not label the remaining definition.

C—Closest **O—Opposite or Nearly Opposite**

1. Afterwards, Parks drove to the police station and turned himself in, <u>murmuring</u>, "I think I have killed some people…."

_______ a. mumbling

_______ b. laughing

_______ c. yelling

2. Somehow, during this stage of sleep, a small part of Parks's brain suddenly <u>roused</u> itself.

_______ a. awoke

_______ b. stopped breathing

_______ c. fell asleep

3. But no other part of his brain was alert enough to <u>counteract</u> the messages.

_______ a. override

_______ b. aid

_______ c. hear

4. Everything Parks did that terrible morning was controlled by just one small, befuddled portion of his brain.

_______ a. clear

_______ b. unused

_______ c. confused

5. But beyond that, the body is temporarily paralyzed.

_______ a. uncomfortable

_______ b. deadened

_______ c. revived

_______ Score 3 points for each correct C answer.

_______ Score 2 points for each correct O answer.

_______ **Total Score:** Using Words Precisely

Enter the four total scores in the spaces below, and add them together to find your Reading Comprehension Score. Then record your score on the graph on page 135.

Score	Question Type	Lesson 14
_______	Finding the Main Idea	
_______	Recalling Facts	
_______	Making Inferences	
_______	Using Words Precisely	
_______	**Reading Comprehension Score**	

Author's Approach

Put an X in the box next to the correct answer.

1. What is the author's purpose in writing "Killers in Pajamas: Sleepwalkers or Murderers?"

☐ a. to persuade readers to accept the "sleepwalking defense"

☐ b. to encourage readers to draw their own conclusions about the "sleepwalking defense"

☐ c. to describe situations in which sleepwalking may be dangerous

2. From the statements below, choose those that you believe the author would agree with.

☐ a. REM sleep disorder can cause people to act out their dreams in a near-panic state.

☐ b. A sleepwalker can be directed by a small, confused part of the brain to do things the rest of the brain is unaware of.

☐ c. Someone known to be violent when awake can use the sleeping defense.

3. What does the author imply by saying, "The man then went on to steal $4,200 worth of goods from neighboring apartments"?

☐ a. The man was acting out a dream.

☐ b. The man was being directed by a small part of his brain.

☐ c. The man was pretending to be sleepwalking.

4. Choose the statement below that best describes the author's position in paragraph 16.

☐ a. Some people will try to use sleepwalking as an excuse to get away with a crime.

☐ b. People should be aware that, in the course of one night, a sleepwalker may repeat the same crime several times.

☐ c. People should warn their neighbors if they see a sleepwalker on the loose.

_______ Number of correct answers

Record your personal assessment of your work on the Critical Thinking Chart on page 136.

Summarizing and Paraphrasing

Follow the directions for question 1. Put an X in the box next to the correct answer for question 2.

1. Look for the important ideas and events in paragraphs 8 and 9. Summarize those paragraphs in one or two sentences.

____

____

____

2. Read the statement about the article below. Then read the paraphrase of that statement. Choose the reason that best tells why the paraphrase does not say the same thing as the statement.

Statement: Although sleepwalking runs in families and many children have episodes of sleepwalking, most people outgrow it by the time they reach adulthood.

Paraphrase: Sleepwalking is hereditary, but most children do not sleepwalk at all.

☐ a. Paraphrase says too much.

☐ b. Paraphrase doesn't say enough.

☐ c. Paraphrase doesn't agree with the statement about the article.

_______ Number of correct answers

Record your personal assessment of your work on the Critical Thinking Chart on page 136.

Critical Thinking

Put an X in the box next to the correct answer for questions 1, 4, and 5. Follow the directions provided for the other questions.

1. From the information in paragraph 15, you can predict that

☐ a. the man in Butler, Pennsylvania, would be cleared of all charges.

☐ b. the man in Butler, Pennsylvania, would not be cleared of murder by using the "sleeping defense."

☐ c. the "sleeping defense" would never be used again.

2. Using what you know about Ken Parks and what is told about the Kentucky girl in the article, name three ways Ken Parks is similar to and different from the Kentucky girl. Cite the paragraph number(s) where you found details in the article to support your conclusions.

Similarities

____

____

____

CRITICAL THINKING

Differences

____

____

____

3. Read paragraph 14. Then choose from the letters below to correctly complete the following statement. Write the letters on the lines.

   According to paragraph 14, __________ has happened because __________.

   a. they suffered from REM sleep disorder
   b. their homes were on fire
   c. women throwing their babies out of windows

4. How is committing a crime in one's sleep an example of a phenomenon?

   ☐ a. It is studied by doctors and other experts.
   ☐ b. It is a rare occurrence and one that is much argued and misunderstood.
   ☐ c. It is used as a defense in some murder cases.

5. What did you have to do to answer question 3?

   ☐ a. draw a conclusion (a sensible statement based on the text and your experience)
   ☐ b. find an effect (something that happened)
   ☐ c. find a cause (why something happened)

__________ Number of correct answers

Record your personal assessment of your work on the Critical Thinking Chart on page 136.

Personal Response

This article is different from other articles about phenomena I've read because

____

____

and Ken Parks is unlike other people in the selections I've read because

____

____

____

Self-Assessment

One good question about this article that was not asked would be

____

____

____

and the answer is

____

____

____

Compare and Contrast

Think about the articles you have read in Unit Two. Pick four articles that you learned something important from. Write the titles in the first column of the chart below. Use information you learned from the articles to fill in the empty boxes in the chart.

Title	What kinds of people were described in the article?	What was most difficult for you to believe?	How does this phenomenon affect people's lives?

Suppose you met one of the people you read about in this unit. Write three questions you might ask that person about his or her work or experience.

____

____

____

Words-per-Minute Table

Unit Two

Directions: If you were timed while reading an article, refer to the Reading Time you recorded in the box at the end of the article. Use this words-per-minute table to determine your reading speed for that article. Then plot your reading speed on the graph on page 134.

Lesson	8	9	10	11	12	13	14	
No. of Words	1232	952	1086	1214	870	1224	1178	
Minutes and Seconds								*Seconds*
1:30	821	635	724	809	580	816	785	**90**
1:40	739	571	652	728	522	734	707	**100**
1:50	672	519	592	662	475	668	643	**110**
2:00	616	476	543	607	435	612	589	**120**
2:10	569	439	501	560	402	565	544	**130**
2:20	528	408	465	520	373	525	505	**140**
2:30	493	381	434	486	348	490	471	**150**
2:40	462	357	407	455	326	459	442	**160**
2:50	435	336	383	428	307	432	416	**170**
3:00	411	317	362	405	290	408	393	**180**
3:10	389	301	343	383	275	387	372	**190**
3:20	370	286	326	364	261	367	353	**200**
3:30	352	272	310	347	249	350	337	**210**
3:40	336	260	296	331	237	334	321	**220**
3:50	321	248	283	317	227	319	307	**230**
4:00	308	238	272	304	218	306	295	**240**
4:10	296	228	261	291	209	294	283	**250**
4:20	284	220	251	280	201	282	272	**260**
4:30	274	212	241	270	193	272	262	**270**
4:40	264	204	233	260	186	262	252	**280**
4:50	255	197	225	251	180	253	244	**290**
5:00	246	190	217	243	174	245	236	**300**
5:10	238	184	210	235	168	237	228	**310**
5:20	231	179	204	228	163	230	221	**320**
5:30	224	173	197	221	158	223	214	**330**
5:40	217	168	192	214	154	216	208	**340**
5:50	211	163	186	208	149	210	202	**350**
6:00	205	159	181	202	145	204	196	**360**
6:10	200	154	176	197	141	198	191	**370**
6:20	195	150	171	192	137	193	186	**380**
6:30	190	146	167	187	134	188	181	**390**
6:40	185	143	163	182	131	184	177	**400**
6:50	180	139	159	178	127	179	172	**410**
7:00	176	136	155	173	124	175	168	**420**
7:10	172	133	152	169	121	171	164	**430**
7:20	168	130	148	166	119	167	161	**440**
7:30	164	127	145	162	116	163	157	**450**
7:40	161	124	142	158	113	160	154	**460**
7:50	157	122	139	155	111	156	150	**470**
8:00	154	119	136	152	109	153	147	**480**

Plotting Your Progress: Reading Speed

Unit Two

Directions: If you were timed while reading an article, write your words-per-minute rate for that article in the box under the number of the lesson. Then plot your reading speed on the graph by putting a small X on the line directly above the number of the lesson, across from the number of words per minute you read. As you mark your speed for each lesson, graph your progress by drawing a line to connect the X's.

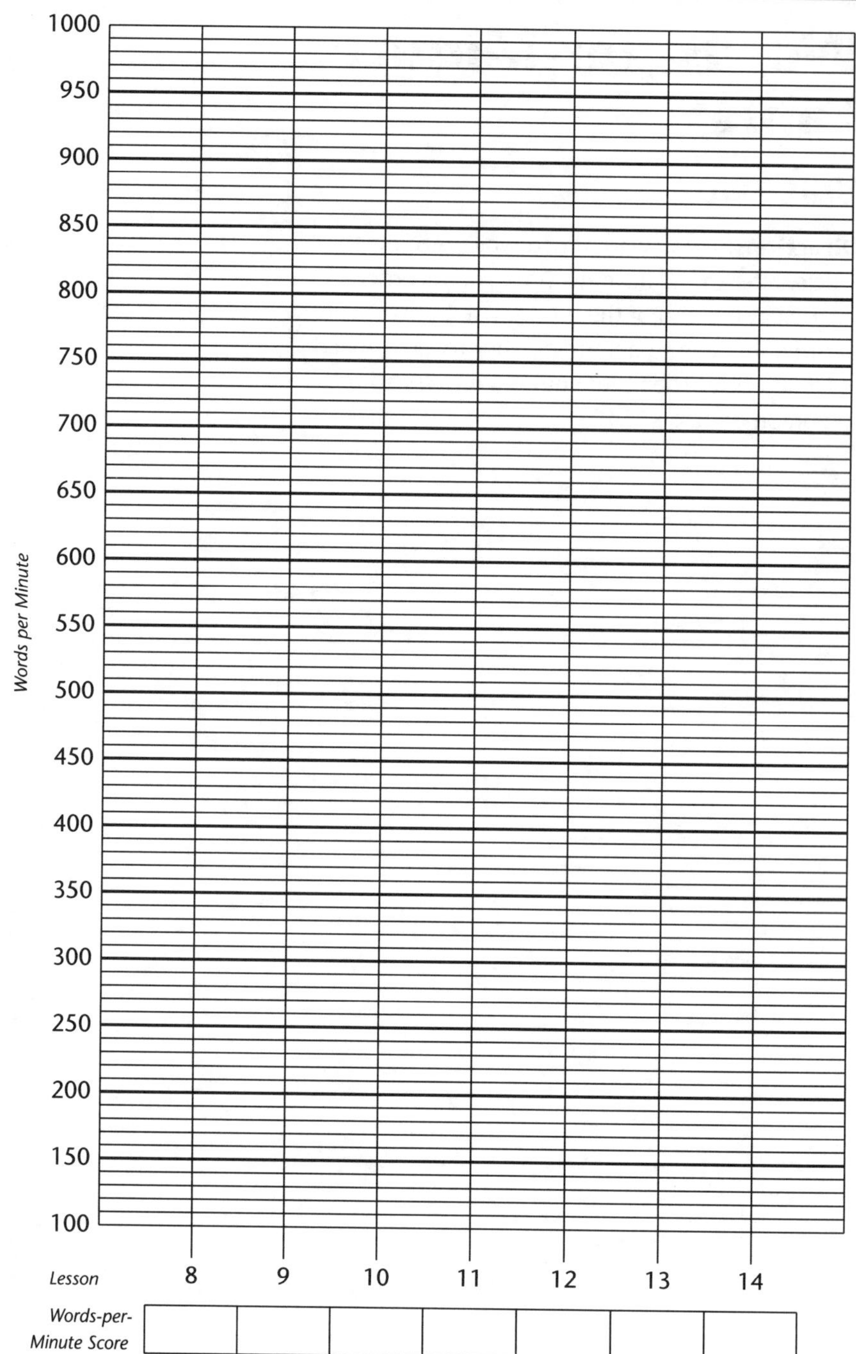

Plotting Your Progress: Reading Comprehension

Unit Two

Directions: Write your Reading Comprehension score for each lesson in the box under the number of the lesson. Then plot your score on the graph by putting a small X on the line directly above the number of the lesson and across from the score you earned. As you mark your score for each lesson, graph your progress by drawing a line to connect the X's.

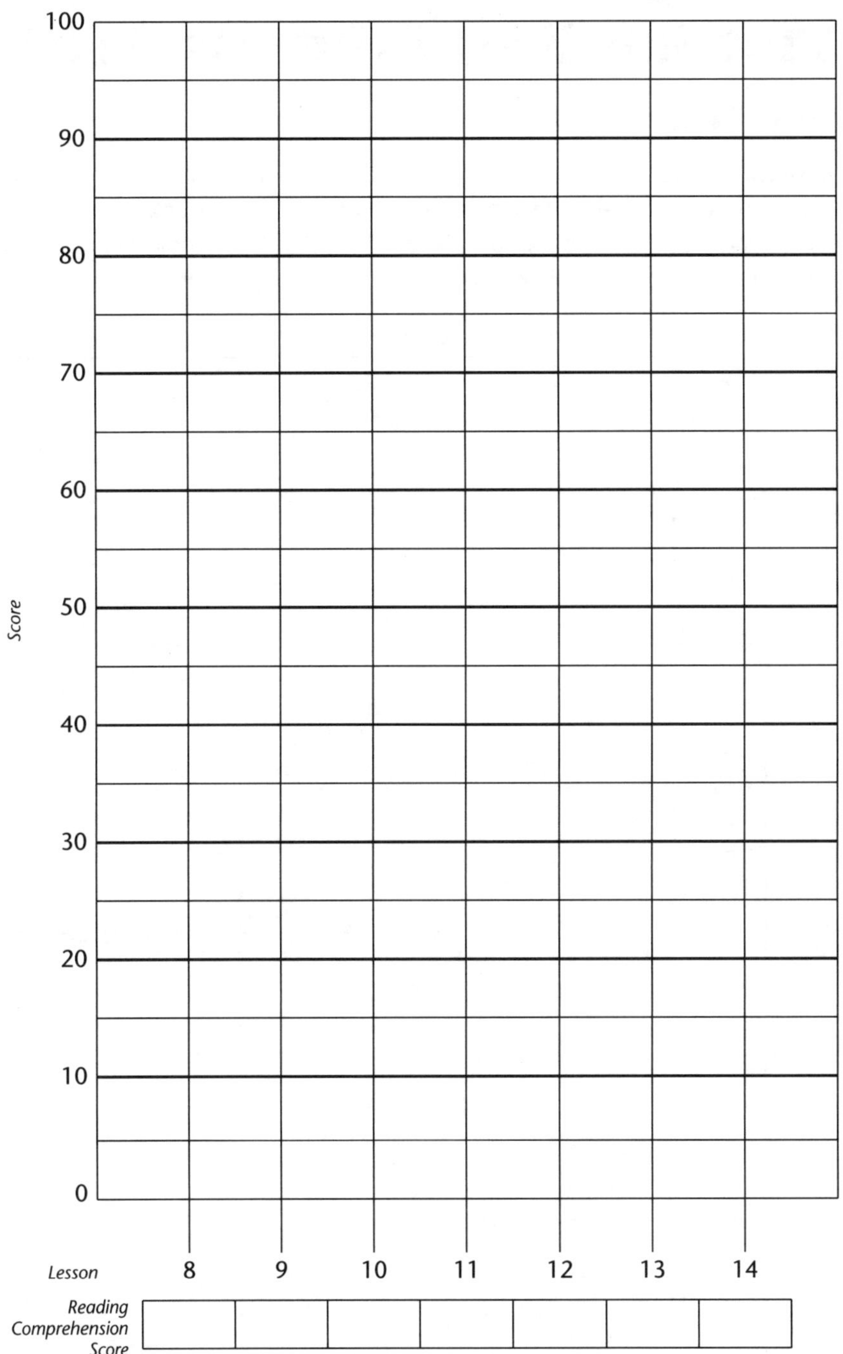

Plotting Your Progress: Critical Thinking

Unit Two

Directions: Work with your teacher to evaluate your responses to the Critical Thinking questions for each lesson. Then fill in the appropriate spaces in the chart below. For each lesson and each type of Critical Thinking question, do the following: Mark a minus sign (–) in the box to indicate areas in which you feel you could improve. Mark a plus sign (+) to indicate areas in which you feel you did well. Mark a minus-slash-plus sign (–/+) to indicate areas in which you had mixed success. Then write any comments you have about your performance, including ideas for improvement.

Lesson	Author's Approach	Summarizing and Paraphrasing	Critical Thinking
8			
9			
10			
11			
12			
13			
14			

UNIT THREE

FIREWALKING
Mind Over Matter

On April 15, 1972, a crowd of 2,000 people gathered in the village of Sunderpur, India, to witness the ritual of fire walking. Attendants had worked all day to ready the fire lanes with red-hot coals. These lanes were dug slightly below ground level. The spectators arranged themselves so that they would have a good view of the walk. Fifteen people had carefully prepared themselves to walk the 20-yard-long pits in their bare feet.

2 Most of the walkers, including the kalasis, or chief fire walker, were experts at this sort of thing. They had walked across hot coals, rocks, logs, and lava for many years without mishap. This time, however, something went wrong. Ten of the 15 fire walkers came scrambling out of the pit in great anguish before they had finished their walk. Their feet were so badly burned that they were rushed to the hospital for treatment.

3 The crowd was both shocked and dismayed. In rural India, as in many other countries, fire walking is a major religious

Firewalkers on the island of Fiji. Firewalking is a major religious event in many parts of the world and is used as a test of an individual's faith.

event. Failure to complete the walk is never taken lightly.

4 Each year, thousands of people test their faith by walking across beds of flaming coals. Most of these walkers are ordinary people who do it by choice. Usually they engage in fire walking during a time of great personal hardship. They walk the coals to please the goddess Kali so that she will cure a disease or cleanse a soul. Failure to complete a walk casts doubt on the power of Kali to protect the walkers, as well as on the power of the kalasis to lead the other fire walkers safely across the coals.

5 To be sure, this failure by 10 fire walkers was an exception. Most fire walkers are successful. Throughout Asia, such trials by fire are repeated regularly. The details of the rituals are different, but the risks are the same. Lava and blazing coals are just as hot in one culture as they are in another.

6 The basic question, however, still remains. How is it possible for anyone, magician or kalasis, to walk over hot coals and not be burned? The true believers have their answer. They say that they are protected against the flames by gods like Kali. For example, the natives of the Fiji Islands believe that the water god sends hundreds of little water babies to spread their bodies over the coals. The natives can then walk on the backs of these water babies.

7 Western scientists, however, are not swayed by such explanations. They want to find a reason that fits into the known laws of physics. Some scientists have suggested that the hot coals are placed in such a way that very little oxygen can reach them. Without oxygen there can be no combustion, and the once-hot coals begin to cool off quickly. This theory has been rejected by many because no one can show how it can be done.

8 Others argue that the fire walkers coat the soles of their feet with some sort of fire-resistant lotion. Many researchers have examined the feet of walkers, however, and have never found anything but ashes picked up on the walk.

9 Friedbert Karger, a West German scientist, was not satisfied with these old answers. He wanted to study the phenomenon firsthand, so in 1974 he went to the Fiji Islands to study and film the ritual of fire walking. There he painted the feet of one of the walkers with heat-sensitive paint, which changes color as the heat gets more and more intense. Karger's film shows the man standing on one rock for seven seconds. When Karger poured paint on the rock, the paint indicated that the rock was 600 degrees Fahrenheit. The man's feet, on the other hand, revealed a temperature of only 150 degrees. That is warm, but not warm enough to burn a person's skin. Karger then tossed a piece of callused skin on the

A Kathakali performer in traditional dress. The intricate makeup takes four hours to apply.

rocks to see what would happen to it. It vaporized in a flash.

10 Karger came away with the same feeling that other researchers have had: fire walking cannot be explained within the realm of known physics. Rather, it appears to be a dramatic example of mind over matter. If a fire walker is not in the right frame of mind, fire walking is an impossible feat. This explains why the 10 walkers in India who were upset by the chief fire walker could not complete their walks. Their anger and frustration caused them to break the trancelike state they needed to be in to walk the coals.

11 If, however, a person is in the right state of mind and has had the proper mental and physical preparation, he or she can succeed. Under such conditions, a person can tolerate direct contact with intense heat for a short period of time.

12 Scientists believe that such "mind power" is aided by a natural physical reaction. When exposed to intense heat, the bottoms of feet will sweat, and this sweat provides a thin layer of insulation from the flames. Nonetheless, the art of fire walking is an impressive display of the magic of the mind.

If you have been timed while reading this article, enter your reading time below. Then turn to the Words-per-Minute Table on page 195 and look up your reading speed (words per minute). Then enter your reading speed on the Reading Speed graph on page 196.

Reading Time: Lesson 15

________ : ________

Minutes *Seconds*

A Finding the Main Idea

One statement below expresses the main idea of the article. One statement is too general, or too broad. The other statement explains only part of the article; it is too narrow. Label the statements using the following key:

M—Main Idea **B—Too Broad** **N—Too Narrow**

_______ 1. In 1972, 10 fire walkers in India failed in their attempts to walk on hot coals.

_______ 2. Many societies have fire walking ceremonies.

_______ 3. Fire walking, a religious ritual that seems to show the power of the mind over the body, continues to baffle scientists.

_______ Score 15 points for a correct M answer.

_______ Score 5 points for each correct B or N answer.

_______ **Total Score:** Finding the Main Idea

B Recalling Facts

How well do you remember the facts in the article? Put an X in the box next to the answer that correctly completes each statement about the article.

1. Most of the walkers at Sunderpur were
   - ☐ a. high-level religious leaders.
   - ☐ b. magicians.
   - ☐ c. experienced fire walkers.
2. People usually engage in fire walking during
   - ☐ a. the harvest season.
   - ☐ b. a time of great personal hardship.
   - ☐ c. a wedding ceremony.
3. Fire walkers in India believe that they are protected by
   - ☐ a. the magician.
   - ☐ b. the kalasis.
   - ☐ c. the goddess Kali and the kalasis.
4. Friedbert Karger was
   - ☐ a. a Fiji Island fire walker.
   - ☐ b. an Indian kalasis.
   - ☐ c. a German scientist.
5. Friedbert Karger tested the Fiji fire walkers by
   - ☐ a. walking the coals himself.
   - ☐ b. painting their feet with a heat sensitive paint.
   - ☐ c. checking to see if their skin was callused.

Score 5 points for each correct answer.

_______ **Total Score:** Recalling Facts

C Making Inferences

When you combine your own experience and information from a text to draw a conclusion that is not directly stated in that text, you are making an inference. Below are five statements that may or may not be inferences based on information in the article. Label the statements using the following key:

C—Correct Inference **F—Faulty Inference**

_______ 1. Fire walking is more common in primitive cultures than in advanced cultures.

_______ 2. Most fire walkers lose their concentration and get burned at some time in their lives.

_______ 3. True believers don't care what scientists think about the impossibility of fire walking.

_______ 4. Scientists who have investigated fire walking have been easily fooled by the natives.

_______ 5. The power of the mind to control the body is unlimited.

Score 5 points for each correct answer.

_______ **Total Score:** Making Inferences

D Using Words Precisely

Each numbered sentence below contains an underlined word or phrase from the article. Following the sentence are three definitions. One definition is closest to the meaning of the underlined word. One definition is opposite or nearly opposite. Label those two definitions using the following key; do not label the remaining definition.

C—Closest **O—Opposite or Nearly Opposite**

1. They had walked across hot coals, rocks, logs, and lava for many years without <u>mishap</u>. This time, however, something went wrong.

_______ a. an accident

_______ b. a burn

_______ c. good fortune

2. Ten of the 15 fire walkers came scrambling out of the pit in great <u>anguish</u> before they had finished their walk.

_______ a. happiness

_______ b. distress

_______ c. embarrassment

3. The crowd was both shocked and <u>dismayed</u>.

_______ a. pleased

_______ b. bored

_______ c. confused and upset

4. Western scientists, however, are not <u>swayed</u> by such explanations. They want to find a reason that fits into the known laws of physics.

_______ a. familiar with

_______ b. influenced by

_______ c. unimpressed by

5. Under such conditions, a person can tolerate direct contact with intense heat for a short period of time.

_______ a. endure

_______ b. enjoy

_______ c. not stand for

_______ Score 3 points for each correct C answer.

_______ Score 2 points for each correct O answer.

_______ **Total Score:** Using Words Precisely

Enter the four total scores in the spaces below, and add them together to find your Reading Comprehension Score. Then record your score on the graph on page 197.

Score	Question Type	Lesson 15
_______	Finding the Main Idea	
_______	Recalling Facts	
_______	Making Inferences	
_______	Using Words Precisely	
_______	**Reading Comprehension Score**	

Author's Approach

Put an X in the box next to the correct answer.

1. The main purpose of the first paragraph is to

☐ a. inform the reader about the power of the kalasis.

☐ b. describe the ritual of fire walking.

☐ c. describe and set a scene.

2. From the statement "lava and blazing coals are just as hot in one culture as they are in another," you can conclude that the author wants the reader to think that

☐ a. some people have claimed that the lava and coals in Asia are not as hot.

☐ b. the fire walkers really do walk over hot coals without getting burned.

☐ c. Kali protects the fire walkers from getting burned.

3. In this article "nonetheless, the art of fire walking is an impressive display of the magic of the mind" means fire walking

☐ a. is a magic trick.

☐ b. impresses everyone who witnesses the spectacle.

☐ c. is an example of the mind's ability to conquer nature.

4. Some people believe that fire walking opposes the laws of physics. The author addresses the opposing point of view in the article by

☐ a. claiming that with the proper mental and physical preparation, a walker can tolerate high heat for a short time.

☐ b. pointing out that the placement of the hot coals allows them to cool off quickly.

☐ c. suggesting that the walkers coat their feet with heat-resistant lotion.

_______ Number of correct answers

Record your personal assessment of your work on the Critical Thinking Chart on page 198.

Summarizing and Paraphrasing

Put an X in the box next to the correct answer for question 3. Follow the directions provided for the other questions.

1. Complete the following one-sentence summary of the article using the lettered phrases from the phrase bank below. Write the letters on the lines.

Phrase Bank:

a. a description of an unsuccessful fire walking
b. the idea that fire walking involves mind over matter
c. some of the theories and beliefs about fire walking

The article about fire walking begins with ________, goes on to explain ________, and ends with ________.

2. Reread paragraph 9 in the article. Below, write a summary of the paragraph in no more than 25 words.

____

____

____

____

Reread your summary and decide whether it covers the important ideas in the paragraph. Next, decide how to shorten the summary to 15 words or less without leaving out any essential information. Write this summary below.

____

____

3. Choose the best one-sentence paraphrase for the following sentence from the article:

"Failure to complete a walk casts doubt on the power of Kali to protect the walkers, as well as on the power of the kalasis to lead the other fire walkers safely across the coals."

☐ a. Many fire walkers doubt that Kali or the kalasis can protect them during a fire walk.

☐ b. A failed fire walk forces the walkers to question the protective powers of both Kali and the kalasis.

☐ c. The kalasis has the power to lead the fire walkers, but Kali is often powerless to protect them.

________ Number of correct answers

Record your personal assessment of your work on the Critical Thinking Chart on page 198.

Critical Thinking

Follow the directions provided for questions 1 and 2. Put an X in the box next to the correct answer for questions 3 and 4.

1. For each statement below, write O if it expresses an opinion or F if it expresses a fact.

________ a. The soles of fire walkers' feet are protected by hundreds of little water babies.

________ b. Most fire walkings are successful.

________ c. The reasons used to explain the possibility of fire walking do not agree with the known laws of physics.

2. Choose from the letters below to correctly complete the following statement. Write the letters on the lines.

   In the article, _________ and _________ are different.

   a. Kali
   b. the chief fire walker
   c. the kalasis

3. What caused the callused skin to vaporize?

☐ a. Karger poured paint on the hot rocks.
☐ b. Karger threw it on the hot rocks.
☐ c. A man stood on a hot rock for seven seconds.

4. How is fire walking an example of a phenomenon?

☐ a. Fire walking is an impressive display of the magic of the mind.
☐ b. Fire walkers go into a trancelike state before they begin their walk.
☐ c. Western scientists cannot explain how someone could walk on hot coals without getting burned.

_________ Number of correct answers

Record your personal assessment of your work on the Critical Thinking Chart on page 198.

Personal Response

What was most surprising or interesting to you about this article?

____

____

____

____

Self-Assessment

What concepts or ideas from the article were difficult to understand?

____

____

____

____

Which concepts or ideas were easy to understand?

____

____

____

____

FROZEN FOR TEN THOUSAND YEARS

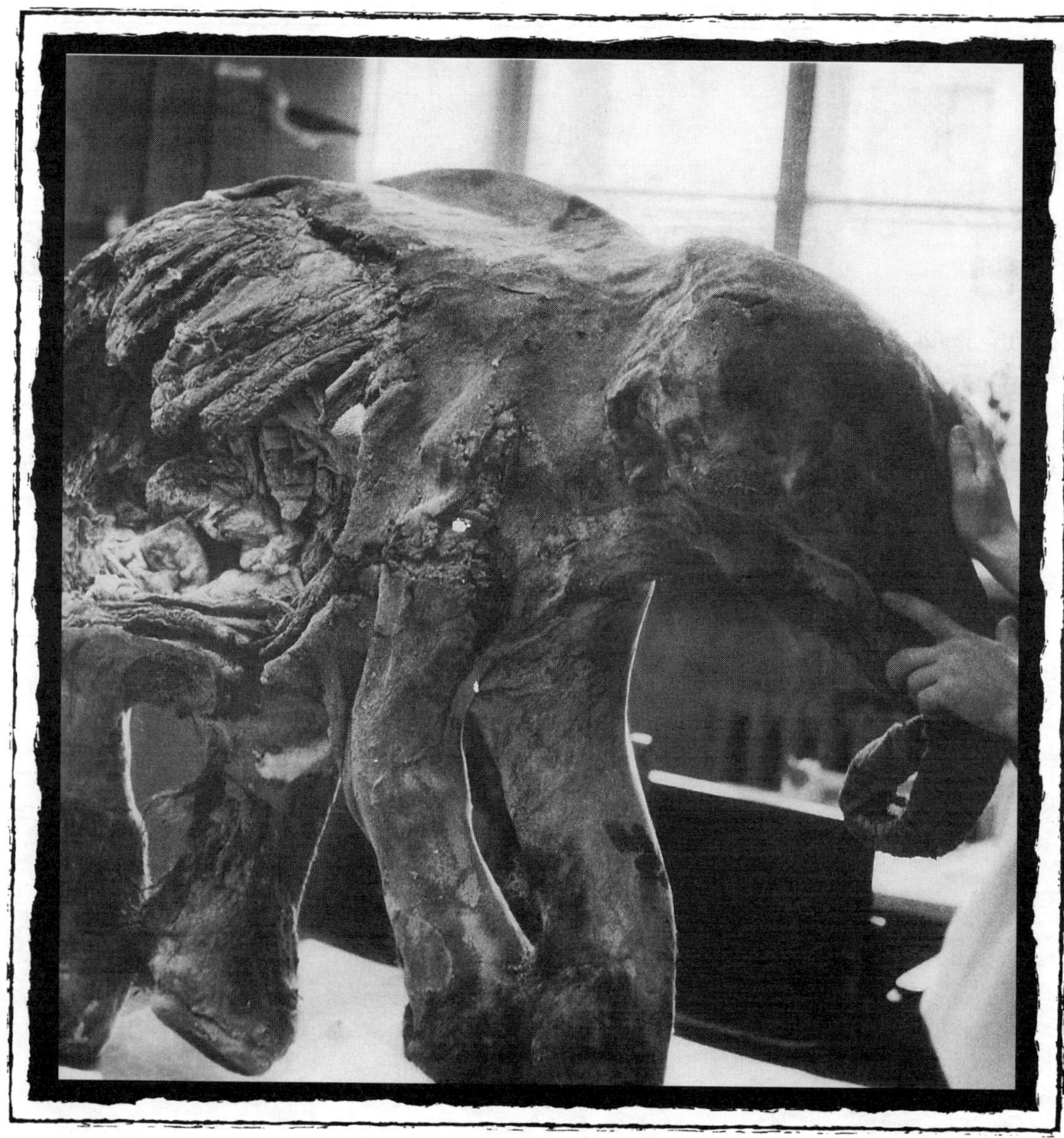

This baby mammoth died 10,000 years ago at the age of nine. The body was found frozen in an excavation area in northeastern Siberia on June 23, 1977.

Ten thousand years ago, enormous hairy creatures roamed the Arctic regions in great herds. The animals moved slowly, lumbering across the frozen tundra in search of food. They were woolly mammoths, and for many years they thrived in their frigid surroundings.

2 In many ways, the woolly mammoth looked like an elephant. The elephant, however, can survive only in warm climates, whereas the mammoth was built to live in a much colder environment. It was slightly bigger than an elephant and had long, curled tusks that it used for digging in the hard dirt. It also had a high hump on its forehead. A coat of long coarse hair and a thick layer of fat kept the mammoth warm during the long winter months.

3 Although the woolly mammoth was well suited to its environment, about 10,000 years ago this awesome animal perished. Like the dinosaurs, which died out 60 million years ago, the mammoth became extinct. The dinosaurs, however, lived and died long before there were people on the earth. The mammoth lived

at the same time as the early cave people. These people made drawings of mammoths on the walls of their caves. Long after these huge animals died out, people told legends of a great wild, woolly elephant.

4 Stories were not all that survived down through the ages. Every now and then a hunter in Siberia or Alaska would come upon a massive tusk as he dug for food. These tusks were too big to have come from elephants. Each time one was found, stories of giant woolly mammoths gained strength.

5 Then, in 1800, the chief of the Tungus tribe in northern Siberia noticed a tusk sticking out of a frozen mound of earth. At first the chief was terribly frightened, because he had never seen a tusk that big before. Like the other members of his tribe, he believed that the center of the Earth was filled with dangerous animals. Even the sight of one of these animals was said to cause death. The chief feared that the tusk belonged to such a creature.

6 It took him months to find the courage to take a closer look at the tusk. By this time it was spring, and the ground had begun to thaw. When the chief returned to the tusk, he was able to clear away some of the dirt that surrounded it. As he dug, the chief was amazed to find that the tusk was still attached to a frozen carcass. The chief had discovered the frozen body of a woolly mammoth.

7 Word of the Tungan chief's discovery spread quickly, and soon many people were digging in the wastelands of Siberia in search of woolly mammoths. They were interested in the ivory tusks of the beasts, which were very valuable. Scientists also became interested and began to search the area, hoping to find out more about the animals themselves.

8 Tons of bones were found in many spots throughout the Arctic, but in the end only 39 frozen mammoths were discovered. While mammoth bones were unearthed in several different places, frozen mammoths were uncovered only in Siberia and northern Alaska. Even among these carcasses, only four were intact. The remaining 35 were incomplete.

9 Still, the discoveries these researchers made were remarkable. They found frozen remains of some mammoths still in an upright position. They found others with green grass, meadow plants, and twigs still in their stomachs. The flesh of some of the mammoths was still quite fresh. The meat had decayed too much for people to eat, but sled dogs were eager to consume it.

10 What did these findings mean? Some scientists concluded that the mammoths must have died very quickly. The upright position of some of the woolly mammoths seemed to support the idea that they had been flash-frozen in place. All of the preserved remains indicated that the mammoths had been healthy and robust when they died. They had not died slowly by starving or freezing.

11 In the late 1800s, a scientist named Henry Howorth suggested that the mammoths had perished in a great flood. There is no evidence, however, that these animals drowned. Not many people today agree with Howorth. Still there are a number of people who do think that all

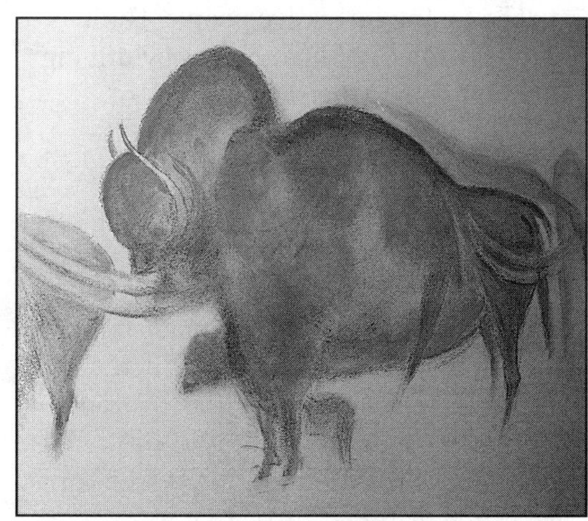

A painting of a mammoth found in Magdalenian Cave, Font de Gaume, France

the woolly mammoths died quickly in a worldwide disaster. These people point to the fact that the blood cells of the mammoths had not burst, indicating that the animals were frozen quickly rather than slowly under the mud and muck of the tundra. The people with this view believe that there must have been a sudden, major change in the world's climate, which could have produced a rapid drop in the temperature.

12 Most experts today, however, have a different idea. They believe that a change in the climate did, indeed, hurt the mammoths. But the scientists also think that people helped to destroy the mammoths by killing too many of them.

13 Ten thousand years ago, in the closing days of the last Ice Age, the world's climate began to change quickly. Apparently the woolly mammoths had trouble adjusting to the changes. In addition to this, the animals were being stalked by the early cave people. Hunters killed hundreds of mammoths by driving them off cliffs. Thus, in the space of only 200 years, the number of woolly mammoths dwindled from over 50,000 to zero.

14 Most scientists think that the mammoths that were found frozen were simply the rare ones that happened to die and then freeze before their bodies could rot. In other words, these frozen mammoths were the victims of freak accidents. Woolly mammoths were giant, awkward creatures. Those that were preserved in the earth could have slipped off the edges of cliffs or cracked through thin layers of late-summer ice. In any event, these few must have sunk into the thick mud of the tundra and become buried. Protected from direct exposure to the air, they did not decay rapidly. As the weather became colder, the soil around them froze and their bodies were trapped. This explanation accounts for the healthy condition and full stomachs of the unearthed carcasses.

15 A final solution to the mystery of the woolly mammoths does not seem likely. Some people like their answers to fit within the known laws of nature; they like to see things evolve slowly. Others look for sudden disasters to explain the mysteries of this planet. Whatever the real answer is, the woolly mammoth is gone forever.

If you have been timed while reading this article, enter your reading time below. Then turn to the Words-per-Minute Table on page 195 and look up your reading speed (words per minute). Then enter your reading speed on the Reading Speed graph on page 196.

Reading Time: Lesson 16

________ : ________

Minutes *Seconds*

A Finding the Main Idea

One statement below expresses the main idea of the article. One statement is too general, or too broad. The other statement explains only part of the article; it is too narrow. Label the statements using the following key:

M—Main Idea **B—Too Broad** **N—Too Narrow**

_______ 1. The woolly mammoth, with its huge size and curved tusks, looked much like an elephant.

_______ 2. Though some people believe that the extinction of the woolly mammoth was caused by a great disaster, most experts believe that the mammoth died out from a combination of changing climate and over-hunting.

_______ 3. Many animals have died as a result of changes in the world's climate.

_______ Score 15 points for a correct M answer.

_______ Score 5 points for each correct B or N answer.

_______ **Total Score:** Finding the Main Idea

B Recalling Facts

How well do you remember the facts in the article? Put an X in the box next to the answer that correctly completes each statement about the article.

1. The woolly mammoth died out
- ☐ a. around 10,000 years ago.
- ☐ b. just before the time of the first cave people.
- ☐ c. around 60 million years ago.

2. The first person who discovered a frozen mammoth in Siberia was
- ☐ a. a scientist.
- ☐ b. an ancient hunter.
- ☐ c. a tribal chief.

3. The number of frozen mammoth carcasses found so far is
- ☐ a. 39.
- ☐ b. 35.
- ☐ c. 200.

4. The frozen mammoths were
- ☐ a. healthy when they died.
- ☐ b. all killed by hunters.
- ☐ c. all found in Siberia.

5. Henry Howorth believed that the mammoths died from
- ☐ a. a sudden change of climate.
- ☐ b. the cold of the Ice Age.
- ☐ c. a huge flood.

Score 5 points for each correct answer.

_______ **Total Score:** Recalling Facts

C Making Inferences

When you combine your own experience and information from a text to draw a conclusion that is not directly stated in that text, you are making an inference. Below are five statements that may or may not be inferences based on information in the article. Label the statements using the following key:

C—Correct Inference **F—Faulty Inference**

_______ 1. The thickness of an animal's coat, or fur, indicates the kind of climate in which it lives.

_______ 2. Woolly mammoths are the only extinct animals whose passing has remained somewhat of a mystery to scientists.

_______ 3. Sudden changes in the climate would wipe out all animal life.

_______ 4. After the first woolly mammoth carcass was uncovered, many members of the Tungas tribe no longer were afraid when they saw tusks in the ground.

_______ 5. The meat of the woolly mammoth was a part of the diet of early cave people.

Score 5 points for each correct answer.

_______ **Total Score:** Making Inferences

D Using Words Precisely

Each numbered sentence below contains an underlined word or phrase from the article. Following the sentence are three definitions. One definition is closest to the meaning of the underlined word. One definition is opposite or nearly opposite. Label those two definitions using the following key; do not label the remaining definition.

C—Closest **O—Opposite or Nearly Opposite**

1. The animals moved slowly, lumbering across the frozen tundra in search of food.

_______ a. stepping clumsily

_______ b. walking carefully

_______ c. slipping

2. Although the woolly mammoth was well suited to its environment, about 10,000 years ago this awesome animal perished.

_______ a. inspired fear

_______ b. died out

_______ c. flourished

3. Even among these carcasses, only four were intact. The remaining thirty-five were incomplete.

_______ a. diseased

_______ b. lacking some parts

_______ c. whole

4. All of the preserved remains indicated that the mammoths had been healthy and <u>robust</u> when they died.

_______ a. strong and vigorous

_______ b. fat and woolly

_______ c. weak and tired

5. In addition to this, the animals were being <u>stalked</u> by the early cave people.

_______ a. protected

_______ b. eaten

_______ c. hunted

_______ Score 3 points for each correct C answer.

_______ Score 2 points for each correct O answer.

_______ **Total Score:** Using Words Precisely

Enter the four total scores in the spaces below, and add them together to find your Reading Comprehension Score. Then record your score on the graph on page 197.

Score	Question Type	Lesson 16
_______	Finding the Main Idea	
_______	Recalling Facts	
_______	Making Inferences	
_______	Using Words Precisely	
_______	**Reading Comprehension Score**	

Author's Approach

Put an X in the box next to the correct answer.

1. The author uses the first sentence of the article to

☐ a. describe a prehistoric setting.

☐ b. describe the qualities of the woolly mammoth.

☐ c. compare woolly mammoths and elephants.

2. Which of the following statements from the article best describes the woolly mammoth?

☐ a. "It was slightly bigger than an elephant and had long, curled tusks that it used for digging in the hard dirt."

☐ b. "In many ways, the woolly mammoth looked like an elephant."

☐ c. "The mammoth lived at the same time as the early cave people."

3. Choose the statement below that is the weakest argument for explaining the extinction of the woolly mammoth.

☐ a. The mammoths died following a sudden, major change in the world's climate.

☐ b. The mammoths perished in a great flood.

☐ c. People destroyed the mammoths by killing too many of them.

4. The author probably wrote this article in order to

☐ a. express an opinion about how the woolly mammoths perished.

☐ b. inform the reader about the relationship between mammoths and the early cave people.

☐ c. encourage the reader to think about what killed the mammoths.

_______ Number of correct answers

Record your personal assessment of your work on the Critical Thinking Chart on page 198.

Summarizing and Paraphrasing

Put an X in the box next to the correct answer.

1. Below are summaries of the article. Choose the summary that says all the most important things about the article but in the fewest words.

- ☐ a. The woolly mammoth, a huge elephant-like creature that roamed the Arctic regions, became extinct about 10,000 years ago. Many scientists believe that a sudden climate change as well as hunting practices led to the animal's destruction.
- ☐ b. Although woolly mammoths were well suited to their environment, the animals perished about 10,000 years ago. Some scientists believe that the mammoths died in a great flood, while others suggest that a sudden change in the world's climate brought about their extinction.
- ☐ c. Woolly mammoths perished about 10,000 years ago. Scientists disagree about what caused the animals' extinction.

2. Read the statement about the article below. Then read the paraphrase of that statement. Choose the reason that best tells why the paraphrase does not say the same thing as the statement.

Statement: Scientists discovered traces of food in the stomachs of the mammoths found frozen in the tundra, and the animals' flesh was still relatively fresh.

Paraphrase: The frozen mammoths that the scientists found were well preserved.

- ☐ a. Paraphrase says too much.
- ☐ b. Paraphrase doesn't say enough.
- ☐ c. Paraphrase doesn't agree with the statement about the article.

________ Number of correct answers

Record your personal assessment of your work on the Critical Thinking Chart on page 198.

CRITICAL THINKING

Critical Thinking

Put an X in the box next to the correct answer for questions 1 and 2. Follow the directions provided for the other questions.

1. Which of the following statements from the article is an opinion rather than a fact?

- ☐ a. "Ten thousand years ago, in the closing days of the last Ice Age, the world's climate began to change quickly."
- ☐ b. "The dinosaurs lived and died long before there were people on the earth."
- ☐ c. "All the woolly mammoths died quickly in a worldwide disaster."

2. From the article, you can predict that if another sudden, major change occurred in the world's climate,

- ☐ a. the woolly mammoths would return.
- ☐ b. some animal species would not survive the change.
- ☐ c. everything on Earth would die instantly.

3. Using what you know about elephants and what is told about woolly mammoths in the article, name three ways an elephant is similar to and different from a woolly mammoth. Cite the paragraph number(s) where you found details in the article to support your conclusions.

Similarities

____

____

____

Differences

___

___

___

4. Think about cause-effect relationships in the article. Fill in the blanks in the cause-effect chart, choosing from the letters below.

Cause	Effect
Mammoths were buried in the tundra.	___
___	Cave dwellers made drawings of mammoths.
___	A Tungan chief fled from a mammoth tusk.

a. Mammoths lived at the same time as people.

b. They did not decay rapidly.

c. He believed that it belonged to an animal that could cause his death.

5. In which paragraph did you find the information or details to answer question 2?

___

___ Number of correct answers

Record your personal assessment of your work on the Critical Thinking Chart on page 198.

Personal Response

I agree with the author because

___

___

___

___

Self-Assessment

Before reading this article, I already knew

___

___

___

___

CAN ANIMALS PREDICT EARTHQUAKES?

For centuries the Japanese noted that catfish leapt madly about in their ponds before an earthquake struck. In 1835, an immense flock of screaming seabirds flew over the city of Concepción, Chile. Hours later, the city was destroyed by an earthquake. Minutes before the devastating San Francisco quake of 1906, dogs ran howling through the streets. In 1963, shortly before an earthquake hit Skopje, Yugoslavia (now the capital of Macedonia), the zoo animals cried out and charged their cage bars.

2 In 1975, a man in Guatemala got up from his bed to prepare a snack shortly after midnight. To his surprise, he saw his two goldfish leap out of their bowl and land on the floor. The man was puzzled, but he placed the fish back in the bowl and returned to his bed. Three hours later an earthquake rocked Guatemala, less than 20 miles from where the man and his goldfish lived. Over 17,000 people were killed.

3 Were these animals somehow aware that an earthquake was coming? Many Asian people have long believed that animals can sense earthquakes about to

Evidence suggests that animals experience radical changes in behavior prior to an earthquake. These changes in behavior can be useful in predicting earthquakes.

strike. Western scientists, however, usually dismissed reports of strange animal behavior as nothing more than tall tales. Yet, in time, the scientists became impressed by the sheer volume of stories concerning animal behavior before earthquakes. So, in recent years, the experts have begun to take a second look. Now most scientists are convinced that there really is something to the idea that animals can sense when earthquakes are about to take place.

4 The event that changed the views of many scientists took place in northeastern China during the early 1970s. Chinese scientists, using an instrument called a seismograph (SIZE-muh-graf), began to record and measure a series of large shocks in the earth. The seismic signals increased so sharply that in 1974 the Chinese experts flatly predicted that a major earthquake would strike the region within two years.

5 Six months later, the animals in the region went crazy. Snakes turned suicidal by climbing out of their cozy underground homes and freezing in the winter cold. Rats ran through the streets in broad daylight. Birds in cages flew wildly about. Chickens refused to enter their coops. In general, the animal kingdom went berserk. Within hours, northeastern China was hit by a series of minor earth tremors.

6 In February 1974, geese began to fly into trees. Pigs attacked each other and tore down their pens. Dogs howled wildly for no apparent reason. Three police dogs suddenly refused to obey the commands of their trainers and began sniffing the ground. These occurrences, too, were followed by a series of minor shocks.

7 Chinese officials were now certain that a major earthquake was coming soon. They ordered the evacuation of Haicheng—a city of over 1 million people. Within a few hours after the evacuation, a huge earthquake reduced the city to rubble. Countless lives were saved because the Chinese listened to the warnings being given by the animals.

8 How is it possible for animals to predict earthquakes? The experts are not exactly sure what happens to upset the animals. Dr. Barry Raleigh, a geophysicist for the United States Geological Survey, said: "The animals are doing great. I only wish they could talk about it and explain what they sense."

9 Since the animals won't discuss their feelings with scientists, the scientists have had to develop their own theories. Some scientists believe that animals can detect low-frequency sounds from early shocks that are so small that even seismic machines cannot pick them up.

10 Other scientists think that some animals are supersensitive to even minute vibrations in the earth. The legs of

Seismographs measure the direction, duration, and strength of ground movement and help scientists predict earthquakes.

pigeons, for example, are highly sensitive. In an experiment done in 1975, the leg nerves of some laboratory pigeons were severed, while the nerves of others were left alone. During a small earth tremor, the pigeons with normal nerves flew wildly about. The ones with severed nerves showed no reaction at all.

11 Thomas Gold, a scientist from Cornell University, feels that he may have found a part of the answer. An earthquake does not happen suddenly. It is caused by a movement in the earth's crust. Before the earthquake actually strikes, gases from within the earth are forced to the surface. These gases, which are odorous, quickly mix with the air and go undetected by humans and most animals. Bottom-dwelling fish and burrowing animals, however, may react strongly to these alien fumes.

12 Helmut Tributsch, along with a number of other scientists, thinks that animals can sense when something is "in the air." Before a quake, the earth releases masses of charged particles called *ions* (I-ons). The air becomes alive with electricity. Humans don't notice it, but many animals do.

13 A final solution to this mystery has not been found. It seems clear, however, that no single explanation explains the reactions of all animals. Different animals respond to different things. Some animals may pick up the faintest sound or detect the slightest shock wave in the earth. Other animals may be alerted by a strange odor or by charged particles in the air.

14 In any event, we can no longer scoff at the idea that animals can help protect us from earthquakes. Animals will not replace our seismographs, but they can still provide a valuable backup system. Their help could mean the difference between life and death. Just ask the people of Haicheng.

If you have been timed while reading this article, enter your reading time below. Then turn to the Words-per-Minute Table on page 195 and look up your reading speed (words per minute). Then enter your reading speed on the Reading Speed graph on page 196.

Reading Time: Lesson 17

_______ : _______

Minutes *Seconds*

A Finding the Main Idea

One statement below expresses the main idea of the article. One statement is too general, or too broad. The other statement explains only part of the article; it is too narrow. Label the statements using the following key:

M—Main Idea **B—Too Broad** **N—Too Narrow**

_______ 1. Many animals can hear, smell, and sense things that humans cannot.

_______ 2. Fish often leap wildly about just before an earthquake strikes.

_______ 3. It appears that some animals can predict when and where an earthquake is likely to hit.

_______ Score 15 points for a correct M answer.

_______ Score 5 points for each correct B or N answer.

_______ **Total Score:** Finding the Main Idea

B Recalling Facts

How well do you remember the facts in the article? Put an X in the box next to the answer that correctly completes each statement about the article.

1. The man who saw his goldfish leap out of the bowl lived in
   - ☐ a. southwest China.
   - ☐ b. Guatemala.
   - ☐ c. northeast China.
2. The event that changed the minds of many scientists about the reports of animal behavior took place in
   - ☐ a. Chile.
   - ☐ b. northeast China.
   - ☐ c. Yugoslavia.
3. Haicheng is a Chinese
   - ☐ a. village.
   - ☐ b. city.
   - ☐ c. scientist.
4. In one experiment, scientists severed the leg nerves of
   - ☐ a. dogs.
   - ☐ b. pigs.
   - ☐ c. pigeons.
5. The charged particles that the earth releases before an earthquake are called
   - ☐ a. ions.
   - ☐ b. shock waves.
   - ☐ c. vibrations.

Score 5 points for each correct answer.

_______ **Total Score:** Recalling Facts

C Making Inferences

When you combine your own experience and information from a text to draw a conclusion that is not directly stated in that text, you are making an inference. Below are five statements that may or may not be inferences based on information in the article. Label the statements using the following key:

C—Correct Inference **F—Faulty Inference**

_______ 1. Animals act crazy before an earthquake because they sense that they are in great danger.

_______ 2. All animals are capable of predicting when an earthquake will strike.

_______ 3. For a long time scientists rejected reports of strange animal behavior because they did not trust the accuracy of the reports.

_______ 4. Western scientists were impressed by the reports from China because the animal behavior there was closely checked by Chinese scientific authorities.

_______ 5. Most scientists agree on how animals are able to predict earthquakes.

Score 5 points for each correct answer.

_______ **Total Score:** Making Inferences

D Using Words Precisely

Each numbered sentence below contains an underlined word or phrase from the article. Following the sentence are three definitions. One definition is closest to the meaning of the underlined word. One definition is opposite or nearly opposite. Label those two definitions using the following key; do not label the remaining definition.

C—Closest **O—Opposite or Nearly Opposite**

1. In 1835, an immense flock of screaming seabirds flew over the city of Concepcion, Chile.

_______ a. tiny

_______ b. beautiful

_______ c. huge

2. Other scientists think that some animals are supersensitive to even minute vibrations in the earth.

_______ a. frequent

_______ b. very small

_______ c. great

3. In an experiment done in 1975, the leg nerves of some laboratory pigeons were severed, while the nerves of others were left alone.

_______ a. cut

_______ b. tested

_______ c. connected

4. Bottom-dwelling fish and burrowing animals, however, may react strongly to these alien fumes.

_______ a. strange

_______ b. common

_______ c. toxic

5. In any event, we can no longer scoff at the idea that animals can help protect us from earthquakes.

_______ a. mention

_______ b. take very seriously

_______ c. mock

_______ Score 3 points for each correct C answer.

_______ Score 2 points for each correct O answer.

_______ **Total Score:** Using Words Precisely

Enter the four total scores in the spaces below, and add them together to find your Reading Comprehension Score. Then record your score on the graph on page 197.

Score	Question Type	Lesson 17
_______	Finding the Main Idea	
_______	Recalling Facts	
_______	Making Inferences	
_______	Using Words Precisely	
_______	**Reading Comprehension Score**	

Author's Approach

Put an X in the box next to the correct answer.

1. What does the author mean by the statement "western scientists, however, usually dismissed reports of strange animal behavior as nothing more than tall tales"?

☐ a. Most Western scientists didn't believe that animals could predict earthquakes.

☐ b. Most Western scientists didn't believe that animals could act in a strange manner.

☐ c. Western scientists who believed that animals could predict earthquakes were ridiculed.

2. What is the author's purpose in writing "Can Animals Predict Earthquakes"?

☐ a. to inform the reader about the destructive power of earthquakes

☐ b. to inform the reader about research on animals' reactions to approaching earthquakes

☐ c. to emphasize the similarities between Asian scientists and Western scientists

3. Choose the statement below that best describes the author's position in paragraph 14.

☐ a. Animals cannot replace seismographs.

☐ b. A backup system could have saved lives in Haicheng.

☐ c. Scientists should use both seismographs and animals' warnings to help predict earthquakes.

4. The author tells this story mainly by

- ☐ a. retelling personal experiences.
- ☐ b. telling different stories about the same topic.
- ☐ c. comparing different topics.

_______ Number of correct answers

Record your personal assessment of your work on the Critical Thinking Chart on page 198.

Summarizing and Paraphrasing

Follow the directions provided for questions 1 and 2. Put an X in the box next to the correct answer for question 3.

1. Complete the following one-sentence summary of the article using the lettered phrases from the phrase bank below. Write the letters on the lines.

Phrase Bank:

a. the studies conducted by Chinese scientists with seismographs and animals
b. a review of the behavior of animals prior to some devastating earthquakes
c. a discussion of how animals might sense earthquakes

The article about animals' reactions to earthquakes begins with _______, goes on to explain _______, and ends with _______.

2. Reread paragraph 2 in the article. Below, write a summary of the paragraph in no more than 25 words.

____

____

____

Reread your summary and decide whether it covers the important ideas in the paragraph. Next, decide how to shorten the summary to 15 words or less without leaving out any essential information. Write this summary below.

____

____

3. Choose the best one-sentence paraphrase for the following sentence from the article:

"Some scientists believe that animals can detect low-frequency sounds from early shocks that are so small that even seismic machines cannot pick them up."

- ☐ a. Some scientists believe that animals react to the same sounds detected by seismographs.
- ☐ b. Some scientists test animals' reactions to earthquakes by giving them small electrical shocks.
- ☐ c. Some scientists believe that animals can hear sounds made by earthquakes so small that seismographs don't register them.

_______ Number of correct answers

Record your personal assessment of your work on the Critical Thinking Chart on page 198.

Critical Thinking

Put an X in the box next to the correct answer for questions 1, 3, and 4. Follow the directions provided for question 2.

1. From what the article told about Haicheng, you can predict that Chinese scientists will

☐ a. no longer use seismographs to detect earthquakes.

☐ b. continue to monitor animals and take their warnings very seriously.

☐ c. no longer listen to the warnings given by animals.

2. Choose from the letters below to correctly complete the following statement. Write the letters on the lines.

In the article, the reactions of the ________ and the reactions of the ________ are alike.

a. seabirds flying over Concepción, Chile, in 1835

b. caged birds in China in 1974

c. pigeons with severed nerves in a laboratory in 1975

3. What was the effect of the snakes' crawling out of their underground homes?

☐ a. The snakes ran through the streets in broad daylight.

☐ b. Northeastern China was hit by a series of minor earthquakes.

☐ c. The snakes froze to death in the winter cold.

4. Of the following theme categories, which would this story fit into?

☐ a. People can learn from animals.

☐ b. People are powerless against earthquakes.

☐ c. Animal instincts are more valuable than scientific machines.

________ Number of correct answers

Record your personal assessment of your work on the Critical Thinking Chart on page 198.

Personal Response

I disagree with the author because

____

____

____

Self-Assessment

From reading this article, I have learned

____

____

____

____

A COLD KILLER

No one knows why little Brittany Eichelberger went outside that frosty morning. But early on December 24, 1990, the three-year-old managed to unlock the front door of her family's West Virginia home and wander out into the 20°F. weather. Dressed just in underwear and a T-shirt, she didn't get far. Her parents found her three hours later, lying in the snow near her house, her body frozen solid. "Have you taken a steak from the freezer?" asked a nurse who was at the hospital when Brittany was brought in. "She was that stiff and hard."

2 Brittany's body temperature had dropped to 74°F. She showed no signs of life. Her pupils were fixed and dilated, her heart was not pumping, and she was not breathing. Medical personnel went to work on her anyway. They remembered a well-known rule about hypothermia: Don't give up on people who are cold and dead. Victims aren't truly gone until they're warm and dead.

3 Hypothermia is a state of low body temperature. Normally, humans maintain a body temperature of 98.6 F. To keep from getting too hot, a person's body

Before venturing out in weather like that in the photo, people need to be certain they are properly dressed to avoid hypothermia.

sweats. As the sweat evaporates, the body cools down. To keep from getting too cold, on the other hand, a person's body shivers. The shivering forces muscles into activity, thereby producing heat. This system works well under most conditions, but sometimes the body can't produce enough heat to maintain an adequate temperature. That's when hypothermia sets in.

4 The first warning sign is the shivering. Brittany Eichelberger would have started shivering as soon as her body temperature began dropping. Her brain would have pushed her muscles into action in a desperate attempt to fight off the cold. When that didn't work, the blood vessels near her skin would have constricted. That is the body's way of keeping blood as far away from the cold as possible.

5 When Brittany's temperature dropped to 95˚F. she was officially hypothermic. At that point the blood flow to her brain would have slowed down. She would have become confused and disoriented. Her coordination would have diminished, so that simple things like walking or talking would have become increasingly difficult. With her brain growing fuzzier, she wouldn't have realized the terrible danger she was in. She would have simply felt cold, tired, and ready for sleep.

6 At 86˚F. Brittany would have stopped shivering and her muscles would have become rigid. That marks the onset of severe hypothermia. From that point, a person slips into unconsciousness. Brittany would have been completely unresponsive, lying in a deep coma on the edge of death. Below 77˚F. no body functions are retained. At that point, Brittany's heart and lungs would have stopped working.

7 Although Brittany collapsed in below-freezing weather, the air does not have to be that cold for hypothermia to set in. Plenty of people have died of hypothermia on crisp, 50˚F. days. Often it happens because people are not properly dressed or because they get wet—or both. A hiker can get into trouble if he or she makes the mistake of wearing cotton clothing. While hiking, the cotton becomes wet with perspiration. If something happens to delay the hiker—for instance, if he or she twists an ankle and must wait for help to arrive—that can spell danger. The combination of wet clothes and a cooling breeze can chill the hiker's body to a dangerously low point.

8 Boating accidents are another prime cause of hypothermia. Once someone has been soaked with cold water, it is hard for his or her body to warm itself. Even long-distance runners bathed in sweat are at risk. The winner of the 1994 City of Pittsburgh Marathon was rushed to a medical tent right after crossing the finish line because he showed signs of hypothermia.

9 About 750 people die each year from hypothermia. It's not surprising that

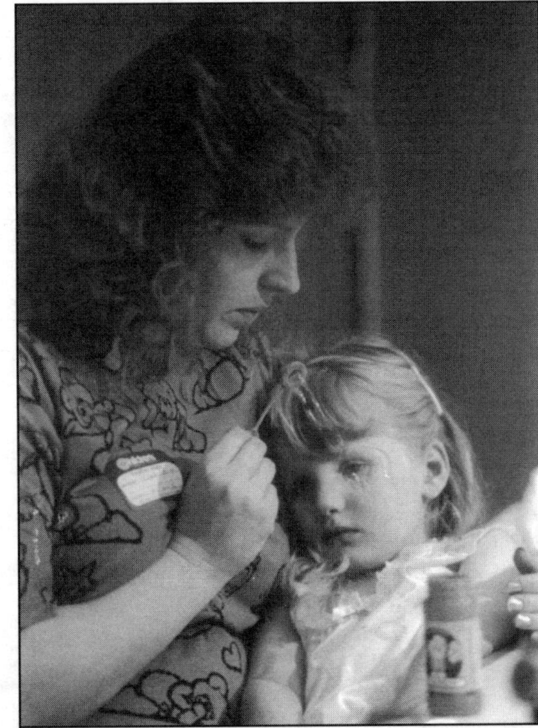

Brittany Eichelberger and her mother two weeks after Brittany wandered out into subfreezing weather

Alaska is the site for many of these deaths. Illinois, too, is a cold-weather state where this kind of death is common. But the other states that make the top 10 list for hypothermia deaths have relatively mild winters. They are Alabama, Arizona, New Mexico, North Carolina, Oklahoma, South Carolina, Tennessee, and Virginia. "Most Southern states are not known for cold winters and that's why people die—because they're not prepared for it," says Dr. Emilio Esteban.

10 More than half of all hypothermia deaths are suffered by people age 64 or older. One reason is that, as people age, they lose their ability to shiver. Their brains have trouble gauging body temperature. Even when they are losing body heat, their brains may not send a signal to the muscles to generate heat. As a result, older people can slide into hypothermia without ever feeling cold.

11 Brittany Eichelberger would have felt cold for a while, but by the time her body was found, she wasn't feeling anything at all. Doctors later said her core temperature had been under 77°F for about 40 minutes. Even after she had been removed from the snow and was surrounded by warm air, her body could not heat itself. Rescue workers quickly began CPR—cardiopulmonary resuscitation. They hoped to restart her heart and get the blood flowing through her body again. At the hospital, doctors trained heat lamps on Brittany's skin. They flushed her stomach with warm water. They heated the oxygen that was being pumped into her lungs.

12 For several hours it was impossible to tell if any life remained in the little girl. At last, after almost three hours in the hospital, doctors detected a weak pulse. As unlikely as it seemed, Brittany's heart was pumping again.

13 In most hypothermia victims, death occurs when the heart stops. Sometimes, as in Brittany's case, the heart can be restarted. But because the brain has been deprived of oxygen, most survivors suffer brain damage. Children have the best chance of fully recovering from severe hypothermia. Doctors think this is because their smaller bodies cool more quickly than those of adults. Before their brains can be damaged by lack of oxygen, their whole system shuts down. The falling body temperature slows metabolism so that the brain, along with the rest of the body's organs, enters a kind of suspended animation.

14 Eight hours after being pulled from the snow, Brittany's body had been warmed to 84°F. She was still unconscious, and there was no way of telling how much brain damage she had sustained. It took another 24 hours before her body had warmed enough for doctors to let her try breathing on her own. When they removed the breathing tube from her lungs, she coughed a bit, then cried out, "Mommy! Mommy!" At that moment, the team of doctors and nurses broke into smiles. They knew little Brittany was going to be okay. Over the next few months, she made a complete recovery. Brittany herself may not remember much of what happened to her. But her parents and the medical personnel who helped save her will never forget how close she came to being killed by the cold.

If you have been timed while reading this article, enter your reading time below. Then turn to the Words-per-Minute Table on page 195 and look up your reading speed (words per minute). Then enter your reading speed on the Reading Speed graph on page 196.

Reading Time: Lesson 18

________ : ________

Minutes *Seconds*

Finding the Main Idea

One statement below expresses the main idea of the article. One statement is too general, or too broad. The other statement explains only part of the article; it is too narrow. Label the statements using the following key:

M—Main Idea **B—Too Broad** **N—Too Narrow**

_______ 1. Many people die each year from hypothermia.

_______ 2. When body temperature drops to dangerously low levels, hypothermia, a potentially deadly condition, sets in.

_______ 3. When Brittany Eichelberger's temperature dropped to 95°F., she was officially hypothermic.

_______ Score 15 points for a correct M answer.

_______ Score 5 points for each correct B or N answer.

_______ **Total Score:** Finding the Main Idea

B Recalling Facts

How well do you remember the facts in the article? Put an X in the box next to the answer that correctly completes each statement about the article.

1. When Brittany arrived at the hospital, her body temperature had dropped to

☐ a. 86°F.
☐ b. 77°F.
☐ c. 74°F.

2. To keep from getting too cold,

☐ a. a person's body shivers.
☐ b. a person's body sweats.
☐ c. the blood vessels near the skin constrict.

3. Hikers should not wear cotton clothing on a cool day because the clothing

☐ a. might cause the hiker to twist an ankle.
☐ b. can become wet with perspiration.
☐ c. isn't warm enough.

4. Most of the people who die from hypothermia are

☐ a. children.
☐ b. 64 years old or older.
☐ c. long-distance runners.

5. In most cases of severe hypothermia, once the heart stops, the patient

☐ a. dies.
☐ b. suffers brain damage.
☐ c. fully recovers.

Score 5 points for each correct answer.

_______ **Total Score:** Recalling Facts

C Making Inferences

When you combine your own experience and information from a text to draw a conclusion that is not directly stated in that text, you are making an inference. Below are five statements that may or may not be inferences based on information in the article. Label the statements using the following key:

C—Correct Inference **F—Faulty Inference**

_______ 1. If Brittany Eichelberger had been left lying in the snow much longer, she would have died.

_______ 2. The doctors would not have been able to save Brittany if she had been 20 years older.

_______ 3. People in warm-weather states never die from hypothermia.

_______ 4. Hypothermia causes a sudden death.

_______ 5. People with hypothermia seem to die in their sleep.

Score 5 points for each correct answer.

_______ **Total Score:** Making Inferences

D Using Words Precisely

Each numbered sentence below contains an underlined word or phrase from the article. Following the sentence are three definitions. One definition is closest to the meaning of the underlined word. One definition is opposite or nearly opposite. Label those two definitions using the following key; do not label the remaining definition.

C—Closest **O—Opposite or Nearly Opposite**

1. Medical <u>personnel</u> went to work on her anyway.

_______ a. customers

_______ b. machines

_______ c. staff

2. This system works well under most conditions, but sometimes the body can't produce enough heat to maintain an <u>adequate</u> temperature.

_______ a. high

_______ b. insufficient

_______ c. satisfactory

3. She would have become confused and <u>disoriented</u>.

_______ a. depressed

_______ b. confused

_______ c. level-headed

4. At last, after almost three hours in the hospital, doctors <u>detected</u> a weak pulse.

_______ a. discovered

_______ b. overlooked

_______ c. inserted

5. But because the brain has been <u>deprived of</u> oxygen, most survivors suffer brain damage.

_______ a. allergic to

_______ b. enriched with

_______ c. denied

_______ Score 3 points for each correct C answer.

_______ Score 2 points for each correct O answer.

_______ **Total Score:** Using Words Precisely

Enter the four total scores in the spaces below, and add them together to find your Reading Comprehension Score. Then record your score on the graph on page 197.

Score	Question Type	Lesson 18
_______	Finding the Main Idea	
_______	Recalling Facts	
_______	Making Inferences	
_______	Using Words Precisely	
_______	**Reading Comprehension Score**	

Author's Approach

Put an X in the box next to the correct answer.

1. Which of the following statements from the article best describes hypothermia?

☐ a. "About 750 people die each year from hypothermia."

☐ b. "Hypothermia is a state of low body temperature."

☐ c. "Plenty of people have died of hypothermia on crisp, 50°F days."

2. From the statement "at last, after almost three hours in the hospital, doctors detected a weak pulse," you can conclude that the author wants the reader to think that the doctors

☐ a. worked long and hard to save Brittany.

☐ b. were frustrated by Brittany's lack of response to treatment.

☐ c. did not have much hope that Brittany would survive.

3. The author probably wrote this article in order to

☐ a. emphasize the similarities between warm-weather and cold-weather states.

☐ b. describe what happens when body temperature drops.

☐ c. inform the reader about the dangers of hypothermia.

4. The author tells this story mainly by

☐ a. telling one person's experience with hypothermia.

☐ b. telling several people's experiences with hypothermia.

☐ c. using his or her imagination and creativity.

_______ Number of correct answers

Record your personal assessment of your work on the Critical Thinking Chart on page 198.

Summarizing and Paraphrasing

Follow the directions provided for question 1. Put an X in the box next to the correct answer for question 2.

1. Complete the following one-sentence summary of the article using the lettered phrases from the phrase bank below. Write the letters on the lines.

Phrase Bank:

a. Brittany's full recovery

b. what happens to the hypothermic victim as body temperature drops

c. the discovery of Brittany's frozen body

The article about hypothermia begins with ________, goes on to explain ________, and ends with ________.

2. Read the statement about the article below. Then read the paraphrase of that statement. Choose the reason that best tells why the paraphrase does not say the same thing as the statement.

Statement: The elderly are more susceptible to hypothermia because, as people age, they lose the ability to shiver.

Paraphrase: Because older people don't shiver as much as younger people, they are more likely to slide into hypothermia without ever feeling cold.

☐ a. Paraphrase says too much.

☐ b. Paraphrase doesn't say enough.

☐ c. Paraphrase doesn't agree with the statement about the article.

________ Number of correct answers

Record your personal assessment of your work on the Critical Thinking Chart on page 198.

Critical Thinking

Put an X in the box next to the correct answer for questions 1, 3, 4, and 5. Follow the directions provided for question 2.

1. From the events in the article, you can predict that the following will happen next :

☐ a. Brittany's parents will make sure that their daughter never wanders out into the cold again.

☐ b. Brittany's parents will be arrested for child neglect.

☐ c. Brittany will never be allowed to wear cotton clothing.

2. Choose from the letters below to correctly complete the following statement. Write the letters on the lines.

On the positive side, ________, but on the negative side ________.

a. a child whose heart is restarted may survive

b. an adult whose heart is restarted may survive

c. the survivor will probably suffer brain damage

3. What causes children to have a better chance than adults of fully recovering from hypothermia?

☐ a. Children's brains are not as severely damaged by a lack of oxygen.

☐ b. Children's hearts are easier to restart.

☐ c. Children's bodies cool more quickly than those of adults.

4. If you were a doctor, how could you use the information in the article to treat someone with hypothermia?

☐ a. Like Brittany's doctors, never give up until the patient slips into unconsciousness.

☐ b. Like Brittany's doctors, never give up until the patient is warm and dead.

☐ c. Like Brittany's doctors, never give up until the patient is cold and dead.

5. What did you have to do to answer question 4?

☐ a. find a cause (why something happened)

☐ b. draw a conclusion (a sensible statement based on the text and your experience)

☐ c. find a comparison (how things are the same)

______ Number of correct answers

Record your personal assessment of your work on the Critical Thinking Chart on page 198.

Personal Response

How do you think Brittany Eichelberger felt when she finally regained consciousness in the hospital?

____

____

____

____

Self-Assessment

The part I found most difficult about the article was

____

____

____

____

I found this difficult because

____

____

____

____

WHAT HAPPENED IN TUNGUSKA?

A peasant testified: "When I sat down to have my breakfast beside my plough, I heard sudden bangs, as if from gun fire. My horse fell to its knees. The wind was so strong that it carried off some of the soil from the surface of the ground."

2 Another witness said: "The sky was split in two and high above the forest the whole northern part of the sky appeared to be covered with fire. A hot wind as if from a cannon blew past the huts from the north. At that moment I felt great heat as if my shirt had caught fire."

3 A woman reported: "Early in the morning when everyone was asleep in the tent, it was blown up into the air, together with the occupants. When they fell back to earth, the whole family suffered slight bruises, but Akulina and Ivan actually lost consciousness."

4 What caused the sky to split in two? Why was the whole family tossed into the air like so many rag dolls? And what could have knocked the peasant's horse to its knees? Well, no one knows for sure exactly what happened. But, on June 30,

Trees scorched and uprooted at the edge of the crater formed by the Tunguska meteorite.

1908, in the Tunguska River basin in remote Siberia, there was an explosion that was heard 744 miles away.

5 The blast was so great that shock waves circled the globe twice. It was so great that it devastated an area 62 miles wide. Its explosive power was 15 hundred times the explosive power of the atom bomb that was dropped on Hiroshima during World War II. It was the Tunguska Event.

6 Fortunately, this huge explosion occurred in an uninhabited region of Siberia. The only known casualties were herds of reindeer and millions of pine trees. The witnesses who heard the explosion or saw the northern sky turn to fire were far enough away to live through the experience.

7 Yet, strangely, the incident went largely unnoticed by the rest of the world. In 1908, Russia was ruled by Czar Nicholas II. When reports of the explosion reached the Czar's government in Moscow, the capital city, they were dismissed as the ramblings of ignorant peasants. The shock waves were thought to be nothing more than an earthquake tremor. No one bothered to check out what had really happened.

8 Even in London, the shock waves were picked up but casually filed away and forgotten. Strange things, however, were reported in the newspapers over the next few days. The sky became so filled with fine dust that people thousands of miles away in the British Isles were able to read the small print of their newspapers at midnight. This was possible because the summer sun was just below the horizon, and its light reflected off the dust particles. No one, however, made any connection between these unusual occurrences and the blast in the wasteland of Siberia.

9 World War I, the Russian Revolution, and the Russian Civil War prevented any investigation into the Tunguska Event for many years. By 1921 not many people were interested in the 13-year-old stories of the monster explosion. But a man named Leonid A. Kulik, a researcher in meteorites, became obsessed with the strange affair and the tales of a handful of illiterate peasants.

10 In the years that followed, Kulik was able to piece together a picture of what had happened. There had indeed been a tremendous explosion in 1908 that created great shock waves and caused enormous forest fires. Trees over a vast area were tossed about like matchsticks. Hundreds of square miles of land were scorched. Had the explosion happened in a populated area, the death toll would have been phenomenal.

11 At first, Kulik thought that the area must have been hit by a meteor. But he searched in vain for the crater that would have been formed. It would later be determined that only an explosion that had taken place above the earth could have caused the unique pattern of devastation found at Tunguska.

12 In fact, the explosion had many of the earmarks of a nuclear blast. Atomic bombs

A comet streaks through the night sky. Scientist Carl Sagan believed that a piece of a comet may have caused the blast at Tunguska.

are often detonated in the air, well above the surface of the earth. Like the blast that took place at Tunguska, an atomic explosion scorches the land and does not make a crater. Those who witnessed the blast at Tunguska said that a mushroom-shaped cloud formed in the atmosphere. The trademark of an atomic bomb is also the mushroom cloud. And, after the atom bomb was dropped on Hiroshima, trees and vegetation began to grow at a much faster rate than normal. The same weird plant growth occurred at Tunguska.

13 What could have caused the destruction at Tunguska? Some of the explanations that have been offered range from the fanciful to the bizarre. Some people take the parallels between nuclear blasts and Tunguska seriously. They suggest that some alien spaceship was forced to crash-land with nuclear weapons on board. Others have considered the possibility that a tiny black hole passed through the earth in Siberia and emerged from the other side. Some scientists have even hinted that antimatter from outer space clashed with the ordinary matter of earth to cause the explosion. None of these ideas, however, is adequately backed by evidence.

14 Carl Sagan, who was then a scientist at Cornell University, thought that the 1908 blast was caused by a piece of Comet Encke. If a large chunk of a comet entered the earth's atmosphere, it would be traveling at a speed of 70,000 miles per hour. At that speed, the comet, which is made up largely of ice, would explode in the air. The effects would be much like those of a nuclear explosion. There would be a fireball and a mushroom cloud. Trees would be burnt and forests leveled. Shock waves would be sent around the world. And no crater would be made.

15 This explanation is the most reasonable one that has been offered. But we will probably never know for sure what devastated the Tunguska area in 1908. If the explosion was caused by a comet entering our atmosphere, could it happen again? Could it happen in an area that is densely populated? If Carl Sagan was right, yes it could. But the chances of something like that happening are slim, since occurrences like the Tunguska Event are extremely rare.

If you have been timed while reading this article, enter your reading time below. Then turn to the Words-per-Minute Table on page 195 and look up your reading speed (words per minute). Then enter your reading speed on the Reading Speed graph on page 196.

Reading Time: Lesson 19

_______ : _______

Minutes *Seconds*

A Finding the Main Idea

One statement below expresses the main idea of the article. One statement is too general, or too broad. The other statement explains only part of the article; it is too narrow. Label the statements using the following key:

M—Main Idea **B—Too Broad** **N—Too Narrow**

_______ 1. Scientist Carl Sagan thought that the Tunguska explosion may have been caused by a comet.

_______ 2. In 1908, a huge explosion that some scientists believe was caused by a comet devastated the Tunguska region of Siberia.

_______ 3. Many scientists try to find explanations for unusual events such as the Tunguska explosion.

_______ Score 15 points for a correct M answer.

_______ Score 5 points for each correct B or N answer.

_______ **Total Score:** Finding the Main Idea

B Recalling Facts

How well do you remember the facts in the article? Put an X in the box next to the answer that correctly completes each statement about the article.

1. The shock wave from Tunguska circled the globe

☐ a. once.
☐ b. twice.
☐ c. five times.

2. Tunguska is a

☐ a. comet.
☐ b. scientist.
☐ c. place in Siberia.

3. The fine dust particles caused by the Tunguska Event

☐ a. alarmed Russian scientists.
☐ b. filled the sky for thousands of miles and reflected sunlight.
☐ c. reduced world temperatures.

4. Leonid A. Kulik was a

☐ a. researcher of meteorites.
☐ b. Russian government official.
☐ c. scientist from Cornell University.

5. The explosion at Tunguska did not

☐ a. cause the formation of a mushroom cloud.
☐ b. leave a crater.
☐ c. concern any of the peasants who saw its effects.

Score 5 points for each correct answer.

_______ **Total Score:** Recalling Facts

C Making Inferences

When you combine your own experience and information from a text to draw a conclusion that is not directly stated in that text, you are making an inference. Below are five statements that may or may not be inferences based on information in the article. Label the statements using the following key:

C—Correct Inference **F—Faulty Inference**

______ 1. If an event like the one that took place in Tunguska were to occur today, it would go unnoticed by the world's press.

______ 2. In 1908 the government in Moscow had little respect for the people of Tunguska.

______ 3. People were not greatly alarmed by the cloud of fine dust particles that made the night sky bright.

______ 4. Even after several years, there was still plenty of evidence that an enormous blast had taken place in Tunguska.

______ 5. Earth will probably experience an explosion similar to the Tunguska Event within the next century.

Score 5 points for each correct answer.

______ **Total Score:** Making Inferences

D Using Words Precisely

Each numbered sentence below contains an underlined word or phrase from the article. Following the sentence are three definitions. One definition is closest to the meaning of the underlined word. One definition is opposite or nearly opposite. Label those two definitions using the following key; do not label the remaining definition.

C—Closest **O—Opposite or Nearly Opposite**

1. Fortunately, this huge explosion occurred in an uninhabited region of Siberia.

______ a. unpopulated area

______ b. crowded area

______ c. distant area

2. The only known casualties were herds of reindeer and millions of pine trees.

______ a. things that escaped harm

______ b. dead and injured

______ c. witnesses

3. No one, however, made any connection between these unusual occurrences and the blast in the wasteland of Siberia.

______ a. boundaries

______ b. fertile area

______ c. barren land

4. It would later be determined that only an explosion that had taken place above the earth could have caused the unique pattern of devastation found at Tunguska.

_______ a. vegetation

_______ b. destruction

_______ c. creation

5. Some people take the parallels between nuclear blasts and Tunguska seriously.

_______ a. similarities

_______ b. incidents

_______ c. differences

_______ Score 3 points for each correct C answer.

_______ Score 2 points for each correct O answer.

_______ **Total Score:** Using Words Precisely

Enter the four total scores in the spaces below, and add them together to find your Reading Comprehension Score. Then record your score on the graph on page 197.

Score	Question Type	Lesson 19
_______	Finding the Main Idea	
_______	Recalling Facts	
_______	Making Inferences	
_______	Using Words Precisely	
_______	**Reading Comprehension Score**	

Author's Approach

Put an X in the box next to the correct answer.

1. The main purpose of the first paragraph is to

☐ a. stimulate the reader's curiosity.

☐ b. describe a Russian peasant's life.

☐ c. convey a mood of terror.

2. Which of the following statements from the article best describes the explosion in Tunguska?

☐ a. "On June 30, 1908, in the Tunguska River basin in remote Siberia, there was an explosion that was heard 744 miles away."

☐ b. "Trees over a vast area were tossed about like matchsticks."

☐ c. "The shock waves were thought to be nothing more than an earthquake tremor."

3. Choose the statement below that is the weakest argument for claiming that the Tunguska Event was caused by a nuclear blast.

☐ a. Similar to an atomic explosion, the blast over Tunguska scorched the land and did not make a crater.

☐ b. The trees and vegetation in Tunguska grew at a much faster rate than normal after the explosion.

☐ c. Some scientists argue that a tiny black hole passed through the earth in Siberia and emerged through the other side.

4. How is the author's purpose for writing the article expressed in paragraph 14?

☐ a. The author emphasizes the similarities between the Tunguska Event and a nuclear explosion.

☐ b. The author informs the reader about the Comet Encke.

☐ c. The author informs the reader about the theory that seems to best explain the Tunguska Event.

_________ Number of correct answers

Record your personal assessment of your work on the Critical Thinking Chart on page 198.

Summarizing and Paraphrasing

Follow the directions provided for question 1. Put an X in the box next to the correct answer for questions 2 and 3.

1. Look for the important ideas and events in paragraphs 5 and 6. Summarize those paragraphs in one or two sentences.

____

____

____

2. Below are summaries of the article. Choose the summary that says all the most important things about the article but in the fewest words.

☐ a. Some scientists believe that the 1908 explosion in Tunguska was caused by a stray piece of Comet Encke.

☐ b. Many scientists have compared the explosion in Tunguska in 1908 to a nuclear blast.

☐ c. In 1908 an explosion rocked the Tunguska region of Siberia. Although the incident was largely ignored at the time, some researchers today believe that the blast was due to a comet chunk exploding in the air.

3. Choose the sentence that correctly restates the following sentence from the article:

"When reports of the explosion reached the Czar's government in Moscow, the capital city, they were dismissed as the ramblings of ignorant peasants."

☐ a. The peasants' report of the explosion was ignored when it reached Moscow because it was wordy and uninformative.

☐ b. Because peasants were considered uneducated and untrustworthy, the government in Moscow ignored their reports of the explosion.

☐ c. The Czar's government in Moscow dissolved after receiving word from the peasants of the Tunguska explosion.

_________ Number of correct answers

Record your personal assessment of your work on the Critical Thinking Chart on page 198.

Critical Thinking

Put an X in the box next to the correct answer for question 1. Follow the directions provided for the other questions.

1. From what Carl Sagan said, you can predict that a comet fragment

☐ a. will probably enter Earth's atmosphere within the next hundred years.

☐ b. would only explode over areas that are not densely populated.

☐ c. exploding over a populated area would kill hundreds of thousands of people.

2. Choose from the letters below to correctly complete the following statement. Write the letters on the lines.

   In the article, the effects of ________ and the effects of ________ are alike.

   a. the Tunguska Event
   b. a meteor striking the earth
   c. a nuclear blast

3. Choose from the letters below to correctly complete the following statement. Write the letters on the lines.

   According to the article, the Tunguska explosion caused ________ to ________, and the effect was ________.

   a. fill the sky thousands of miles away
   b. people could read by the light reflected off the particles
   c. fine dust

4. In which paragraph did you find the information or details to answer question 3?

____

________ Number of correct answers

Record your personal assessment of your work on the Critical Thinking Chart on page 198.

Personal Response

What new question do you have about this topic?

____

____

____

Self-Assessment

When reading the article, I was having trouble with

____

____

____

____

MIND GAMES

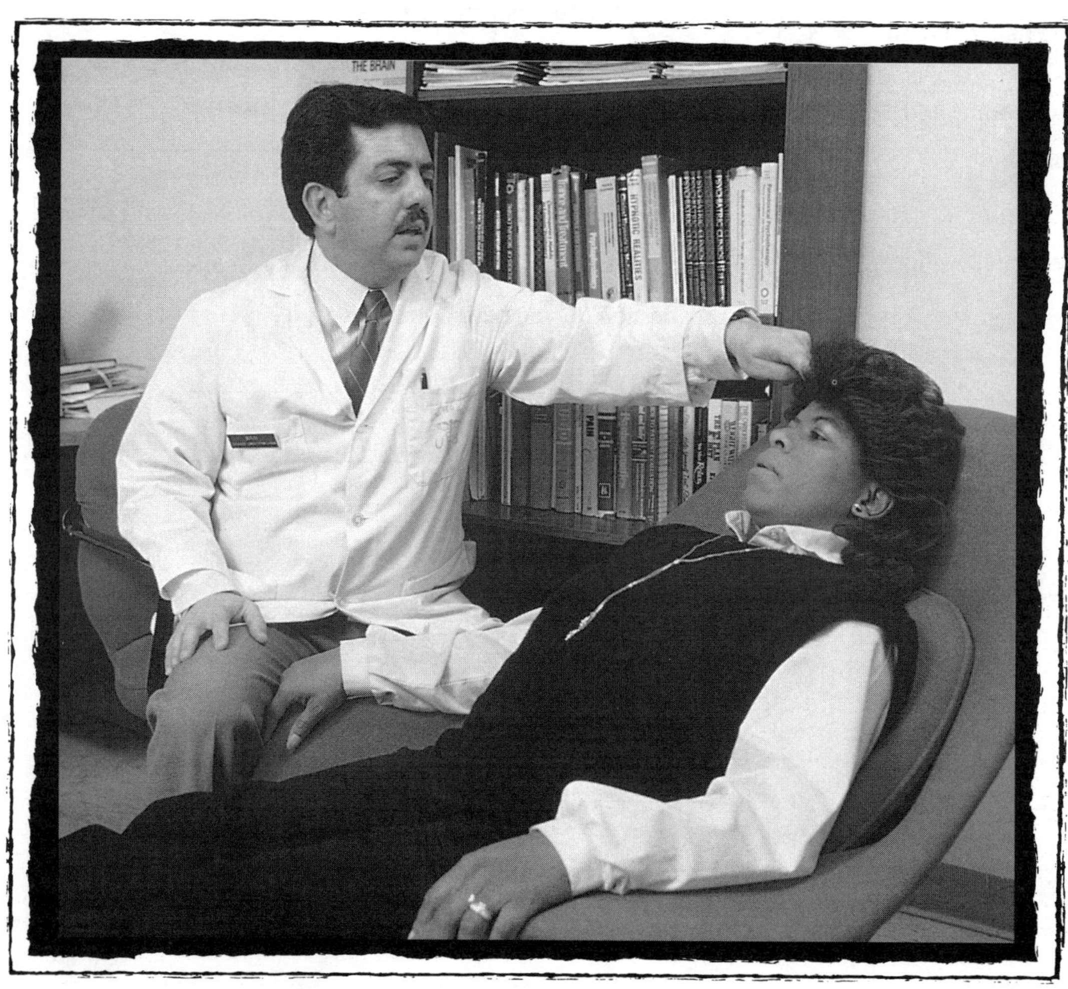

Hypnosis can help people alter behaviors, overcome fears, or retrieve lost memories.

"Your eyes are getting heavy...you are becoming sleepy...." The calm, soothing voice drones on and on. "Concentrate hard on the beam of light. Your eyes are becoming very heavy.... You are getting sleepy, *very* sleepy."

2 Hypnotists use these or similar words to induce a trance called hypnosis. For a long time, hypnosis was considered a trick, a kind of parlor game. A few enthusiasts believed it could be used to heal the sick, but most doctors scoffed at such notions. They had no faith in what they called "mind games." Now, however, times have changed. Doctors understand the importance of the mind-body connection and are willing to take a second look at hypnosis.

3 Just what is hypnosis? Most reference books define it as an altered state of consciousness. Some people believe that definition is accurate. Others say it is all wrong. Doctor Robert Baker of the University of Kentucky has been practicing hypnosis for more than 20 years, but he doesn't believe it produces an altered state. "It's nonsensical to argue

that hypnosis involves some sort of special state," Baker says, "when we can't find it no matter how long we look." Indeed, researchers have found no evidence that the brain changes during hypnosis. People like Baker think that the hypnotized mind plays a trick on itself. Hypnosis, they say, occurs when one part of the brain shuts down and another part remains highly focused.

4 Other people define hypnosis as a state of repose. The body relaxes, the mind is more open and attentive, and breathing becomes more regular. Doctor Robert Fisher, a psychiatrist, says hypnosis is like going to the movies. You are aware of everything when you enter the theater. You can hear the crackle of candy wrappers. You notice the head of the person in front of you. You feel the spilled popcorn under your feet. But, says Fisher, "Once the screen fills with images, you gradually become absorbed and you're in a state of focused concentration."

5 Most people don't care whether or not hypnosis is an altered state of consciousness. They are not looking for the perfect definition. They only ask: Will it work for me? Will hypnosis help me stop smoking or lose weight? Will it allow me to overcome phobias such as a fear of flying? Can hypnosis ease the pain of giving birth or getting a tooth extracted? Can it help me retrieve lost memories?

6 On this practical level, there is lots of evidence that hypnosis works. There is proof that it can change certain behaviors. Cigarette smoking is one example. Psychotherapist Laura Foster Collins uses hypnosis to help her clients kick the habit. Ina Josephson had been puffing away on two packs of cigarettes a day for 18 years. She had tried to quit smoking several times but had always failed. At last, she asked Collins to hypnotize her.

7 First, Collins made sure Josephson really wanted to quit. Without that motivation, says Collins, hypnosis will never work. Then while hypnotized, Josephson was asked to see herself as a nonsmoker. She envisioned a situation in which she would normally reach for a cigarette. But under hypnosis she could say, "No, thanks. I don't smoke."

8 The hypnosis worked. Josephson gave up smoking completely and even lost the urge to smoke. Still, only about one smoker in five quits for good as a result of hypnosis. Anyone who has ever smoked knows how difficult it is to break the habit. Hypnosis can help, but it must be combined with a strong desire to quit.

9 Helping a person give up a bad habit is one thing, but can hypnosis be used to block pain during surgery? Most experts agree that it can at least minimize such pain. A few surgeons have used it during operations to help reduce their patients' pain. Some dentists have also reported some success. In about 10 to 20 percent of

While it doesn't work for everyone, hypnosis has been used to help people quit smoking.

cases, hypnosis can eliminate the sensation of pain completely. When that happens, the results can be pretty spectacular.

10 Take the case of Victor Rausch, a young man from Canada. Rausch needed to have his gallbladder removed. But he decided to skip the anesthetic and rely solely on hypnosis. He even refused to take an aspirin. Just before the surgeon sliced open his abdomen, Rausch hypnotized himself. In his mind, he heard his favorite piano music and envisioned peaceful scenes. His pulse rate and blood pressure remained steady throughout the procedure. From time to time Rausch even talked and joked with the surgeon. The entire operation lasted 75 minutes. When it was over, Rausch got up off the table and walked away. He swore he felt no pain, just a little tugging.

11 Self-hypnosis can also help in other situations. Patients can use it to ward off asthma attacks or epileptic seizures. In 1996, the National Institute of Health reported that hypnosis can ease headaches. It can also reduce the pain caused by cancer.

12 Self-hypnosis can be a wonderful healing tool for those skilled enough to practice it. It can be performed anywhere and at any time. It has no side effects and doesn't cost a thing. And most important, hypnosis gives the patient a sense of control over what is happening to his or her body.

13 Hypnosis has also been used to jog lost or suppressed memories. The police have often used it to solve violent crimes. Eyewitnesses or victims of crimes might be badly traumatized. These people might be too fearful to speak about what they saw or to identify the criminal. But under hypnosis, people often can overcome such fears. They can then relate what happened.

14 How accurate are these memories? Can the testimony of a hypnotized eyewitness or victim be trusted? In recent years, more and more state courts have said no. In 1983, for instance, the New York Supreme Court ruled that hypnosis created a "mixture of accurate recall [and] fantasy." And it was impossible to tell one from the other.

15 Hypnosis is not for everyone. Some people are naturally better subjects than others. Who is the ideal subject? There are no barriers based on intelligence, age, or sex. Dr. Herbert Spiegel says, "Artists and writers often make good subjects because they are comfortable with fantasy and new things." Still, all good subjects should be motivated. And most of all, they must have an open mind and a willingness to concentrate.

If you have been timed while reading this article, enter your reading time below. Then turn to the Words-per-Minute Table on page 195 and look up your reading speed (words per minute). Then enter your reading speed on the Reading Speed graph on page 196.

Reading Time: Lesson 20

________ : ________

Minutes *Seconds*

Finding the Main Idea

One statement below expresses the main idea of the article. One statement is too general, or too broad. The other statement explains only part of the article; it is too narrow. Label the statements using the following key:

M—Main Idea **B—Too Broad** **N—Too Narrow**

_______ 1. Hypnosis demonstrates the mind-body connection.

_______ 2. Victor Rausch relied solely on hypnosis to block pain when he had his gallbladder removed.

_______ 3. Hypnosis can be an effective and inexpensive tool for changing behavior, blocking pain, and jogging memories.

_______ Score 15 points for a correct M answer.

_______ Score 5 points for each correct B or N answer.

_______ **Total Score:** Finding the Main Idea

B Recalling Facts

How well do you remember the facts in the article? Put an X in the box next to the answer that correctly completes each statement about the article.

1. Today, many doctors view hypnosis as a

☐ a. trick.
☐ b. parlor game.
☐ c. technique worth looking into.

2. People who want to use hypnosis to quit smoking must

☐ a. be motivated to change.
☐ b. be able to hypnotize themselves.
☐ c. listen to music during the procedure.

3. Most experts agree that hypnotism

☐ a. can completely block surgical pain.
☐ b. has no effect on surgical pain.
☐ c. can at least minimize surgical pain.

4. Hypnosis is a wonderful healing tool particularly because

☐ a. there are no barriers to its use based on intelligence, age, or sex.
☐ b. it gives the patient a sense of control over what is happening to his or her body.
☐ c. it provides an altered state of consciousness.

5. Under hypnosis, eyewitnesses or victims of crime

☐ a. can sometimes overcome their fear and relate what happened.
☐ b. may be badly traumatized.
☐ c. may be too fearful to speak about they saw.

Score 5 points for each correct answer.

_______ **Total Score:** Recalling Facts

C Making Inferences

When you combine your own experience and information from a text to draw a conclusion that is not directly stated in that text, you are making an inference. Below are five statements that may or may not be inferences based on information in the article. Label the statements using the following key:

C—Correct Inference **F—Faulty Inference**

_______ 1. More and more people are using hypnosis to help them with many different kinds of problems.

_______ 2. An important thing that hypnosis can do is help people "see" themselves change unwanted behavior.

_______ 3. Experts are unable to agree on a precise definition of hypnosis.

_______ 4. Many doctors will soon use hypnosis instead of anesthesia during surgery.

_______ 5. The testimony of a hypnotized crime victim would be admissible in most courts.

Score 5 points for each correct answer.

_______ **Total Score:** Making Inferences

D Using Words Precisely

Each numbered sentence below contains an underlined word or phrase from the article. Following the sentence are three definitions. One definition is closest to the meaning of the underlined word. One definition is opposite or nearly opposite. Label those two definitions using the following key; do not label the remaining definition.

C—Closest **O—Opposite or Nearly Opposite**

1. Hypnotists use these or similar words to induce a trance called hypnosis.

_______ a. alert condition

_______ b. dreamlike state

_______ c. skeptical attitude

2. A few enthusiasts believed it could be used to heal the sick, but most doctors scoffed at such notions.

_______ a. dentists

_______ b. supporters

_______ c. opponents

3. Other people define hypnosis as a state of repose.

_______ a. agitation

_______ b. forgetfulness

_______ c. peacefulness

4. Most experts agree that it can at least minimize such pain.

_______ a. cause

_______ b. greatly lessen

_______ c. increase

5. Eyewitnesses or victims of crimes might be badly traumatized.

_______ a. harmed

_______ b. benefited

_______ c. misunderstood

_______ Score 3 points for each correct C answer.

_______ Score 2 points for each correct O answer.

_______ **Total Score:** Using Words Precisely

Enter the four total scores in the spaces below, and add them together to find your Reading Comprehension Score. Then record your score on the graph on page 197.

Score	Question Type	Lesson 20
_______	Finding the Main Idea	
_______	Recalling Facts	
_______	Making Inferences	
_______	Using Words Precisely	
_______	**Reading Comprehension Score**	

Author's Approach

Put an X in the box next to the correct answer.

1. From the statements below, choose those that you believe the author would agree with.

☐ a. Experts should continue to explore hypnosis and its usage.

☐ b. The testimony of hypnotized crime victims should be allowed in court.

☐ c. In some cases, patients should be given the option of using either anesthesia or self-hypnosis during surgery.

2. What does the author imply by saying "And most important, hypnosis gives the patient a sense of control over what is happening to his or her body"?

☐ a. The patient, not the doctors, should be in control during a surgical procedure.

☐ b. Hypnosis allows patients to cure themselves without relying on doctors.

☐ c. Very often, patients don't feel that they have any control over what is happening to them.

3. The author probably wrote this article in order to inform the reader about the

☐ a. correct definition of hypnosis.

☐ b. many applications of hypnosis.

☐ c. limitations of hypnosis.

4. The author tells this story mainly by

☐ a. comparing different topics.

☐ b. using his or her imagination and creativity.

☐ c. telling different stories about the same topic.

_______ Number of correct answers

Record your personal assessment of your work on the Critical Thinking Chart on page 198.

Summarizing and Paraphrasing

Follow the directions provided for questions 1 and 2. Put an X in the box next to the correct answer for question 3.

1. Look for the important ideas and events in paragraphs 13 and 14. Summarize those paragraphs in one or two sentences.

____

____

____

2. Reread paragraph 10 in the article. Below, write a summary of the paragraph in no more than 25 words.

____

____

____

____

Reread your summary and decide whether it covers the important ideas in the paragraph. Next, decide how to shorten the summary to 15 words or less without leaving out any essential information. Write this summary below.

____

____

____

3. Choose the best one-sentence paraphrase for the following sentence from the article:

   "Hypnosis, they say, occurs when one part of the brain shuts down and another part remains highly focused."

☐ a. Some people believe that hypnosis occurs when the brain becomes highly focused on sleep.

☐ b. Some people believe that hypnosis occurs when a part of the brain sleeps while another concentrates intensely.

☐ c. Some people believe that hypnosis occurs when the brain completely goes to sleep.

_______ Number of correct answers

Record your personal assessment of your work on the Critical Thinking Chart on page 198.

Critical Thinking

Follow the directions provided for questions 1–3. Put an X in the box next to the correct answer for question 4.

1. For each statement below, write O if it expresses an opinion or F if it expresses a fact.

_______ a. The hypnotized mind plays a trick on itself.

_______ b. Some surgeons have used hypnosis during operations to minimize a patient's pain.

_______ c. Hypnosis is a state of repose.

2. Choose from the letters below to correctly complete the following statement. Write the letters on the lines.

   On the positive side, ________, but on the negative side ________.

   a. their memories may not be accurate
   b. hypnosis can help victims of crime overcome their fears and jog their memories
   c. hypnosis doesn't always help people change their behavior

3. Read paragraph 7. Then choose from the letters below to correctly complete the following statement. Write the letters on the lines.

   According to paragraph 7, ________ because ________.

   a. hypnosis helped Ina Josephson quit smoking
   b. she envisioned herself as a nonsmoker
   c. she had a strong desire to quit

4. How is hypnosis an example of a phenomenon?

☐ a. Hypnosis produces an altered state of consciousness in its subjects.
☐ b. Hypnosis causes brain changes.
☐ c. Experts don't really know how hypnosis works but cannot deny the technique's effectiveness and usefulness.

________ Number of correct answers

Record your personal assessment of your work on the Critical Thinking Chart on page 198.

Personal Response

Begin the first five to eight sentences of your own article about hypnosis. It may tell of a real experience or one that is imagined.

____

____

____

____

____

Self-Assessment

A word or phrase in the article that I do not understand is

____

____

____

____

KILLER BUGS

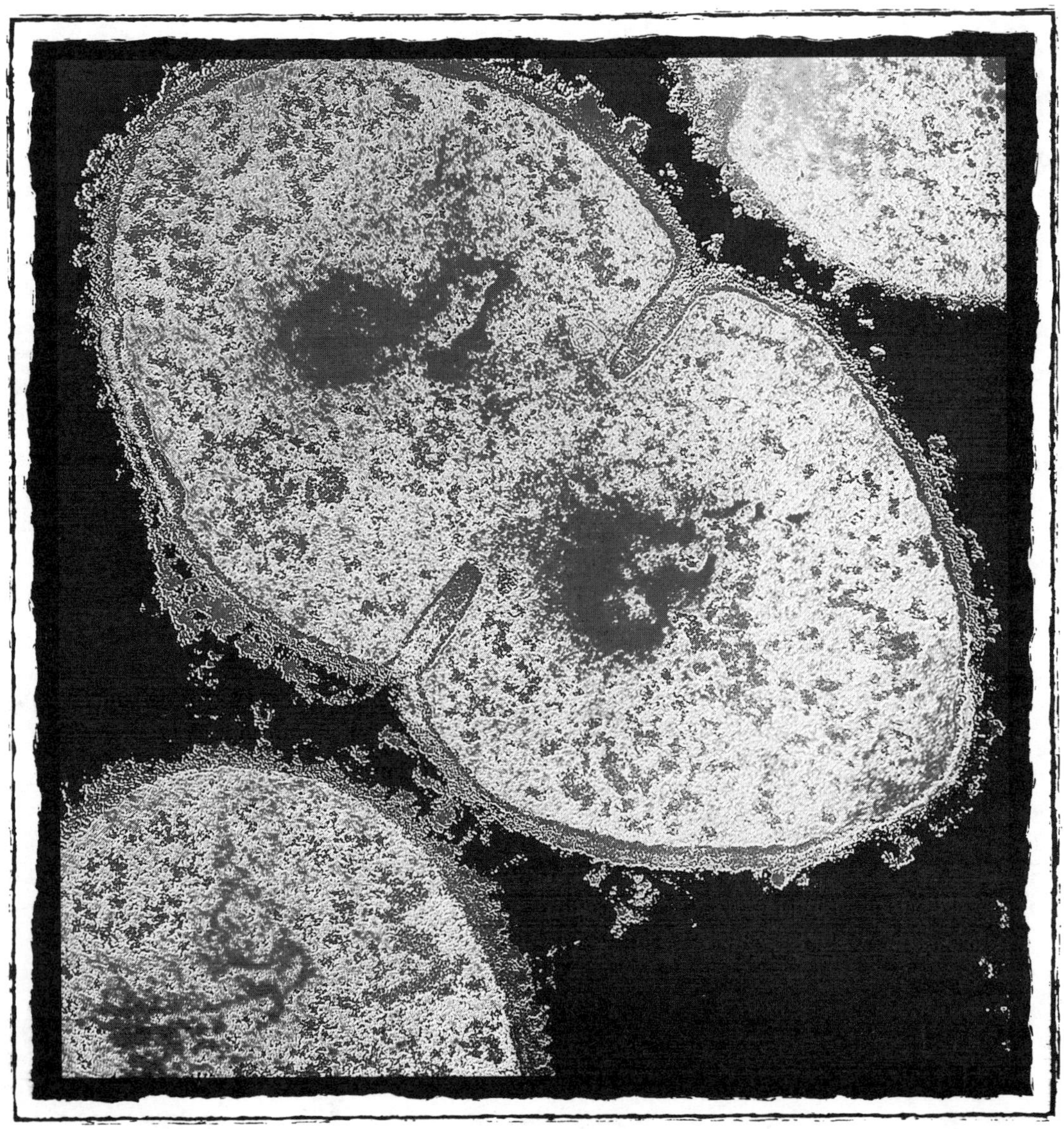

Streptococcus pyogenes *group A bacterium, believed to be responsible for an outbreak of flesh-eating bacteria in England in 1994*

The British newspaper splashed a picture of a hideously deformed face across page one. If the tabloid's photograph didn't grab readers' attention, the headline certainly did. It read: KILLER BUG ATE MY FACE. The huge headline of another tabloid screamed: EATEN ALIVE.

2 Such headlines caused a near panic in England in 1994. All kinds of horror stories began circulating. The tabloids featured gruesome details of faces melting away and limbs rotting. It was reported that victims needed to have their arms or legs amputated to save their lives. To many people, such ghoulish reports sparked real fears that a new form of the black plague was at hand. This time, however, the damage wasn't being caused by flea-bitten rats but by flesh-eating bacteria.

3 The English tabloids are notorious for making up stories out of thin air, but this time they had facts to support their claims. Some people really were dying from "killer bugs," known as flesh-eating bacteria. In less than five months, 11 people had died in England alone. Most

had been perfectly healthy before being attacked by the bugs. One was a two-year-old boy. Another was a 64-year-old doctor.

4 The victims died quickly. After 43-year-old Brian Bounds experienced leg pains, he went to the doctor, believing he had strained a muscle. Eighteen hours later, he was dead. One morning 39-year-old Terry Bowden stood in the kitchen making breakfast for his four children. He noticed that his legs had started to swell. He lived just 36 more hours. The disease spread through his body too quickly for his doctors to save him. "It got hold of him so fast," said his wife, Christine. "In the end I don't think he really knew who I was. He was just staring at me, looking really frightened."

5 The tabloids were also correct when they said that some doctors had sacrificed patients' limbs to save their lives. That almost happened to John Jeffs, a 43-year-old Canadian man who one day felt an excruciating pain under his right arm. The pain traveled rapidly across his chest and up his neck. Hours later, with the killer bug attacking his heart and liver, doctors put Jeffs on life support systems. The man's flesh was literally melting away. "The skin was coming off his hands and feet in thick chunks," recalled his wife.

6 Doctors considered amputating his arm. Luckily, that wasn't necessary. The antibiotics they used stopped the infection just in time. Still, serious damage had been done to his body. It would be many months before Jeffs could go back to work.

7 In the case of Canadian Lucien Bouchard, the antibiotics were given too late. He delayed going to the hospital because he thought he had only pulled a

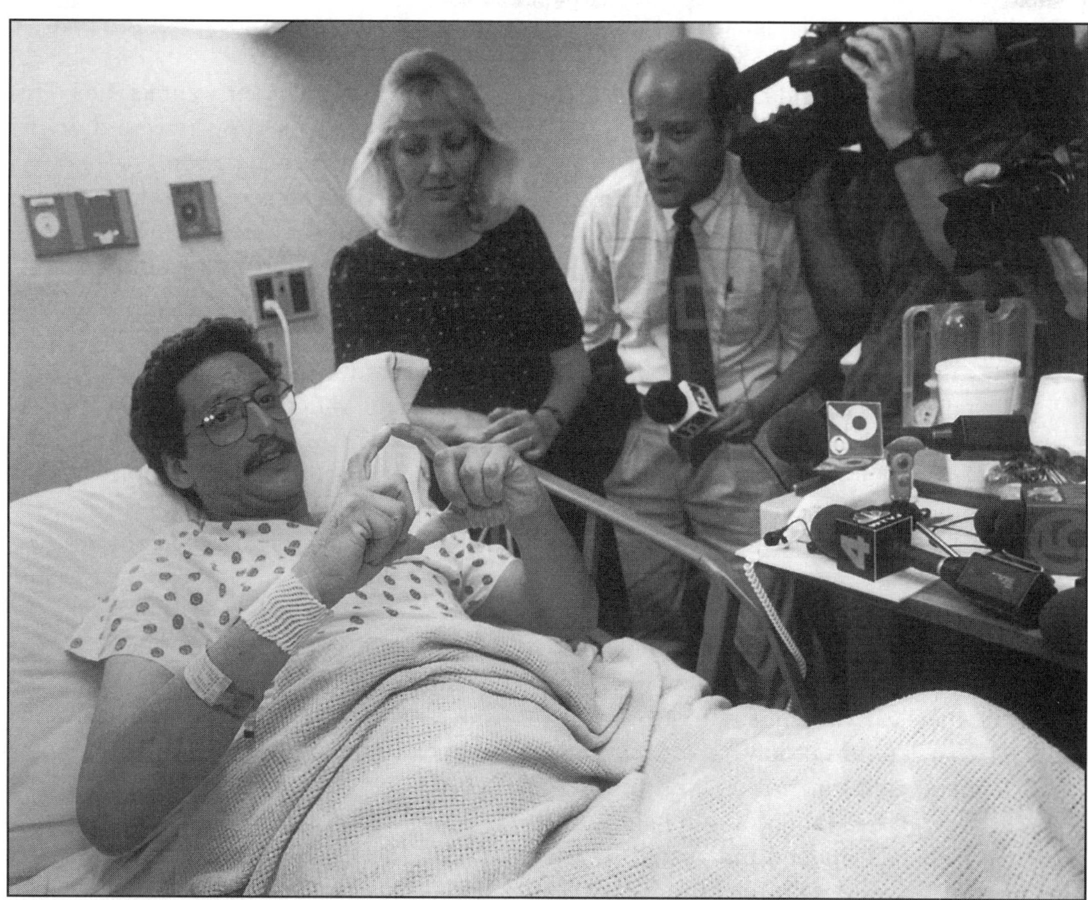

Steve Hillman shows the size of a rash caused by a flesh-eating bacteria.

leg muscle. The doctors were forced to amputate his left leg in order to save his life. Still, Bouchard was fortunate just to survive. The flesh-eating bacteria spreads with amazing speed. It can eat away at fat and muscle at the incredible rate of an inch an hour! In severe cases, it destroys tissue as rapidly as doctors can cut it out.

8 Is the human race facing a horrifying new scourge? We can relax—the answer is no. All the stories you have just read are true, but they are also exceedingly rare. The killer bug is not contagious and affects only one person in a million.

9 Also, despite the lurid headlines and the fear they caused, the killer bug is nothing new. It has been around for centuries. It may even go all the way back to Hippocrates, the Greek "father of medicine" who lived nearly 2,500 years ago. Since then, the killer bug has only occasionally developed into fatal, runaway infections.

10 The bug is still around. In fact, at any given moment, about 10 percent of all individuals have it in their systems. It is called Group A streptococcus bacteria. Most of the time, this bacteria is not a "killer." It usually causes nothing more serious than strep throat or a mild skin infection. Some people have it without becoming ill at all.

11 Still, there is a virulent strain of Group A strep that can turn deadly. (The strain's official name is necrotizing fasciitis. In earlier times, it had more colorful names, such as hospital gangrene and putrid ulcer.) Doctors aren't sure why the bacteria sometimes gets so ugly, but they can see the results. The disease starts in the tissue between the skin and the muscle. Then it attacks muscles and organs throughout the body. Group A strep can also cause scarlet fever, toxic shock, and severe pneumonia.

12 One famous victim of Group A streptococcus was Jim Henson, the creator of the Muppets. In 1990, he became desperately ill from the bacteria. The disease developed into severe pneumonia and then into toxic shock. Henson died soon after.

13 The disease frequently enters the body through a small cut or open wound. So it sometimes strikes people who are recovering from surgery. Hospitals may look clean, but they are not always the healthiest places to be. With all those sick people, blood samples, and test tubes, there are bound to be lots of germs floating around.

14 Roseann Millar discovered that the hard way. The 41-year-old nurse went into a hospital in Scotland for a simple operation. At home a few days later, she felt a pain in her left leg. Millar didn't give it much thought. She thought she was just tired so she went to bed. But the next morning she got the shock of her life. "I could see the bruises through my skin," she recalled. "My abdomen was black and the color extended all the way down my left side and deep into my leg."

15 Millar was rushed back to the hospital. Luckily, her doctors realized right away that they were dealing with flesh-eating bacteria. They cut away a mass of dead tissue in her leg. Miraculously, they saved her leg as well as her life. "I count myself very, very lucky that I'm still here," Millar said.

16 The odds are heavily in your favor that you will never have your body destroyed by flesh-eating bacteria. Still, why take any chances? Even a seemingly trivial cut can lead to a deadly infection. So it is strongly recommended that if you see redness or swelling around a cut or if you develop a fever after suffering a cut, call a doctor.

17 Medicines, such as penicillin, are very effective against the bacteria. They can stop the disease dead in its track. But they have to be given quickly. No one wants his or her melting face shown on the front page of a tabloid. And you won't—if you use common sense and don't give the killer bug too much of a head start.

If you have been timed while reading this article, enter your reading time below. Then turn to the Words-per-Minute Table on page 195 and look up your reading speed (words per minute). Then enter your reading speed on the Reading Speed graph on page 196.

Reading Time: Lesson 21

________ : ________

Minutes *Seconds*

Finding the Main Idea

One statement below expresses the main idea of the article. One statement is too general, or too broad. The other statement explains only part of the article; it is too narrow. Label the statements using the following key:

M—Main Idea **B—Too Broad** **N—Too Narrow**

_______ 1. Some strains of bacteria can be deadly.

_______ 2. In some cases, doctors amputated limbs to stop the deadly bacteria.

_______ 3. In 1994 a rare but deadly strain of flesh-eating bacteria attacked victims' skin, muscles, and organs.

_______ Score 15 points for a correct M answer.

_______ Score 5 points for each correct B or N answer.

_______ **Total Score:** Finding the Main Idea

B Recalling Facts

How well do you remember the facts in the article? Put an X in the box next to the answer that correctly completes each statement about the article.

1. Tabloid headlines about the flesh-eating bacteria
   - ☐ a. caused a near panic in England in 1994.
   - ☐ b. were disregarded by the general population.
   - ☐ c. were disproved by medical experts.
2. Most of the victims of the flesh-eating bacteria had
   - ☐ a. just recovered from surgery.
   - ☐ b. long histories of illness.
   - ☐ c. been perfectly healthy.
3. Infection from the flesh-eating bacteria can be successfully stopped with
   - ☐ a. diet and exercise.
   - ☐ b. penicillin and other antibiotics.
   - ☐ c. a simple operation.
4. Group A strep
   - ☐ a. is always a deadly bacteria.
   - ☐ b. has existed for centuries.
   - ☐ c. showed up for the first time in 1994.
5. The disease frequently enters the body through
   - ☐ a. the respiratory system.
   - ☐ b. contaminated food.
   - ☐ c. a small cut or wound.

Score 5 points for each correct answer.

_______ **Total Score:** Recalling Facts

Making Inferences

When you combine your own experience and information from a text to draw a conclusion that is not directly stated in that text, you are making an inference. Below are five statements that may or may not be inferences based on information in the article. Label the statements using the following key:

C—Correct Inference **F—Faulty Inference**

_____ 1. In 1994 instances of killer bug infections reached epidemic proportions.

_____ 2. Victims of the killer bug should stay away from hospitals since they are not always the healthiest places to be.

_____ 3. The people who contracted the disease had no idea they were so sick.

_____ 4. To avoid infection, you should keep away from people who have been attacked by the killer bug.

_____ 5. If administered promptly, antibiotics can stop the bacteria.

Score 5 points for each correct answer.

_____ **Total Score:** Making Inferences

D Using Words Precisely

Each numbered sentence below contains an underlined word or phrase from the article. Following the sentence are three definitions. One definition is closest to the meaning of the underlined word. One definition is opposite or nearly opposite. Label those two definitions using the following key; do not label the remaining definition.

C—Closest **O—Opposite or Nearly Opposite**

1. The tabloids featured gruesome details of faces melting away and limbs rotting.

_____ a. ghastly

_____ b. supporting

_____ c. attractive

2. Is the human race facing a horrifying new scourge?

_____ a. blessing

_____ b. affliction

_____ c. conflict

3. All the stories you have just read are true, but they are also exceedingly rare.

_____ a. fortunately

_____ b. extremely

_____ c. somewhat

4. Also, despite the <u>lurid</u> headlines and the fear they caused, the killer bug is nothing new.

_______ a. modest

_______ b. boldface

_______ c. sensational

5. Still, there is a <u>virulent</u> strain of Group A strep that can turn deadly.

_______ a. deadly

_______ b. unknown

_______ c. benign

_______ Score 3 points for each correct C answer.

_______ Score 2 points for each correct O answer.

_______ **Total Score:** Using Words Precisely

Enter the four total scores in the spaces below, and add them together to find your Reading Comprehension Score. Then record your score on the graph on page 197.

Score	Question Type	Lesson 21
_______	Finding the Main Idea	
_______	Recalling Facts	
_______	Making Inferences	
_______	Using Words Precisely	
_______	**Reading Comprehension Score**	

Author's Approach

Put an X in the box next to the correct answer.

1. What does the author mean by the statement "to many people, such ghoulish reports sparked real fears that a new form of the black plague was at hand"?

☐ a. People feared that the flesh-eating bacteria would kill many people.

☐ b. People were afraid that the flesh-eating bacteria would attack their hands.

☐ c. People feared that the flesh-eating bacteria was caused by a form of witchcraft.

2. The main purpose of the first paragraph is to

☐ a. inform the reader about the killer bug.

☐ b. describe the qualities of the killer bug.

☐ c. grab the reader's attention.

3. What is the author's purpose in writing "Killer Bugs"?

☐ a. to encourage the reader to guard against infection

☐ b. to inform the reader about the history and deadly potential of the Group A streptococcus bacteria

☐ c. to emphasize the similarities between the killer bug and the black plague

4. Choose the statement below that best describes the author's position in paragraph 16.

☐ a. People shouldn't worry at all about being infected by the flesh-eating bacteria.

☐ b. Even though the flesh-eating bacteria is rare, people should take basic precautions to avoid infection.

☐ c. People should always be on the alert against infection by the flesh-eating bacteria.

_________ Number of correct answers

Record your personal assessment of your work on the Critical Thinking Chart on page 198.

Summarizing and Paraphrasing

Put an X in the box next to the correct answer.

1. Below are summaries of the article. Choose the summary that says all the most important things about the article but in the fewest words.

☐ a. Even though the Group A streptococcus bacteria has been around for centuries, it has only occasionally developed into fatal, runaway infections.

☐ b. Many people in 1994 were killed by a flesh-eating bacteria.

☐ c. A rare but deadly form of the Group A streptococcus bacteria attacks skin tissue as well as muscles and organs throughout the body.

2. Choose the sentence that correctly restates the following sentence from the article:

"So it is strongly recommended that if you see redness or swelling around a cut or if you develop a fever after suffering a cut, call a doctor."

☐ a. You should call a doctor every time you cut yourself.

☐ b. You should call a doctor if you develop swelling or a fever as a result of a cut.

☐ c. You should call a doctor when you have a rash, swelling, or a fever.

_________ Number of correct answers

Record your personal assessment of your work on the Critical Thinking Chart on page 198.

Critical Thinking

Put an X in the box next to the correct answer for questions 1, 3, and 4. Follow the directions provided for the other questions.

1. From the information in paragraph 8, you can predict that

☐ a. very few people will ever become infected with the killer bug.

☐ b. many people will become infected with the killer bug.

☐ c. a cure for the killer bug will be found soon.

2. Choose from the letters below to correctly complete the following statement. Write the letters on the lines.

In the article, the _________ and the _________ are different.

a. killer bug

b. flesh-eating bacteria

c. black plague

3. What was the effect of John Jeffs's receiving antibiotics?

- ☐ a. His arm was amputated.
- ☐ b. The infection was stopped just in time.
- ☐ c. He could not go back to work for many months.

4. If you were a doctor or nurse, how could you use the information in the article to treat someone infected with the flesh-eating bacteria?

- ☐ a. Like the doctors who treated John Jeffs, administer penicillin or other antibiotics immediately.
- ☐ b. Like the doctors who treated Lucien Bouchard, amputate an infected limb immediately.
- ☐ c. Like Roseann Millar, realize that hospitals are potentially dangerous places.

5. In which paragraph did you find the information or details to answer question 3?

____

_______ Number of correct answers

Record your personal assessment of your work on the Critical Thinking Chart on page 198.

Personal Response

A question I would like answered by Roseann Millar is

____

____

____

____

Self-Assessment

I can't really understand how

____

____

____

____

Compare and Contrast

Which articles in Unit Three did you learn the most from? Write the titles of three of those articles in the first column of the chart below. Use information from the articles to fill in the empty boxes of the chart.

Title	What kind of animals or people was the article about?	How was information gathered about this phenomenon?	What question still needs to be explored?

Suppose you were a scientist. On the lines below write at least two ways you could learn more about one of the phenomena you read about in this unit.

____

____

____

Words-per-Minute Table

Unit Three

Directions: If you were timed while reading an article, refer to the Reading Time you recorded in the box at the end of the article. Use this words-per-minute table to determine your reading speed for that article. Then plot your reading speed on the graph on page 196.

Lesson	15	16	17	18	19	20	21	
No. of Words	856	1074	892	1168	1049	1074	1129	
Minutes and Seconds								*Seconds*
1:30	571	716	595	779	699	716	753	**90**
1:40	514	644	535	701	629	644	677	**100**
1:50	467	586	487	637	572	586	616	**110**
2:00	428	537	446	584	525	537	565	**120**
2:10	395	496	412	539	484	496	521	**130**
2:20	367	460	382	501	450	460	484	**140**
2:30	342	430	357	467	420	430	452	**150**
2:40	321	403	335	438	393	403	423	**160**
2:50	302	379	315	412	370	379	398	**170**
3:00	285	358	297	389	350	358	376	**180**
3:10	270	339	282	369	331	339	357	**190**
3:20	257	322	268	350	315	322	339	**200**
3:30	245	307	255	334	300	307	323	**210**
3:40	233	293	243	319	286	293	308	**220**
3:50	223	280	233	305	274	280	295	**230**
4:00	214	269	223	292	262	269	282	**240**
4:10	205	258	214	280	252	258	271	**250**
4:20	198	248	206	270	242	248	261	**260**
4:30	190	239	198	260	233	239	251	**270**
4:40	183	230	191	250	225	230	242	**280**
4:50	177	222	185	242	217	222	234	**290**
5:00	171	215	178	234	210	215	226	**300**
5:10	166	208	173	226	203	208	219	**310**
5:20	161	201	167	219	197	201	212	**320**
5:30	156	195	162	212	191	195	205	**330**
5:40	151	190	157	206	185	190	199	**340**
5:50	147	184	153	200	180	184	194	**350**
6:00	143	179	149	195	175	179	188	**360**
6:10	139	174	145	189	170	174	183	**370**
6:20	135	170	141	184	166	170	178	**380**
6:30	132	165	137	180	161	165	174	**390**
6:40	128	161	134	175	157	161	169	**400**
6:50	125	157	131	171	154	157	165	**410**
7:00	122	153	127	167	150	153	161	**420**
7:10	119	150	124	163	146	150	158	**430**
7:20	117	146	122	159	143	146	154	**440**
7:30	114	143	119	156	140	143	151	**450**
7:40	112	140	116	152	137	140	147	**460**
7:50	109	137	114	149	134	137	144	**470**
8:00	107	134	112	146	131	134	141	**480**

Plotting Your Progress: Reading Speed

Unit Three

Directions: If you were timed while reading an article, write your words-per-minute rate for that in the box under the number of the lesson. Then plot your reading speed on the graph by putting a small X on the line directly above the number of the lesson, across from the number of words per minute you read. As you mark your speed for each lesson, graph your progress by drawing a line to connect the X's.

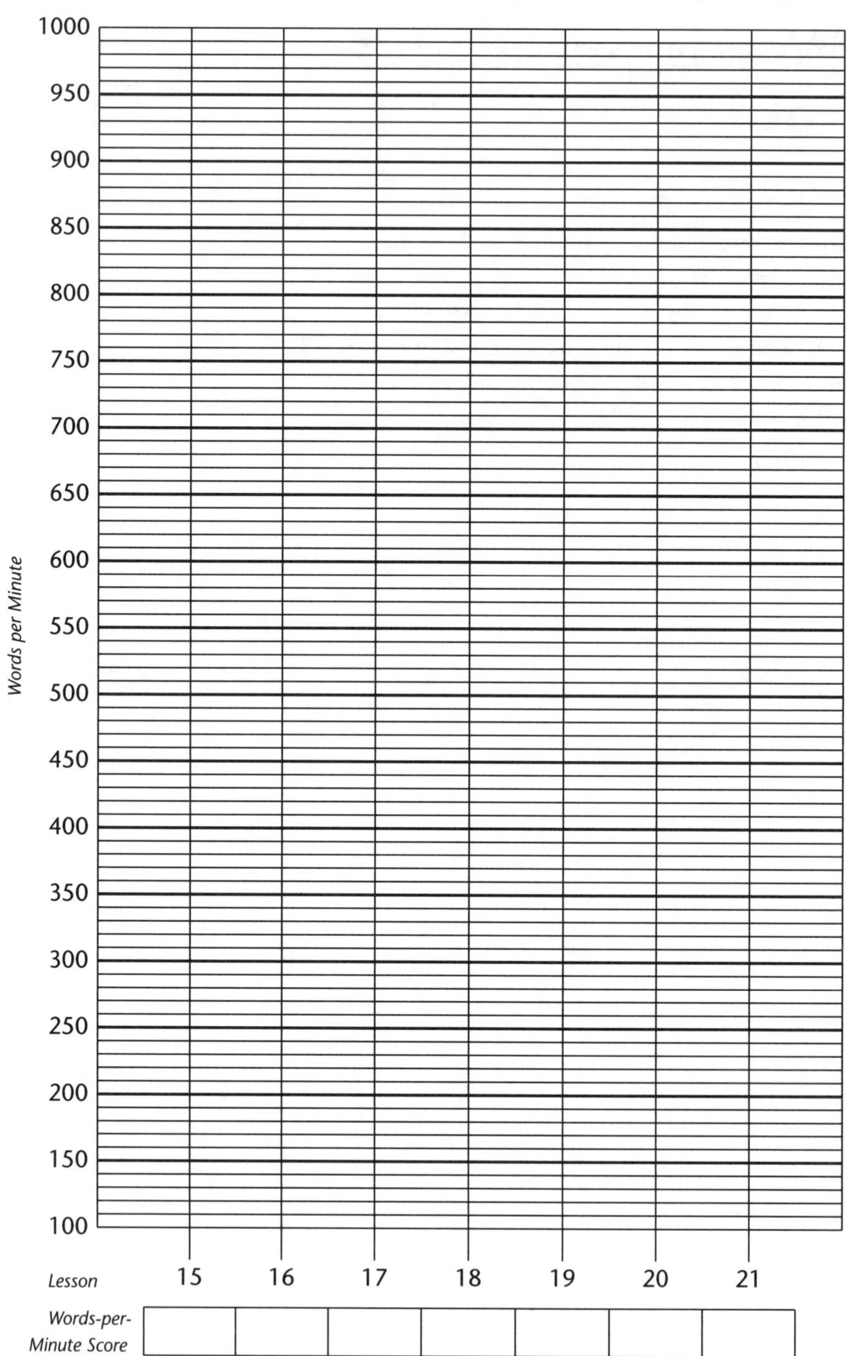

Plotting Your Progress: Reading Comprehension

Unit Three

Directions: Write your Reading Comprehension score for each lesson in the box under the number of the lesson. Then plot your score on the graph by putting a small X on the line directly above the number of the lesson and across from the score you earned. As you mark your score for each lesson, graph your progress by drawing a line to connect the X's.

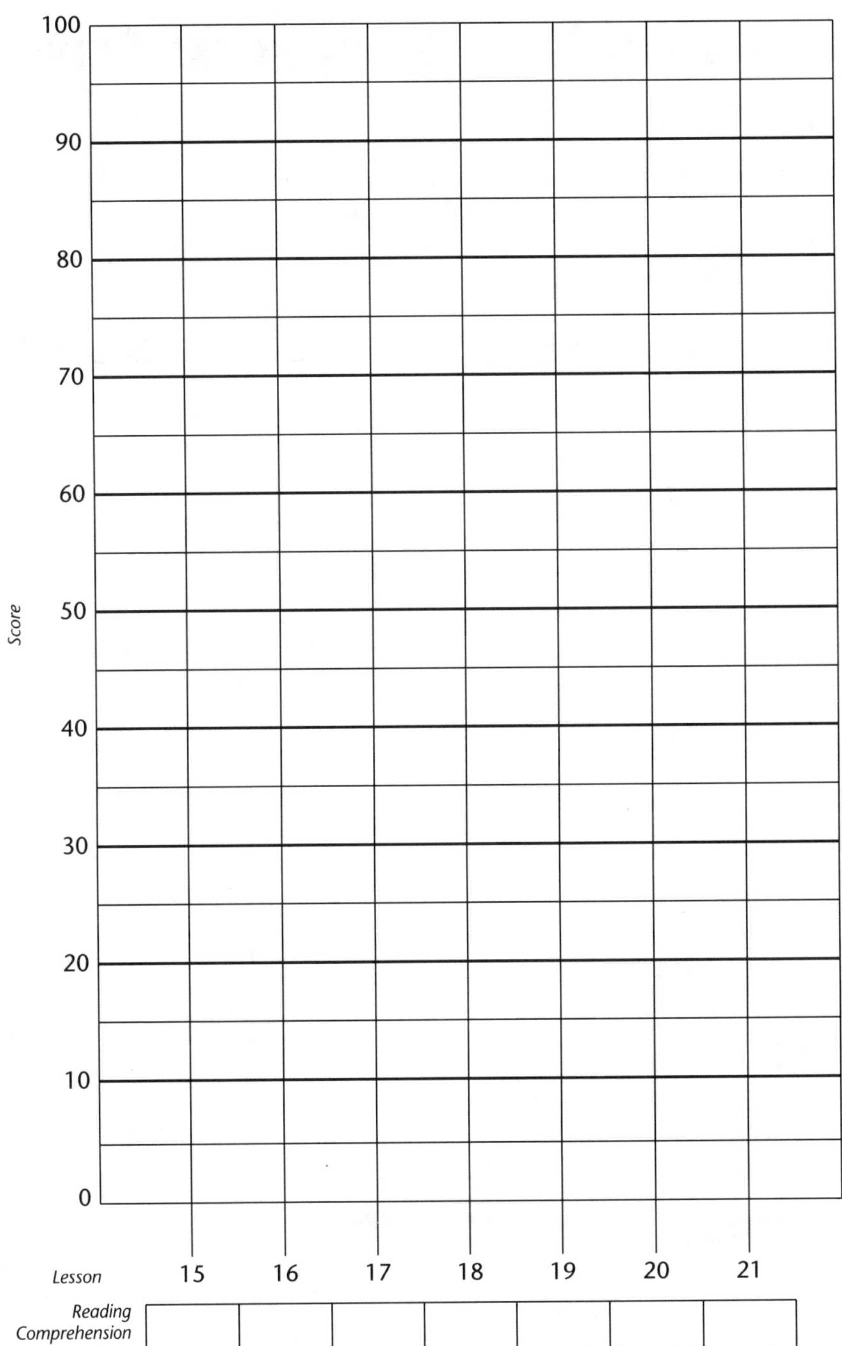

Plotting Your Progress: Critical Thinking

Unit Three

Directions: Work with your teacher to evaluate your responses to the Critical Thinking questions for each lesson. Then fill in the appropriate spaces in the chart below. For each lesson and each type of Critical Thinking question, do the following: Mark a minus sign (–) in the box to indicate areas in which you feel you could improve. Mark a plus sign (+) to indicate areas in which you feel you did well. Mark a minus-slash-plus sign (–/+) to indicate areas in which you had mixed success. Then write any comments you have about your performance, including ideas for improvement.

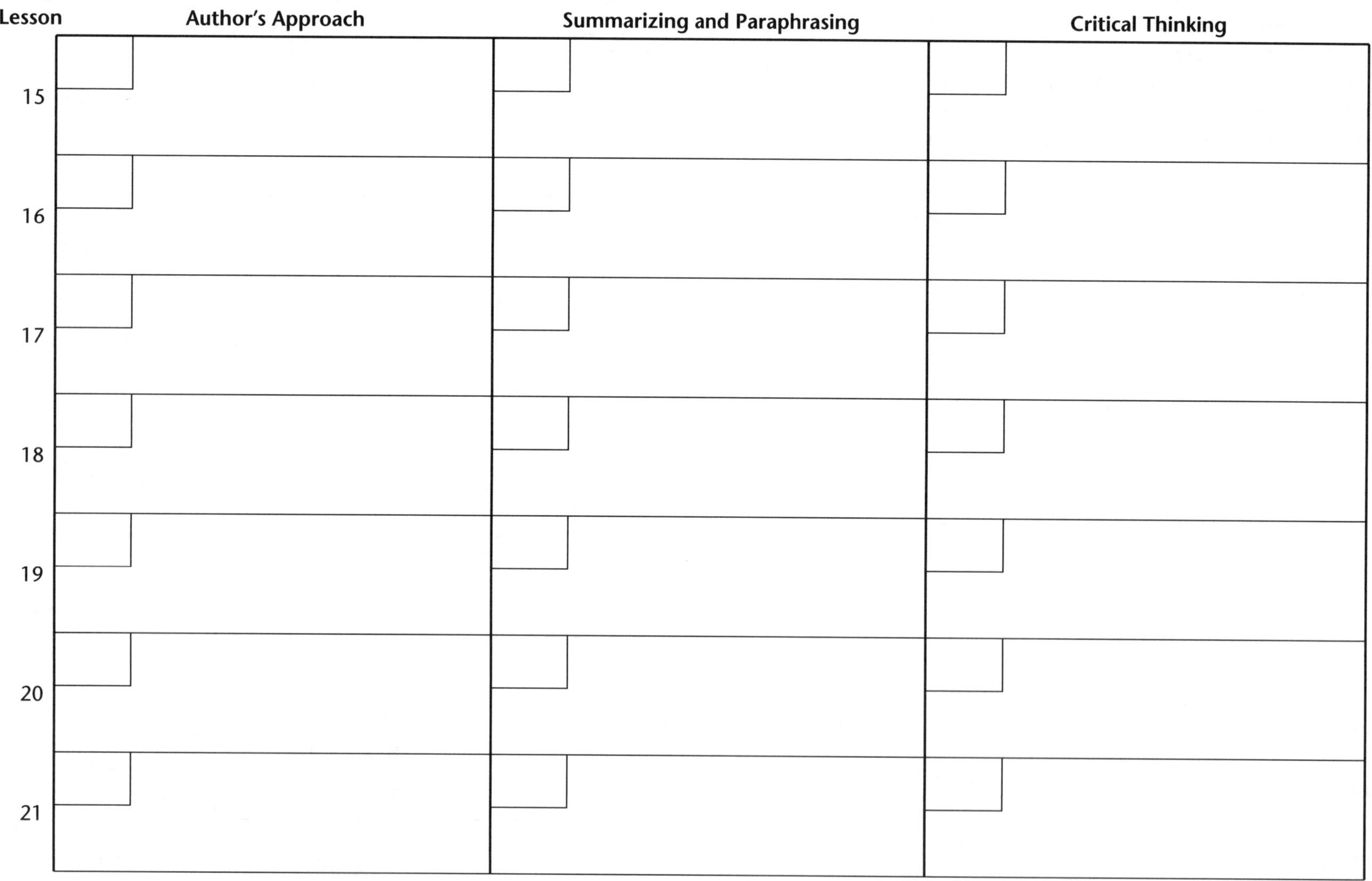

Lesson	Author's Approach	Summarizing and Paraphrasing	Critical Thinking
15			
16			
17			
18			
19			
20			
21			

Picture Credits

Cover Photo: Pekka Parviainen/Science Photo Library/Photo Researchers

Sample Lesson: p. 3, 4 Tom Hollyman/Photo Researchers; p. 5 David Weintraub/Photo Researchers

Unit 1 Opener: p. 13 Roberto Thoni/Corbis-Bettmann

Lesson 1: p. 14 Giraudon/Art Resource, New York; p. 15 The Granger Collection, New York

Lesson 2: p. 22 The Kobal Collection; p. 23 Werner Forman Archive, Ben Heller Collection/Art Resource, New York

Lesson 3: p. 30 Roberto Thoni/Corbis-Bettmann; p. 31 François Lochon/Gamma Liaison

Lesson 4: p. 38 Space Telescope Science Institute/NASA/Science Photo; p. 39 Julian Baum/Science Photo Library/Photo Researchers

Lesson 5: p. 46 Navy Department; p. 47 AP/Wide World Photos

Lesson 6: p. 54 Craig Orsini/Light Sources; p. 55 Courtesy of the State of Florida

Lesson 7: p. 62 Chuck O'Rear/Woodfin Camp & Associates; p. 63 David Nunuk/Science Photo Library/ Photo Researchers

Unit 2 Opener: p. 75 David Hardy/Science Photo Library/Photo Researchers

Lesson 8: p. 76 NASA/Mark Marten/Photo Researchers; p. 77 Pekka Parviainen/Science Photo Library/Photo Researchers

Lesson 9: p. 84 UPI/Corbis-Bettmann; p. 85 © The Board of Trustees of the Victoria & Albert Museum, Art Resource

Lesson 10: pp. 92, 93 from *Nadia: A Case of Extraordinary Drawing Ability in an Autistic Child* © 1977 by Academic Press Inc. (London), Ltd.

Lesson 11: p. 100 David Hardy/Science Photo Library/Photo Researchers; p. 101 Reuters/Corbis-Bettmann

Lesson 12: p. 108 Tom Pantages; p. 109 Dan McCoy/Rainbow

Lesson 13: p. 116 AP/Wide World Photos; p. 117 Dick Rowan/Photo Researchers

Lesson 14: p. 124 J. A. Hobson, Harvard Medical School/Photo Researchers; p. 125 Ed Young/Science Photo Library/Photo Researchers

Unit 3 Opener: p. 137 Spencer Swanger/Tom Stack & Associates

Lesson 15: p. 138 Jack Fields/Photo Researchers; p. 139 Photo Researchers

Lesson 16: p. 146 UPI/Corbis-Bettmann; p. 147 Tom McHugh/Photo Researchers

Lesson 17: p. 154 Superstock; p. 155 Russell D. Curtis/Photo Researchers

Lesson 18: p. 162 Spencer Swanger/Tom Stack & Associates; p. 163 AP/Wide World Photos

Lesson 19: pp. 170 Itar-Tass/Sovfoto; 171 NASA

Lesson 20: p. 178 John Fincara/Woodfin Camp & Associates; p. 179 Tom Pantages

Lesson 21: p. 186 Dr. Kari Lounatmaa/Science Photo Library/Photo Researchers; p. 187 AP/Wide World Photos